First (and Second) Steps in Statistics

First (and Second) Steps in Statistics

2nd edition

Daniel B. Wright and Kamala London

Los Angeles | London | New Delhi
Singapore | Washington DC

First edition published 2002
Reprinted 2002
This second edition published 2009

SAGE Publications Ltd
1 Oliver's Yard
55 City Road
London EC1Y 1SP

SAGE Publications Inc.
2455 Teller Road
Thousand Oaks, California 91320

SAGE Publications India Pvt Ltd
B 1/I 1 Mohan Cooperative Industrial Area
Mathura Road
New Delhi 110 044

SAGE Publications Asia-Pacific Pte Ltd
33 Pekin Street #02-01
Far East Square
Singapore 048763

Library of Congress Control Number: 2008933445

British Library Cataloguing in Publication data
A catalogue record for this book is available from
the British Library

ISBN 978-1-4129-1141-2
ISBN 978-1-4129-1142-9 (pbk)

Typeset by C&M Digitals (P) Ltd, Chennai, India
Printed in Great Britain by TJ International Ltd, Padstow, Cornwall
Printed on paper from sustainable resources

Contents

Preface

So what does '*and second*' in the title of this new edition mean? What has changed so that you should buy this new edition rather than search eBay for the original? There are three areas where we focused. First, there is the general updating of some examples and adding some new ones. We received feedback on which examples worked and which did not, and made changes accordingly. We also go into a little more depth on some topics than in the original edition. If these were the only changes then it would have just been a second edition without the title change. We have two new steps. The chapter in the original edition on robust methods has been taken and spread throughout the other chapters. This change was due to many people writing and saying that they taught, for example, the Wilcoxon tests in the same week as the *t* tests and therefore they wanted them in the same chapter. We also added more tests based on the median because the median often gets discussed in the initial chapters of textbooks, but then is not mentioned again. There are tests for the median, and we wanted to include these. The second extra step is factorial ANOVA. Again, this was in response to public demand (yes, people are demanding factorial ANOVA). This is Chapter 9 in the current edition.

The aim of this book remains the same as in the original edition. It is to teach the conceptual issues about introductory statistics to bright social and behavioural science students, but recognizing that these students may not have taken a mathematics class for several years.

Illustrations

FIGURES

TABLES

one of the toppings has to be meat. It is worth noting that the order of the toppings is irrelevant: mushrooms & pepper is the same as pepper & mushrooms

Acknowledgements

The authors and publishers wish to thank the following for permission to use copyright material:

We thank *The Psychologist* for granting us permission to reproduce material from Wright, D.B. & Williams, S. (2003). How to ... produce a bad results section. *The Psychologist*, *16*, 646–648.

We thank Wiley-Blackwell Publishing for granting us permission to reproduce material from Taylor, S.E., Welch, W.T., Kim, H.S., and Sherman, D.K. (2007). Cultural differences in the impact of social support on psychological and biological stress responses. *Psychological Science*, *18*, 831–837.

1

Univariate Statistics 1: Summarizing Data with Histograms and Boxplots

The art of statistics is both about discerning patterns in data and about communicating information about these patterns to an audience. Statistics is an art, but that does not mean that anything goes. Like other artists you need to learn technical skills and guidelines in order for your art to be any good. To take an extreme example: go to GOOGLE and IMAGE and put in 'Jackson Pollock'. Jackson Pollock was considered one of America's best twentieth-century artists and was most well known for a brand of abstract expressionism where he appeared to drip paint in a chaotic and undisciplined manner over a canvas. However, his technical abilities are clearly shown in his earlier paintings, and it was only with these skills that he could venture into an unexplored artistic genre. This book will not turn you into the Jackson Pollock of statistics, but it will help you to learn the basic tools of the trade and how to apply them. While painters, sculptors and poets have certain tools at their disposal, as a statistical artist you have various tools to facilitate both the discovery and the dissemination of your findings. Statistics is not just about what you can do with data; it is also about how you describe what you found to your expected audience. Therefore, your toolbox must include knowledge about your audience, as well as the more traditional tools like a pen and paper, and some computer software.[1]

This book introduces a language that allows us to talk about statistics, and science more generally. This is not a completely foreign language. Statistical phrases permeate our daily lives. Usually these are not the 'formal' statistics that appear in statistics books and in scientific reports, but they are embedded, very innocently, in our conversations. Examples include phrases like 'I will *probably* have a bagel today' and 'It takes *about* 20 minutes to cook rice'. The aims of this book are to enhance your awareness of these natural language statistics, to allow you to translate these into 'formal' statistics and, in so doing, to enable you to conduct, interpret and describe these statistics.

Consider the two examples mentioned above. Regardless of how likely you think it is that you will have a bagel today, you know roughly what the above statement means. When we use words like 'probably' we are not usually worried about the precise meaning of the phrase. Translating from natural language to formal statistics often involves becoming more precise. Here we might say that the *probability* of having a bagel is more than 0.50 or 50%. Probability is at the heart of statistics and will be described throughout this book. If you had a standard deck of 52 cards, shuffled them thoroughly and were about to draw one card, the probability of it being red is 0.50. So using this analogy, the above statement means that it is more likely that you will have a bagel than randomly choosing a red card from a well-shuffled deck of cards.

The second statement, 'It takes *about* 20 minutes to cook rice', is a statistical phrase because of the word 'about'. Depending on the amount and type of rice, the initial heat of the water, the type of stove and even the altitude at which you are cooking, the amount of time it takes to cook rice is not constant, but varies. Translating this into statistics it becomes 'Twenty minutes is the *central tendency* for the time to cook rice, but the exact time may vary from this'. 'Central tendency' is what the statisticians would call the instructions written on the side of the rice box suggesting how long to cook the rice. It is the value that, across all situations, the rice manufacturers think is the best guess for proper cooking time. There are different and more precise ways of calculating the central tendency including the median, which is discussed in this chapter, and the mean, which is discussed in Chapter 2.

---

1 This book is not tied to any specific statistics software. The accompanying web page provides examples from two of the main packages (mainly SPSS and R). The web also includes the data sets used in this book and much other useful information.

For most of you, the main concern with regards to statistics is not to help you to become a better rice chef, but how statistics are used and reported in the social and behavioural sciences. The point of these examples is to show how frequently statistics are encountered in our lives. During the course of your studies you will come across other 'everyday statistics' and also more formal statistics. This book describes various procedures for creating these statistics.

EXAMPLE: DNA EXONERATIONS

Imagine you are walking home one evening. You can hear police sirens in the background, but you don't think much of them. A police officer approaches and asks you a few questions. A woman has been raped and the police are looking for her attacker. You say you were at a friend's house and have been walking home. The police officer takes your name and contact details, and you go home. The next day another officer arrives at your home, and tells you that you match a rough description that the victim gave of the culprit. They ask you if you will take part in an identification parade. You agree, after all, you're not guilty; the victim won't choose you. Perhaps you would be less calm if you knew what the US Attorney General, Janet Reno, said in the preface to a report about eyewitness accuracy: 'Even the most honest and objective people can make mistakes in recalling and interpreting a witnessed event' (Technical Working Group for Eyewitness Evidence, 1999: iii). The victim identifies you as her assailant, and because jurors trust eyewitness testimony (a lot more than they should), you are convicted and spend years in prison. You may not feel lucky, but in one way you are. The crime that you were falsely convicted of is one that often includes a biological marker, semen. A DNA test is done, which shows that you are not the culprit, and, after some further legal arguments, you are eventually exonerated and released.

Your case is a tragedy of injustice, but you are not alone. The Innocence Project in the US reports hundreds of people who have been falsely convicted but later exonerated based on DNA evidence (www.innocenceproject.com). We will look at the first 163 which we downloaded on 17 November 2005. Each of these individuals' cases is a tragedy, and it is important that when you report your statistics you do not lose sight of the meaning of each case. Each individual spent years in prison, falsely accused. As voiced by Uncle Tupelo: 'Handcuffs hurt worse when you've done nothing wrong' ('*Grindstone*' by Farrar and Tweedy).

The length of time in prison of these 163 people (the data file, dnayears.sav, is on this book's website) will be used to illustrate some of the basic statistical concepts and graphs.

Each of the individuals in the DNA file is a *case*. The *sample* is composed of the 163 cases. The larger *population* in this example would be all falsely convicted individuals exonerated by DNA evidence. There is information about several attributes for each of the

Table 1.1 *The DNA cases from the Innocence Project*

Caseno$_i$	firstn$_i$	lastn$_i$	state$_i$	year1$_i$	year2$_i$	time$_i$
1	Gary	Dotson	Illinois	1979	1989	10
2	David	Vasquez	Virginia	1985	1989	4
3	Edward	Green	DC	1989	1990	1
⋮	⋮	⋮	⋮	⋮	⋮	⋮
162	Leo	Waters	North Carolina	1981	2005	24
163	George	Rodriquez	Texas	1987	2005	18

cases. Each of these attributes is called a *variable*. For this example there are seven variables: the case number, the person's first and last name, the state where they were convicted, the year they were convicted, the year they were released, and the time between conviction and release. Each person has a *value* for each variable, thus for the first person, Gary Dotson, the value for state is 'Illinois' and for time is 10 years. Most of the values that are used in this book are numeric, but the values can also be words, pictures, etc. The way that we will refer to variables is by giving them a name that describes them, writing them in *italics*, and including a subscript which tells us that people may have different values for this attribute. So, the variables $state_i$ and $time_i$ refer to the variables denoting the state in which the person was convicted and the time they spent in prison. The subscript i shows that there are different values for these variables, the i referring to different people in the sample. If you are referring to the first person the subscript 1 is used. Thus, $state_1=$ 'Illinois' and $time_1=10$ years. For numeric values it is important to include the units of measurement so that it is clear that Gary Dotson spent 10 years in prison, rather than, say, 10 months in prison.

The values for all the people in the sample, when placed together, form a *data set*. Most of the common statistical packages hold the data set in a spreadsheet format, like Table 1.1. Each row represents a single individual. The ':' means that the values for cases 4 to 161 are not included. It is a big data set, so would take up a lot of room to print and would be difficult to get a summary feeling for the data. This is one of the purposes of statistics, to identify useful summary information and to describe this to others.

One of the major objectives of statistics is to accurately summarize large quantities of data so that the reader can understand the overall patterns of responses. Two main types of techniques for summarizing data will be described in this chapter. The first technique is a histogram. Several variations are discussed. First a dot histogram and a stem-and-leaf diagram are shown. Then we present a generic histogram and a name histogram. The second technique is based on the *five-point summary* and is called a box-and-whiskers plot (or just boxplot). Both of these methods are appropriate for describing *quantitative data* (where the variable itself is on a numerical scale, such as number of years imprisoned, or score on a measure of anxiety symptoms). Methods for describing *qualitative data* (data that describe category membership such as being in the Republican Party versus the US Democratic Party or as having cats versus dogs) are described in Chapter 3.

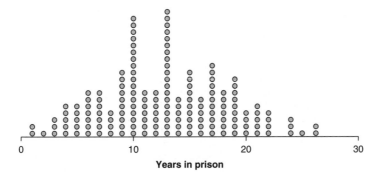

Figure 1.1   A dot histogram of the amount of time spent in prison for the 163 people from the DNA data file

HISTOGRAMS

We go through a series of histograms that vary in how much information is embedded within the histogram. The first type is a dot histogram. Here each individual is shown with a dot. The stem-and-leaf diagram is the next type. Here, numeric information is included. While this type is much lauded by statisticians, it is not as popular as the final histogram we present, the generic histogram. The generic histogram, or just histogram, is the most commonly used type. Finally, we present a name histogram as an example of an extension to the generic histogram.

The Dot Histogram

Figure 1.1 shows a dot histogram. Each case is shown with a dot. Because there are four people that spent eight years in prison, four dots are placed in a column above eight years on the *x* axis. This can be done in a word processing package, or it can be done in some statistics packages.

Stem-and-Leaf Diagram

The dots in Figure 1.1 each represent a person. Their placement shows how long that person spent in prison, but the dot itself provides no other information. A stem-and-leaf diagram (Tukey, 1972, 1977) allows the individual 'dot' to provide information. A stem-and-leaf for the DNA data is shown in Figure 1.2. The variable is divided into two-year bins. The numbers on the far left are the number of people in each bin. The next number is the first digit. Each

Freq.	Stem	Leaf
2	0	**11**
4	0	2333
10	0	4444455555
14	0	66666667777777
14	0	88889999999**9**999
25	1	00000000000000000001111111
26	1	2222222**3**3333333333333333333
16	1	4444445555555555
17	1	66666677777777777
16	1	8888888999999999
9	2	000011111
4	2	2222
4	2	4445
2	2	**66**

Figure 1.2 A stem-and-leaf diagram of the amount of time spent in prison for the 163 people from the DNA data file. The values in **bold** are the minimum, maximum, the median and the two hinges, which are the five numbers of the five-number summary and described in the next section

digit on the right stands for an individual person, and gives the value for that person. Thus, there are two people who spent one year in prison, one who spent two years in prison, and three who spent three years in prison.

Tukey (1977) goes into much detail about how to make these plots, how to use them to help check the data, and what can be added to them. Until recently they had been used rather sparingly, but have become more popular because they are often used when reporting *meta-analyses*. These are studies which combine the results of different studies. A particular statistical result from each study would be represented by each digit.

In Figure 1.2 multiple stems are the same because the bins are only two years wide. In many stem-and-leaf diagrams each stem is unique. For example, consider the following data from Wright and Osborne (2005) on 80 people's scores on a dissociation measure. Dissociation, which means having difficulty integrating mental images, thoughts, emotions and memories into consciousness (the word 'spaciness' is sometimes used, but this does not capture the full meaning of the term), has scores which can vary from 0 to 100. The stem-and-leaf diagram, as printed by SPSS, is shown in Figure 1.3. It shows that there were four people with scores of less than 10 (scores of 3, 7, 9 and 9), a couple of scores of 60 or above, but that most of the scores are between 20 and 60.

The Generic Histogram

The two types of histogram shown above are alternatives to the generic histogram. If you squint looking at these, this is what a generic histogram is. It focuses solely on the macro

Freq.	Stem	Leaf
4	0.	3799
4	1.	0267
18	2.	113455556688888899
20	3.	01112222223357888889
18	4.	0111135566677788889
14	5.	00002223346779
2	6.	04

Figure 1.3   A stem-and-leaf diagram of the amount of self-reported dissociation (0–100 scale) for 80 participants (from Wright & Osborne, 2005)

information. The DNA data, with two-year bins, is shown in Figure 1.4. If doing this by hand, the *x* axis scale is made in the same way as with the other histograms. You need to calculate the number of people in each bin (which can be done with the 'Frequencies' command in many statistics packages). You draw the *y* axis from 0 to above the maximum number in any bin. You then draw a horizontal line for each bin corresponding to the number of people in those bins. Use this to make a rectangular box. Make sure that you label the axes properly. All of the main statistics packages allow you to make

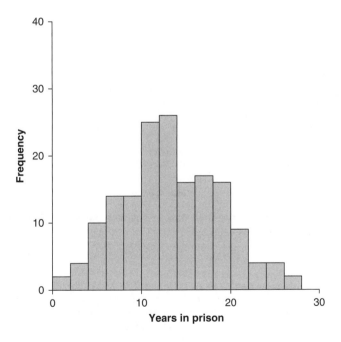

Figure 1.4   A histogram of the amount of time spent in prison for the 163 people from the DNA data file

histograms. The most common mistake is using a 'bar chart' option instead of the histogram option. Bar charts are discussed in Chapter 3. While some of them look like histograms, they are a different graphical technique (Wilkinson, 2005). Notice with the histogram, the bars are touching one another, which denotes that the data are quantitative.

Deciding about Bins

When making a histogram the critical decision is the size of the bins. Many software programs set the number of bins by default, according to the number of cases and variety of their responses. Often, the program's default settings are fine but if needed you can adjust their selected number of bins.

As you increase the number of bins, you increase the amount of numeric information, but sometimes this is providing too much information and it breaks Grice's maxim of quantity. Figures 1.5 (a–c) show the same data as Figure 1.4 but with bins of one year, four years or eight years. Figure 1.5 (a) probably provides too much information. Readers may concentrate on the peaks at 10 and 13 years, and the dips at 11 and 12 years, which probably are not important. Figure 1.5 (c) provides too little information. The reader would probably want to have more precision. Figure 1.5 (b) provides about the right amount of information for most readers. Either this or Figure 1.4 (bin width of two years) is probably the best.[2]

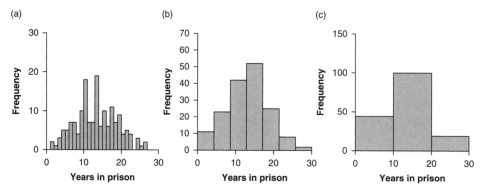

Figure 1.5 (a–c)   Histograms for the DNA data cases with bin widths of (a) one year, (b) four years and (c) eight years

---

2 There are statistical procedures that provide a guide for how wide the bins should be. Wand (1997) describes several of these, and different computer packages use different algorithms. Some of these are complicated and all require some statistical concepts that we have yet to encounter. For the present purpose it is just worth knowing that these procedures suggest widths of between two and four years.

A Name Histogram

A phrase often attributed to, but probably never said by, Stalin is: 'A single death is a tragedy, a million deaths is a statistic' (http://www.time.com/time/personoftheyear/archive/photohistory/stalin.html; 25 October 2005). There is a distrust of statistics because numbers can appear to deny the humanity deserving of each individual represented by those numbers. Turning data, like that in Table 1.1, into a graph, can sometimes remove the humanity from the individual datum (datum is the singular of data). The final histogram we show helps to highlight the importance of each of the individual data points. We call it a *name histogram* and it is based on Tufte's micro/macro distinction (1990, see pp. 140–141). This is like the dot histogram shown in Figure 1.1, but instead of printing dots we print the person's name. We made this in Word (details on the book's web page). We show it to emphasise the types of graphs that you can produce.

Summary of Histograms

Several types of histogram were shown. They vary in how much information they provide. It is important to think about how much information you wish to provide to your audience. The dot histogram shows each case as a dot, but provides no further information. It is useful because it makes clear the number of people in each bin. The stem-and-leaf diagram also provides this, but gives extra information about the numeric value. Stem-and-leaf diagrams are liked by methodologists, and appear in scientific journals, but not in the popular press. Hopefully this will increase. The generic histogram, which does show up in the popular press, focuses only on the macro level. The name histogram provides lots of individual information and for examples like the DNA cases reinforces to your audience the gravity of each datum. It is also useful with smaller data sets, but providing the names for all 163 cases is too much for most purposes.

The information provided in all histograms is about the distribution of the variable, for most of the graphs in this chapter this is the variable $time_i$. The distribution of a variable is an important aspect of the variable. These graphs show that there were a few people who just spent a couple of years in prison for crimes that they did not commit, and a few who spent more than 20 years in prison, but that most spent between five and 20 years in prison. They also show us if any particular values are more prevalent than others. The histograms also reveal the shape of the distribution. Many distributions have a shape like that shown in these figures, where most of the values are in the centre and the figure looks kind of 'bell shaped'. One particular shape that has these characteristics is called the Normal distribution. We will discuss this in more detail in Chapter 5.

Figure 1.6   A name histogram for the data in Table 1.1

0–1	2–3	4–5	6–7	8–9	10–11	12–13	14–15	16–17	18–19	20–21	22–23	24–25	26–27
						Toney							
					Rollins	Webb							
					Mercer	Sarsfield							
					Danziger	Watikns							
					Fritz	Robinson							
					Williamson	Ochoa							
					Jimerson	Velasquez							
					Kotler	Green							
					Holland	Bradford							
					Johnson	Ollins		Adams					
					Krone	Ollins	Holdren	Rainge	Brown				
					Criner	Saunders	Youngblood	Williams	Jean				
			Gonzalez		Miller	McSherry	Lavernia	Charles	Anderson				
			Gregory		Richardson	McGee	Pierce	Butler	Mayes				
			Mitchell		Jones	McCray	Pope	Lloys	Webster				
			Webb	Dixon	Miller	Richardson	Thomas	Sutherlin	Maher				
		Matthews	Scruggs	Wardell	Smith	Salaam	Godschalk	Erby	Charles				
		Sutton	Snyder	Reynolds	Hernadez	Santana	Bromgard	Avery	Hunt	Townsend			
		Salazar	Dabbs	Moto	Cruz	Wise	Echols	Harrison	Doswell	Lowery			
		Callace	Cowans	Davis	Cotton	Ortiz	Scott	Moon	Nesmith	Willis			
		Woodall	Reid	Davis	Shepard	Byrd	Bauer	Green	Waters	Yarris			
		Durham	Cromedy	Nelson	Bullock	Mahan	Mitchell	Johnson	Fain	Woods			
	Alexander	Johnson	Willis	Gray	Honaker	Mahan	Smith	Abdal	Johnson	Gray	Mcmillan	Diaz	
	Piszczek	Alejandro	Hicks	Harris	Daye	Atkins	Washington	Washington	Goodman	Scott	Ruffin	Gray	
Villasana	Bravo	Brison	Saecker	Chalmers	Linscott	Dominguez	Webb	Bibbins	Booker	Good	Dedge	Williams	Evans
Green	O'Donnell	Vasquez	Jones	Bloodsworth	Dotson	Powell	Kordonowy	Laughman	Rodriguez	Brown	Whitefield	Waters	Terry

Years in prison

THE FIVE-NUMBER SUMMARY

The five-number summary shows five numbers that are used in a popular graphical technique called a boxplot (or box and whiskers). The five numbers are the minimum, maximum, the middle number (called the median), the number that splits the lowest 25% of the sample from the highest 75% of the sample (the first quartile), and the number that splits the lowest 75% of the sample from the highest 25% of the sample (the third quartile). The focus in this section will be on what these values mean and how to use them in graphs. Computing them is straightforward for certain sample sizes, but complex for most sample sizes. Nowadays computers are usually used to calculate them.

Statistics is about reducing the vast amount of data into a smaller amount of information. While the histograms allow important aspects of the data to be understood, they are not reducing the data. The techniques described in this section will allow to you calculate five important values that can be used to summarize an entire distribution. The five numbers of the five-number summary are: the minimum and the maximum, the median, and the two quartiles (sometimes called 'hinges').[3]

The *minimum* is the lowest number. Suppose you went to a playground and wanted to see if it was age-appropriate for a young relative and that there were nine children of the following ages (and some adults):

Values: 2   4   8   3   8   7   2   2   12

First, we sort these from smallest to largest:

Values:	2	2	2	3	4	7	8	8	12
Ranks:	1	2	3	4	5	6	7	8	9

	Minimum	First quartile	Median	Third quartile	Maximum

Each value has a rank. Because some children are the same ages (at least when their ages are just in years), we have just assigned the lowest number (2 years old) with a rank of 1, the second number (2) with a rank of 2, and the third number (2) with a

---

3 The definitions for certain statistics evolve. What this chapter is guided in large part by Tukey's discussion, his term 'hinge' is slightly different from 'quartile'. Nowadays most people use these terms interchangeably.

rank of 3, and similarly with the two cases with the value 8. The minimum value is the one with a rank of 1. This is the value 2 years. The *maximum* is the largest number and has a rank equal to the total number of cases. The total number of cases is often denoted with the letter n, so in this example $n = 9$. The case with rank $= 9$ has a value of 12 years old so this is the maximum. The *median* is the middle value. With $n = 9$, the median is the value with rank 5. Here the value is 4 years. When n is odd, the rank of the median is $(n + 1)/2$, here $(9 + 1)/2 = 10/2 = 5$. Notice this is the ranking of the value i.e., the fifth value, which in this example equals 4 years old. This is observation such that half the people score above it and half score below it. The situation when n is even is discussed below. The quartiles are the 'medians' of the lower and upper halves of the data. They separate out the upper and lowest 25% of the values. The word 'quartile' is based on 'quarter'; the quartiles divide the data into quarters. The five-point summary can be written as:

$n = 9$

	4	Units = years
2	8	IQR = 6
2	12	Range = 10

Within the box are the five numbers. The median is shown and then below it the quartiles and then below them the extreme values (the minimum and maximum). Some additional information is often included with the five-number summary. The number of cases is shown above the box. To the right of the box are three additional pieces of information. First, the units of the variables, here years of age, is printed. Below this the interquartile range (IQR) is shown.[4] This is the difference in values between the upper and lower quartiles and can be calculated from the information in the box ($8 - 2 = 6$). Below this is the range, the difference between the maximum and minimum values ($12 - 2 = 10$). The IQR and the range will always be positive values.

When you have larger datasets it can be easier to calculate the five-number summary using a stem-and-leaf diagram. Figure 1.7 redraws the stem-and-leaf diagram from Figure 1.3, but marking off the quartiles (technically, the median is a quartile since it takes all three points to divide the variable into quarters). Each quarter has 40 cases. When presented like this it is easy to see the five numbers. The five-number summary is shown in Figure 1.7. The quartiles and the IQR are important concepts; they show that approximately half of the cases lie between nine and 17.

---

4 You may come across the *semi-interquartile* range, which is the IQR divided by 2.

	Freq.	Stem	Leaf
40 cases	2	0	11
	4	0	2333
	10	0	4444455555
	14	0	66666667777777
	10	0	8888999999
	1	0	**9**
40 cases	3	1	999
	25	1	0000000000000000001111111
	12	1	222222233333
	1	1	**3**
40 cases	13	1	3333333333333
	16	1	4444455555555555
	11	1	66666677777
	1	1	**7**
40 cases	5	1	77777
	16	1	888888889999999999
	9	2	000011111
	4	2	2222
	4	2	4445
	2	2	66

$n = 163$

	13	
9		17
1		26

Units = years
IQR = 8
Range = 25

Figure 1.7 A stem-and-leaf diagram, split by quartiles, and a five-point summary box for the DNA data

Having 163 cases here makes calculating the five-number summary relatively simple because these can be divided into four equally sized groups of 40 plus the median and two quartiles. When there is an even number of cases the median is more difficult to calculate. Consider calculations of the median. The formula, $(n + 1)/2$, produces non-whole numbers. If there are 10 values, the median rank is 5.5. To calculate the median you need to take the average of the 5th ranked case and the 6th ranked case. If the data are:

Values:	1	3	3	5	7	9	9	11	13	17
Ranks:	1	2	3	4	5	6	7	8	9	10

Median

The 5th case has the value 7 and the 6th the value 9. Thus, the median is equal to halfway between these, or 8. This is called the mid-rank of the two numbers. In Chapter 2 you will learn about a statistic called the 'mean'. It is also the mean of these two numbers. Half the values fall above eight-years-old and half fall below eight-years-old.

Similarly, finding the quartiles is more difficult and there are some subtle differences in how some packages and books define quartiles and IQR. Luckily, statistics computer programs calculate these values for you, which leaves us to focus on the concepts. The concepts are: the first quartile separates the lowest 25% of the data from the rest, the third quartile separates the highest 25% of the data from the rest, and the IQR includes the middle 50% of the data. The rank for the first quartile is $n/4$ and for the third quartile is $3n/4$, both of which will usually be a non-whole numbers. For ease when doing these by hand, you should round the first quartile up to the next highest rank, and round the third quartile down to the next lowest rank. For example, with $n = 10$, the rank of first quartile is $10/4 = 2.5$ so the 3rd value (3) should be used, and the rank of the third quartile is $3 \times 10/4 = 7.5$, so the 7th value (9) should be used.

While quartiles divide the values into four equally sized groups, for different purposes you may wish to divide the values into different numbers of groups. Quartiles are one of the most useful. Another popular method is to divide the values into 100 equally sized groups. These are called *percentiles* (dividing the data into percentages). You may hear parents saying their child is in the 98th percentile on some standardized test. This means only 1–2% of children who take this test do better.

Box-and-Whiskers Plots, or Boxplots

Figure 1.8 shows Ruby. On one of our web pages we described how this cunning feline devised the box-and-whiskers plot (as seemed obvious from the photo), not the great statistician John Tukey. Many people wrote who appeared not have grasped *sarcasm*.

Figure 1.8   Resolving the debate about the origin of the box-and-whiskers plot:
Ruby versus Tukey

While there were some precursors (for example, Spear, 1952, as cited in Tufte, 2001),
let us use these pages to set the record straight. Ruby is a loveable cat, but is insignifi-
cant in the history of statistics. John Tukey (1977) is generally credited as the creator
of box-and-whiskers plots. In fact, aspects of Tukey's original description of the box-
and-whiskers plot and a plot which he called a schematic plot (Tukey, 1972: Fig. 18.8)
are often incorporated together, and go under the more general term *boxplots* (McGill
et al., 1978). Therefore we will use this term.

The boxplot is a graph of the five-number summary. We will describe two versions, one
created by the computer (an actual boxplot) and a simplified version that can be drawn
easily by hand, called a quartile plot (Tufte, 2001). Details for drawing a boxplot are shown
in Box 1.2. Many of the computer packages use slightly different ways of making boxplots
(Reese, 2005), but they all produce the same basic diagrams. A rectangular box is drawn
from the lower quartile to the upper quartile and a vertical line is placed within the box to
denote the median. The possible length of the whiskers are defined as 1.5 x IQR. For the
DNA data the IQR is 8 so the maximum whisker length is 12. The whiskers *could* go from
the lower quartile, 9, to −3 and from the upper quartile, 17, to 29. But, the whiskers stop at
the most extreme observed value that is within the possible length. Here it stops at 1 and 26.
The points where these whiskers end are called *adjacent* points. A boxplot for these data is
shown in Figure 1.9.

Tufte (2001) is the most influential person on creating good graphs. He described how
the basic boxplot was difficult to draw by hand and also used more ink than is necessary
(he stresses that good graphs should use as little ink as possible). He pointed out that a boxplot could be drawn without the box. He describes several alternatives. The one we like

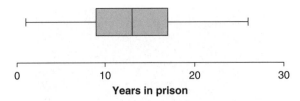

Figure 1.9   A boxplot for the DNA data. This shows the five-number summary in graphical form

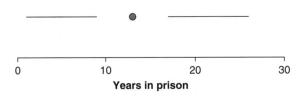

Figure 1.10   A simplified boxplot called a quartile plot (Tufte, 2001). When drawing by hand this is easier to draw than a standard boxplot

best replaces the median with a dot, leaves out the box, but keeps the whiskers. Tufte calls this a 'quartile plot'. An example is shown in Figure 1.10.

When there are values outside the whiskers they should be shown. Sometimes it is useful to distinguish cases just outside the whiskers from those far outside the whiskers. Tukey (1977) gives various rules for doing this, calling points more than 1.5 IQR from the median as *outside* points and those 3.0 IQR from the median as *far outside* points. Suppose the following were annual salaries in $1000 for 25 people:

Values: 3 12 12 15 15 15 15 15 18 21 22 22 22 22 22 27 28 30 30 30 32 33 38 75 150
Ranks: 1 2 3 4 5 6 7 8 9 10 11 12 13 14 15 16 17 18 19 20 21 22 23 24 25

The five-number summary is:

$$n = 25$$

22		Units = $1000
15	30	IQR = 15
3	150	Range = 147

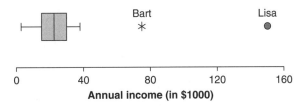

Figure 1.11   A boxplot of annual income (in $1000) for 25 people. The outside point (Bart) and far outside point (Lisa) are both labelled. These are usually referred to as *outliers*

The resulting boxplot is shown in Figure 1.11. The possible whisker length is $1.5 \times$ IQR. The lower adjacent point is $3000 and the upper adjacent point is $38,000, so this is where the whiskers end. The value $75,000 is more than 1.5 IQR from the median so it is an outside point, and is labelled with a star. The value $150,000 is more than 3.0 IQR from the median so it is a far outside point. It is denoted with a circle. Particularly with small data sets it is often useful to label these points. This allows some of the micro information in Figure 1.1 to be included. People are likely to be most interested in these extreme points so this provides micro information where it is most useful.

Box 1.2   Making a Boxplot by Hand

There are some slight variations that can be used when constructing a boxplot. Here are the rules for a fairly simple version. Before beginning this you should have sorted all the data in order from lowest to highest, found the median, the upper and lower quartiles, and the IQR.

1 On graph paper, make the horizontal axis so that the values cover the range of values in the same way as was done for histograms in Chapter 2.
2 Draw short vertical lines, above the axis, to denote the medians for the different groups (or the median if you have a single group).
3 Draw a short vertical line for each quartile, and join these as a box (see Figure 1.9).
4 Calculate the values for the whiskers as follows:

Lower whisker = lower quartile 1.5 IQR
Higher whisker = higher quartile 1.5 IQR

Draw these as lines extending from the box to the furthest data point (called the adjacent point) that is within this 'inner fence'.
5 Denote any data points outside these whiskers, but within 3.0 IQR of the median, with some character (a star in Figure 1.11), and those beyond this point with a different character (a circle in Figure 1.11).

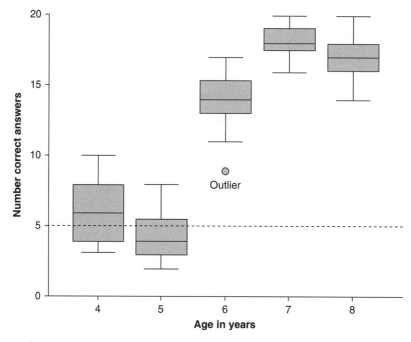

Figure 1.12 Boxplots for the number of correct answers on a test by the participants' ages. The dashed line shows the prediction for random guessing

Boxplots are most useful when comparing groups. Suppose a developmental psychologist asked 20 children from each of five different age groups to solve some mathematics problems. Suppose there were 20 multiple-choice questions and each question had four options. The data might look like that depicted in Figure 1.12. We have changed this to vertical boxplots; most packages give you the choice of having them horizontal or vertical. If people were guessing randomly, they would probably get somewhere near five correct answers because the probability of correctly guessing for any individual question is 25% (this level is shown with a dashed line in the figure). Most four- and five-year-olds are at about this level, so clearly have not mastered whichever mathematical techniques are involved. The seven- and eight-year-olds get most of the questions right. They are at the *ceiling*, meaning they cannot do much better. The scores on these mathematics problems differentiate among the six-year-old children. Some do poorly, some do well, and most are in the middle. If an educational psychologist wanted a test to discriminate among children, these problems would be most useful with the six-year-olds. Figure 1.13 shows this graph using the quartile plots (Tufte, 2001). When there are several groups this is often useful. Further, we have added a dashed line between all the medians. This is appropriate if the grouping variable is based on some type of scale, like age.

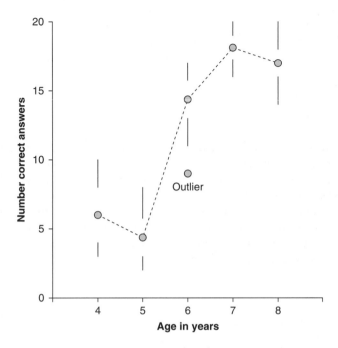

Figure 1.13   Quartile plots, as developed by Tufte (2001), showing the same data as Figure 1.12

SUMMARY OF THE FIVE-NUMBER SUMMARY AND BOXPLOTS

Histograms provide much information about the distribution of a data set. Often it is useful to summarize this information in a few numbers, in order to give the reader more detail about the distribution. The five-number summary is a good set of numbers for this. They summarize the data well and are easy to explain to other people. Most people know what the minimum and maximum are (the lowest and highest numbers). The median is the number that half of the people scored above this value and half of the people scored below it. The lower quartile has 25% of the values lower and the upper quartile has 25% of the values higher. The area between the lower and upper quartiles contains 50% of the data.

The *boxplot* refers to a collection of techniques based on the five-number summary. Most statistics packages produce them. The box shows where about 50% of the cases are. The whiskers are a length which Tukey chose that should include most of the remaining data. Those outside the whiskers are outliers. Tukey distinguished outside points from far outside points, though often people just label all of these as outliers. Reese (2005) notes that boxplots frequently occur in scientific publications, because they accurately and clearly display important characteristics about the distribution and allow different groups of people to be easily compared, but at present they are not included in many popular magazines and newspapers. He argues that this should change because the five-number summary can be easily comprehended by most people.

CONCLUSIONS

Histograms and boxplots both convey information about single variables. They are univariate (uni, from the Latin *unus* meaning one) procedures. How much of the information that is displayed in a histogram depends on the type of histogram and the bin size. Procedures like the stem-and-leaf diagram display more precise information than the generic histogram. As the width of the bin increases, information is lost. With boxplots most of the information is lost. It is assumed that the key points of the distribution can be summarized with a small set of numbers and including information on only a few outlying cases. It is possible to display histograms and boxplots together, as in Figure 1.14. This shows the distribution of scores on a variable that measures dissociation on a 0–100 scale and it shows that most people have low scores, but a few have high scores.

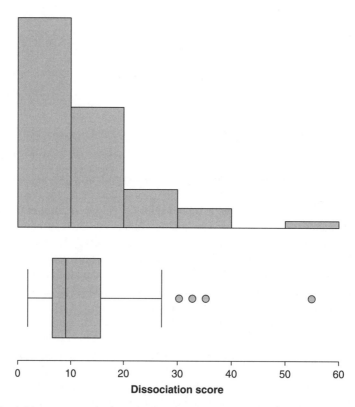

Figure 1.14   A histogram and a boxplot for responses to DES II (Wright & Loftus, 1999), a questionnaire measuring dissociative experiences

EXERCISES

1.1 How is Grice's (1975) maxim of quantity relevant to graphing data? (*Hint*: see discussion of histograms.)

1.2 Why is the number of bins, or the bin width, an important decision when constructing a histogram?

1.3 Find an 'everyday' statistical phrase from a newspaper. Say what the phrase means and why it is a statistical phrase.

1.4 Describe what the following four terms mean: variables, values, sample and cases. How can you write the value of a variable for a single case?

1.5 Four types of histograms were introduced. They were: dot plots, stem-and-leaf diagrams, generic histograms and name histograms. When would each be used? What additional information is included in the name histogram that is not in the dot histogram? Which procedure would be best if you had only 10 cases? Which if you had 2000 cases?

1.6 What are the five numbers in the five-number summary and what does each mean? What other information is usually printed with the five-number summary?

1.7 If the distribution provides more information than the five-number summary, why is five-number summary of value?

1.8 When might you prefer to use boxplots as opposed to histograms?

1.9 In the table below there is a restaurant bill for 10 people. They decided to split the bill evenly for their dinners.

(a) Make a histogram of these data. Say which type of histogram you made.

(b) If you were asked how much it costs for a typical meal at this restaurant, what amount would you give? What is the statistical term for it called?

Meal prices at DK's Curry Palace (prices are in UK pounds; (£1 ≈ $2, where '≈' means approximately)

Name	Price
Louise	£4.50
Steve	£13.00
Alice	£5.50
Susan	£4.50
Dave	£6.00
Joanne	£5.50
Mel	£5.00
Tom	£5.00
Andy	£5.50
Alexa	£6.00

(Cont'd)

1.10 If you had data on 18,000 people's scores on a life quality measure, which type of histogram would you use?

1.11 The following exam marks, out of 100, were awarded to 23 students:

54 65 63 75 81 32 0 69 48 38 19 68 55 67 70 72 76 0 74 47 61 65 88

(a) Find the five-number summary.
(b) Make a boxplot. Say which type you have made.

 **FURTHER READING**

Brief online works:

Gould, S.J. (1985). The median isn't the message. *Discover*, 6 (June), 40–42.
Available on several websites including: http://cancerguide.org/median_not_msg.html. All the praise given to this essay is well deserved.

Tufte, E. (2003). PowerPoint is evil. *Wired*, 11.09, http://www.wired.com/wired/archive/11.09/ppt2.html.
The title really says it all. What would happen if Microsoft could afford lawyers? An updated version is in his 2006 book *Beautiful Evidence*. See also http://www.edwardtufte.com/bboard/q-and-a-fetch-msg?msg_id=0001yB&topic_id=1.

wikipedia has pages on many of the concepts, like histogram, boxplot, five-number summary, median and quartile. Although *wikipedia* gets the occasional bad press, it is usually accurate and a good source of information. Most other web resources are less reliable. In general, to learn about academic subjects it is best to use academic websites.

Books

There are several good books about graphing. We decided to be very selective and choose two.

Tufte, E.R. (2001). *The Visual Display of Quantitative Information* (2nd ed.). Cheshire, CT: Graphics Press.
A truly marvellous book! See http://www.edwardtufte.com/tufte/ for more on Tufte.

Tukey, J.W. (1977). *Exploratory Data Analysis*. Reading, MA: Addison-Wesley.
This is a 'how-to' book which allowed serious scientists to talk about graphics. Tukey was one of the top twentieth-century scientists. Although there is an emphasis on constructing graphs by hand, which thanks to computers is no longer necessary, the logic and fluency of this text is still excellent. Unfortunately it is out of print, but most university libraries will have copies.

2

Univariate Statistics 2: The Mean and Standard Deviation

The four main learning outcomes of this chapter are to:

1   be able to calculate the mean of a variable
2   be able to calculate the standard deviation of a variable
3   think about possible transformations and
4   remember to use the correct units

Much psychological research concerns calculating and comparing values of one statistic, the *mean*. The mean is also used and referred to in popular culture as the average. Like the median, it is a measure of the centre of a variable's distribution, but it has become more popular. Another important statistic, the standard deviation, is also introduced in this chapter. It shows how spread out the data are around the mean. In later chapters we use the standard deviation to help to calculate the precision of the estimate of the mean.

THE MEAN: LANGUAGE ACQUISITION

He was born in Oklahoma in 1973, but at two weeks was uprooted from Oklahoma to live most of his early life in student digs in New York City. At nine months Nim Chimpsky began personalized tuition at Columbia University. Following the apparent acquisition of language by other non-human primates, Herbert Terrace and colleagues (Terrace, 1987; Terrace et al., 1979) tried to teach sign language to Nim under laboratory conditions. The name *Nim Chimpsky* is with reference to the great linguist Noam Chomsky (see p. 29 of Terrace, 1987, for how they came up with the name).

Language requires using words with meaning and applying rules to combine words, and must go beyond mimicry and cannot be due to even unconscious prompting from the human observers. Terrace's research set strict standards trying to make sure that Nim truly was producing language. Thomas Sebeok, one of the best known semioticians (i.e., people who study signs and meaning), is alleged to have said: 'In my opinion, the alleged language experiments with apes divide into three groups: one, outright fraud; two, self-deception; three, those conducted by Terrace' (http://en.wikipedia.org/wiki/Nim_Chimpsky, accessed 26 June 2006).

Terrace and colleagues documented several of the two- and three-word phrases that Nim used. Table 2.1 (data from Terrace, 1987: Table 7) shows the number of times Nim signed for 18 different types of food, and how often he gave that sign either with the sign for *Nim* versus for *Me* (so, *apple* + *Nim* or *Nim* + *apple* versus *apple* + *Me* or *Me* + *apple*). Terrace called each use of a particular type of phrase a 'token', hence Table 2.1 gives the number of tokens. We are interested in whether Nim used *Nim* or *Me* more. The simplest approach to this is to count the number of *Nim* tokens and the number of *Me* tokens. This is called the *sum* of them. For the *Nim* phrases this is:

$$90 + 91 + 1 + 24 + 2 + 17 + 26 + 68 + 80 + 4 + 2 + 4 + 24 + 29$$
$$+ 98 + 21 + 12 + 65 = 658$$

The variable for the number of tokens using the word *Nim* for each type of food can be denoted Nim_i, where the subscript i tells the reader that the variable Nim_i can have a different value for each food (note that *Nim* is a variable, Nim is the chimpanzee's name). So, banana is the first food. Thus, $Nim_1 = 91$ tokens. Note that it is always important to include the units that are being measured, here 'tokens' of the particular linguistic type. There is a shorthand way to write 'add up all the values' and that is using the summation sign which is the capital Greek letter sigma: Σ. Write: $\Sigma Nim_i = 658$ tokens to mean the sum of all the values of Nim_i. For the *Me* tokens the sum is: $\Sigma Me_i = 378$ tokens. So, for this set of 18 foods, Nim, used his own name about twice as often as the pronoun *Me*. Comparing the sums of each of these variables is informative.

Figure 2.1 shows stem-and-leaf diagrams (see Chapter 1) presented back-to-back to allow the distributions of the two variables to be compared. It is clear that, for most of the food types, Nim uses his own name more than the pronoun *Me*, but there is one outlier for Me_i values. For some reason when referring to *banana* he tends to use his own name. In Chapter 1 we discussed using the median to describe the centre of a distribution. Because there are 18 foods, the median is halfway between the 9th and 10th values; the mid-rank is 9.5. These have been printed in **bold** in the stem-and-leaf diagram. The median for Nim_i is 24 tokens. The median for Me_i is halfway between the 9th and 10th values, halfway between 4 and 9. This is (4 + 9)/2 or 6.5 tokens. Because the median is higher for Nim_i, it appears Nim uses his name more than the pronoun *Me*.

An alternative to the median is the mean.[1] It is probably the most used statistic both in science and in the popular press. Like the median, it is a measure of central tendency; it provides a single number for the centre of the distribution. It is sum of all the values divided by the number of items in the sample. In symbols, we write: $\bar{x} = \Sigma x_i/n$, where n is the sample size. The notation $\bar{x}$ is pronounced 'x bar'. To denote the mean of a variable it is common practice to draw a line over the variable name, so the mean of Nim_i is $\overline{Nim}$. There are several alternatives for denoting the mean. Another method is to denote it with the capital letter M, so that the mean of Nim_i would be M_{Nim}. These are the two most common ways to denote the mean of a variable. For our example:

$$\overline{Nim} = \frac{\Sigma Nim_i}{n} = \frac{658}{18} = 36.56 \text{ tokens and } \overline{Me} = \frac{\Sigma Me_i}{n} = \frac{378}{18} = 21.00 \text{ tokens}$$

This shows that the mean number of times Nim used his own name for those 18 foods was 36.56 times per food type compared with only 21.00 times for the pronoun *Me*. So, the mean for Nim_i is higher than the mean for Me_i.

The means for both of these are larger than their respective medians, particularly for the uses of *Me*. This is because of one very large value. For whatever reason, Nim used the pronoun *Me* 131 times to get a banana. The mean is greatly affected by extreme points, while the median is not. This is one of the reasons why people often choose the median, rather than the mean.

---

1 The word 'average' is often used in the press instead of 'mean', for things like a batting average. Statisticians often talk about different types of 'means'. The full name for the mean we describe is the 'arithmetic mean', and it is the most common 'mean' and is what people (even statisticians) are referring to when they say mean. We are often asked if the statistical word 'mean' derives from either the English word that has the synonym cruel or the word with the synonym signify. The answer is: neither. According to the *Oxford English Online Dictionary*, the word 'mean' has several meanings, including sexual intercourse (so if your instructor asks you to find a mean ...). The statistical term is more similar with the word mean as used in music for the middle note than with these other uses (see http://dictionary.oed.com/).

Table 2.1 *The number of times that Nim used his name versus the pronoun Me in response to 18 foods. The foods are in descending order of the total number of tokens used*

Food type	*Nim* tokens	*Me* tokens	Total
Banana	91	131	222
Apple	90	44	134
Gum	68	62	130
Sweet	98	31	129
Nut	80	20	100
Yogurt	65	3	68
Tea	21	30	51
Grape	26	14	40
Raisin	29	9	38
Water	12	18	30
Cracker	24	4	28
Pear	24	4	28
Fruit	17	1	18
Peach	4	1	5
Egg	2	2	4
Orange	4	0	4
Pancake	2	2	4
Berry	1	2	3

Nim tokens	Stem	*Me* tokens
44221	0	011223**449**
72	10	48
96**441**	20	0
	30	01
	40	4
85	50	
	60	2
0	70	
810	80	
	90	
	100	
	110	
	120	
	130	1

Figure 2.1 A stem-and-leaf diagram of the distribution of *Nim* tokens and *Me* tokens in response to 18 foods. The values in **bold** are the middle two values

Consider the data from Exercise 1.9 on the amount spent by 10 people at DK's Curry Palace. The values were (all in £, and £1 ≈ $2): 4.50, 13.00, 5.50, 4.50, 6.00, 5.50, 5.00, 5.00, 5.50 and 6.00. The total bill was £60.50. If they decided to split this bill equally, then they would calculate the mean: £60.50/10 people = £6.05 per person. This is different from the median (which you had to find in Exercise 1.9, so we will not give you the answer here). Steve would be paying a lot less than he should since he got £13 worth of food. We say Steve is an outlier and that he has a large positive *residual*. A residual is how far off the observed value is from the estimated value. All the other people have fairly small, but negative residuals. Louise and Susan have negative residuals of £1.50, the largest in magnitude, which means they are subsidizing Steve's gluttony the most. Residual is a concept that is brought up in other chapters, particularly on regression, where more complex methods could be used to estimate how much each person should pay.

THE VARIANCE AND STANDARD DEVIATION

The mean and median are measures of the central tendency of a distribution. In Chapter 1 you were introduced to the *range* and the *IQR* as measures of the spread of the distribution. In this chapter you are introduced to the two most popular statistics to describe the spread of a distribution. These are the *variance* and the *standard deviation*, and they are closely related. We will begin with the variance and then describe how to calculate the standard deviation from this.

When one thinks about how spread out a distribution is, one way to think of it is how far away most of the points are from the mean. If they are all close to the mean, then the distribution is not spread out and we would want a measure of spread to reflect this. If the points are far from the mean then we would want a measure of spread to be large. The variance of a variable can be calculated in four steps, providing that you have already calculated the mean.

1   Subtract the mean of the variable from *each* value, $(x_i - \bar{x})$.
2   Multiply this value by itself; in other words, square it, $(x_i - \bar{x})^2$.
3   Add these values together, $\Sigma (x_i - \bar{x})^2$.
4   Divide by the number of cases minus one, $\Sigma (x_i - \bar{x})^2/(n-1)$.

The following shows the equation in full:

$$\text{var}\, x_i = \frac{\sum (x_i - \bar{x})^2}{n-1}$$

Table 2.2 *Calculating the residuals* $(x_i - \bar{x})$, *the squared residuals* $(x_i - \bar{x})^2$, *and the sum of the squared residuals* $\Sigma(x_i - \bar{x})^2$, *which is often just called the sum of squares. To find the variance divide by n–1 (here 10 – 1 = 9), and you get 1.79*

$(x_i - \bar{x}) =$	$(x_i - \bar{x})^2 =$
(4–4.7) = – 0.7	0.49
(3–4.7) = – 1.7	2.89
(4–4.7) = – 0.7	0.49
(5–4.7) = 0.3	0.09
(3–4.7) = – 1.7	2.89
(7–4.7) = 2.3	5.29
(4–4.7) = – 0.7	0.49
(6–4.7) = 1.3	1.69
(6–4.7) = 1.3	1.69
(5–4.7) = 0.3	0.09
Sum(Σ) 0	16.10 minutes squared

Consider the following example with just 10 data points. There is much interest in how people's ability on various physical and mental tasks declines as they get older. Here 10 young adults and 10 much older adults were asked a series of current affairs questions and the times taken to complete these were recorded. The scores, rounded to the nearest minute, were:

Younger:	4	3	4	5	3	7	4	6	6	5
Older:	5	1	9	6	4	4	10	7	4	10

Table 2.2 shows some of the calculations of the variance for the younger people. Notice that the sum of $(x_i - \bar{x})$, called the *sum of the residuals*, is equal to zero (all the negative values are counterbalanced by the positive ones). This is because of the way that the mean is calculated. Notice also that when each residual is squared it is positive. To get the variance we divide the sum of squared residuals (16.10) by the number of cases minus one (10 –1 = 9) and get 16.10/9 = 1.79.

In other sciences, much care is taken with the units of measurement. For example, physicists are very careful differentiating nine metres per second, which describes a velocity, from nine metres per second squared, which describes a *change* in velocity (an acceleration).

Social scientists sometimes are less careful about this, but it can be important. Consider the data in Table 2.2. The value for x_1 is four minutes. The residual is –0.7 minutes; adding or subtracting does not change that these values are in minutes (if it takes five minutes to preheat the oven, and 10 minutes to cook the pie, it takes 15 minutes in total). You cannot add or subtract items that do not have the same units (e.g., you cannot add five minutes to preheat the oven with two cups of sugar and get seven anything). The only time you can add together values with different units is when you can transform the units of one into the other. For example, 15 minutes to cook a cake plus 45 seconds to eat it, produces a total of: 15 minutes × 60 seconds/minute + 45 seconds = 945 seconds for the entire experience.

When a value is squared, so are the units. Items can be multiplied and divided even if they do not have the same units, as in miles travelled being divided by hours taken to achieve miles per hour. The squared residual of the first person is thus 0.49 minutes squared. Summing all these values does not change the units, so the sum of the squared residuals is 16.10 minutes squared. Dividing by $n -1$ (9) gives a variance of 1.79 minutes squared. The variance is a kind of average squared residual. This value gives information about the overall amount of spread, or variability, in the data.

If people are thinking about the spread of response times, it is difficult to think in terms of minutes squared. A measure that is closely related to the variance is the *standard deviation*. The standard deviation, denoted *sd*, is simply the square root of the variance.[2] By taking the square root the units return to minutes.

$$sd = \sqrt{var\,x_i} = \sqrt{\frac{\sum (x_i - \bar{x})^2}{n - 1}}$$

For the above data, the variance is 1.79 minutes squared and the standard deviation is 1.34 minutes. The standard deviation is a measure of how far away observations are from the mean in the same units (here minutes) of the original variable. On average, an observation falls 1.34 minutes from the mean. As you can see by the prior sentence, the standard deviation is much easier to interpret compared with the variance that reports the spread in terms of square units.

Because standard deviations are in the same units as the original variables they can be placed onto many graphs. The most common usage, showing standard deviation bars with means, is shown in the next section. Here, consider Figure 2.2. This is a DNA histogram of Figure 1.5 but with a bar showing the mean (the dot) and bars to show how many people are within one standard deviation of the mean. For most distributions there should be at least 50% of the cases within the standard deviation bars. For a particular type of distribution, the Normal distribution (discussed more in Chapter 5), two-thirds of the cases are within this region.

---

2 The square root is the opposite of squaring. For example, if we square 3 minutes we get 9 minutes squared (3 minutes × 3 minutes = 9 minutes squared). So, the square root of 9 minutes squared is 3 minutes. Both the variance and standard deviation will be positive.

OPTIONAL BOX 2.1

When calculating the variance and the standard deviation you have to square the difference between the mean and each individual value (i.e., the residuals). The reason for squaring this difference given in many textbooks is so that all of the values are positive. As said above, simply summing the residuals would make 0 because the positive and the negative values would balance each other. However, it would be much simpler just to take the absolute value (i.e., ignore any minus signs) and sum these as a measure of spread. In fact, this procedure pre-dates squaring the residuals and is known as the 'least absolute values' approach as compared with the 'least squares' approach. The 'least squares' approach caught on about 200 years ago because, when the analyses become more complex, it is much simpler computationally. In fact, it is only with recent computer advances that the 'least absolute values' approach can be used more widely.

   As only astute inquisitive students read 'optional' boxes, you will have noticed the word 'least' was added to the names of the two approaches and wondered why. Suppose you had a variable, say age_i and you wanted to find the value X which meant that $\Sigma(age_i - X)^2$ was as small as possible. It turns out that value is the mean. The mean is the value that makes the sum of the squared deviations from it the smallest. Now, suppose instead you wanted to find the value X which minimized $\Sigma|age_i - X|$, where $|x|$ means the absolute value of x (so $|3| = |\text{-}3| = 3$). It turns out the value that minimizes the sum of the absolute values is the median. When problems get more complex in future chapters, it turns out that the method of least squares has a pretty straightforward solution, but the method of least absolute values does not.

EXAMPLE: FUEL EFFICIENCY

Let's consider one more example. Companies building and people driving fuel-efficient automobiles are vital for controlling pollution levels and delaying the more cataclysmic consequences of global warming. We looked up fuel efficiencies on several new makes of cars, mostly produced in 2007, from the site http://www.fueleconomy.gov/feg/findacar.htm. Manufacturers of a few vehicles, like the Hummer H2, are not *required* to list their fuel efficiency because they are so large they are classified as heavy-duty vehicles. General Motors does not list it on their web page because they presumably do not think the consequences of global warming are that bad (why else would they make Hummers?). Various Hummer websites give estimates of about 10mpg. To give Hummer a tiny bit of credit, they have created a run-of-the-mill SUV, the H3, which has slightly better fuel efficiency. Anyway, we sampled the automobiles being bought in two fictitious

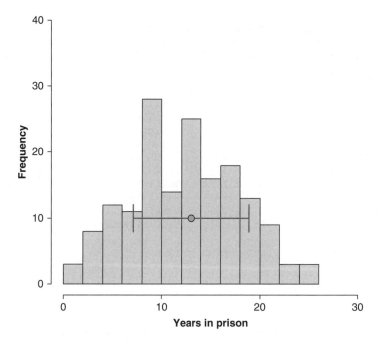

Figure 2.2 A histogram of the amount of time spent in prison before exoneration (like Figure 1.5) with the mean and standard deviation bars added. The circle is the mean and the bars go from one standard deviation below the mean to one standard deviation above the mean

towns, *Arnieville* and *Baltimore*. *Arnieville* has an odd mixture of people, some who buy automobiles specifically because of good fuel efficiency and some who buy automobiles that tend to have very poor fuel efficiency for unknown reasons, although Wainer's (2005: 94–95) 'penis substitution theory of automobile acquisition' (PEST) might be applicable. *Baltimore* has a mix of people, some nice, some less nice, and they buy a range of automobiles.

The mean mpg for *Arnieville* is:

$$\frac{63 + 39 + 33 + 31 + 26 + 21 + 18 + 15 + 11 + 10 + 13 + 13}{12} = \frac{293}{12} = 24.42 \; mpg$$

and for *Baltimore* is:

$$\frac{31 + 28 + 28 + 26 + 26 + 24 + 21 + 18 + 18 + 16 + 35 + 21}{12} = \frac{292}{12} = 24.33 \; mpg$$

Table 2.3 *Automobiles from two fictitious towns with their fuel efficiencies*

Arnieville automobiles	mpg	gp100m	*Baltimore* automobiles	mpg	gp100m
Honda Insight 2006	63	1.59	Ford Escape Hybrid 4WD	31	3.23
Toyota Camry Hybrid	39	2.56	Saturn Ion	28	3.57
Honda Fit	35	2.86	Toyota Camry	28	3.57
Hyundai Accent	33	3.03	Lexus GS 450h	26	3.85
Ford Focus	31	3.23	Volkswagen Passat	26	3.85
Mitsubishi Eclipse	26	3.85	Mercury Mariner FWD	24	4.17
Jaguar XK Convertible	21	4.76	Ford 500 AWD	21	4.76
Buick Rainier 2WD	18	5.56	Mazda CX-7 2WD	21	4.76
Mercedes-Benz SL65 AMG	15	6.67	BMW 550i	18	5.56
Jeep Grand Cherokee 2006	13	7.69	Chevy Trailblazer 4WD	18	5.56
Lamborghini Murcielago	11	9.09	Audi Q7	16	6.25
Hummer H2 2004	10	10.00	Jeep Grand Cherokee 2006	13	7.69

Notes: mpg = miles per gallon; gp100m = gallons per 100 miles.

So, the means in miles per gallon are approximately the same. This might give the false impression that the two towns have similar automobile buying behaviours. It appears from Table 2.3 that the values for *Arnieville* are more spread out than for *Baltimore*. The standard deviation for each town can be calculated by: (1) subtracting the mean from each value to get the residual, (2) squaring each of these residuals, (3) adding all these values together, (4) dividing by $n-1$ which in this case is 12-1 or 11, and finally (5) taking the square root of this value. For *Arnieville* the standard deviation is: 15.41 mpg; for *Baltimore* it is 5.74 mpg.

As shown in Figure 2.2, standard deviations can be placed onto graphs depicting means to show additional information. This is because, unlike the variance, they are in the same units as the original variable. This extra information is about the spread of the data. Figure 2.3 shows the means and the standard deviations for fuel efficiency for these two fictitious towns. This graph was done on the computer, but it can be made without a computer in six steps:

1 Draw a horizontal line and give a label for each group (here, *Arnieville* and *Baltimore*).
2 Draw a vertical line on the left of the graph. Label it and put some values on this axis. The values should go either from the minimum and maximum values attainable (here 0 mpg and there is no maximum possible) or from some value lower than the mean minus one standard deviation and the mean plus one standard deviation. As with other graphs, it is useful to use round numbers, so we go from 0 mpg to 50 mpg in 10mpg increments.
3 Draw a point where the mean is for each variable.

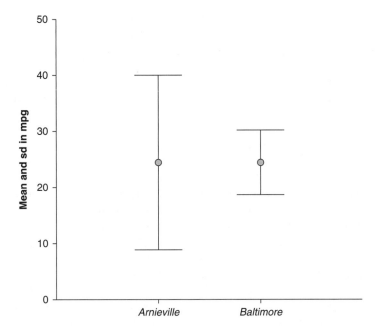

Figure 2.3   The mean fuel efficiency in miles per gallon (mpg) for automobiles from *Arnieville* and *Baltimore*. The bars show one standard deviation (sd) from the mean

4   Subtract the standard deviation of each group from that group's mean. Draw a short horizontal line at this point below the dot. This becomes the lower bound.
5   Add the appropriate standard deviation to each mean and draw a line above the point to make the upper bound.
6   Join these two bounds with a vertical line. The point for the mean should be exactly in the middle of this line.

TRANSFORMING DATA

One of the defining features of a science is that objects are measured. As such, there is much concentration on things like how to measure an attitude or intelligence, and we have stressed the importance of reporting your units. After the data have been collected it is often useful to transform the data either so it makes the data easier to understand (which often makes them more amiable to some of the assumptions of statistical tests discussed in later chapters) or so it changes the data into a form which is more useful for your purposes. The two main examples of this chapter provide examples for each of these.

The stem-and-leaf diagram of Figure 2.1 shows that distributions of tokens for Nim's use of his name and pronoun *Me* are *positively skewed*. This means that most of the values are on the lower end of the scale and there are a few values that are much higher. This is a common situation for many variables within psychology. For example, in testing how much time people take to solve a cognitive task, often a few people get very high scores, taking much longer than most to complete the task.

It is often beneficial to spread out the values at the bottom of the scale and lessen the differences at the top of the scale. Two common methods for positively skewed data like this are to take the square root of the values and to take the natural logarithm of the values. Here we will use the latter approach. The natural logarithm (often denoted *ln* or just *log*) is a mathematical function that is appropriate for values above zero.[3] Because Nim never used some tokens, we have added 0.5 to each value and then taken the natural logarithm. In equations: $\log Nim_i = \ln(Nim_i + 0.5)$. Figure 2.3 shows the effect of taking the logarithm of the values for the histogram for both these variables. Note that the scale changes. The important change is that the shape of the distribution looks more evenly spread. Tukey's (1977) *Exploratory Data Analysis* provides the most lucid rationale for using transformations, though his descriptions for making graphs and calculating some of the transformations are now dated.

It is worth looking specifically at the variable Me_i and its single extremely high value for *banana*. An important question is: what is the impact of this single value on the estimates of the mean and standard deviation? The mean with *banana* is 21.00 tokens, but this drops to 14.53 tokens when this outlier is excluded. The standard deviation is 32.47 tokens with this value, and 17.87 tokens without it. While the mean becomes about a third smaller, the standard deviation drops by about half. The fact that the standard deviation drops more than the mean has important consequences when we discuss inference in Chapter 5. For the logged variable log *Me*, the mean is 2.093 log-tokens. To return to the original units you to back-transform this value using the inverse of the earlier transformation. Here this means exponentiating the value ($e^{2.093}$) which is 8.11 and subtracting 0.5. Thus, the estimate for the centre of the distribution using this method (which many statisticians would prefer for skewed data) is 7.61 tokens. If *banana* is excluded from these calculations the estimate drops 6.38 tokens. Thus, the impact of this outlier is much less. Throughout this book we will describe other methods that can be used to lessen the impact

---

3 The $\ln(x)$ is the power to which the number e has to be raised to get x. e is a special number within mathematics (another special number is $\pi = 3.14$); e is approximately 2.72. If you square (which means taking to the power of 2) this value you get: $2.72^2 = 7.40$. Thus, $\ln(7.40) = 2$. This transformation pulls in high positive values. It does not work for negative values and is equal to negative infinity for 0, so if you have any cases with the value 0 it is common practice to add a small number, like 0.5, to each value before you log the variable. This small value is called a flattening constant.

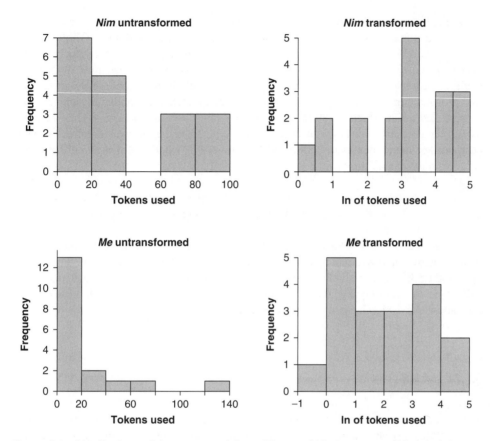

Figure 2.4   Distributions of the amount of times Nim used his own name (*Nim*) and the pronoun *Me*. The untransformed variables are shown to the left, their values after the ln(variable + 0.5) transformation are shown to the right

of outliers. It is important to realize that these methods are often still addressing the same questions as the traditional methods. They are used when traditional methods become less reliable.

For negatively skewed data, which are less common in psychology, the inverse transformations that are used for positively skewed data can be used. Thus, you can square a negatively skewed variable and this usually improves its shape. Similarly, you can exponentiate a variable. There are lots of other methods for transformations to improve the shape of the distribution, but this set is enough for most psychologists.

The second use of transformations is to change the variable into something more useful. The fuel-efficiency data were presented in miles per gallon (mpg) as is the standard in the

USA, the UK, and many other places. This would be the appropriate measurement if you had a certain amount of fuel and wanted to know how far you could travel. Think back to your childhood holidays. Did your mother say: 'We have 30 gallons, where shall we go?' Probably not. In France, fuel efficiency is measured in kilometres per litre. We will not make you completely adopt the French system, but would it make more sense to measure fuel efficiency in gallons per mile? This would equate with your mother saying: 'We are going to Lake Kita which is 100 miles away; how much will the fuel cost?' This is a more useful way to think about fuel efficiency. Table 2.3 shows the number of gallons it takes each of the automobiles to go 100 miles. The question is whether it makes a difference if we look at the data in this way.

Mean *Arnieville* = 5.48 gallons sd *Arnieville* = 2.74 gallons
Mean *Baltimore* = 4.33 gallons sd *Baltimore* = 1.05 gallons

If we assume that everybody has about 100 miles to drive each week, the average *Arnieville* resident uses a gallon more fuel than the average *Baltimore* resident. While there appeared no difference in fuel efficiency between the two fictitious towns using *mpg*, using gallons per 100 miles makes *Baltimore* appear the more efficient town. With this example, the gallons per 100 miles conclusion is more appropriate (Hand, 2004: 45).

SUMMARY

The mean and the standard deviation are two of the most important statistics for psychologists. Whenever you measure any variable you should be interested in where the centre of the distribution is and how spread out the distribution is. While the median and IQR, discussed in Chapter 1, are good measures of this, the mean and standard deviation are much more popular. They are reported in nearly every psychology article. For computational reasons they became the main statistics in the beginning of the twentieth century and many of the statistics designed for more complex problems with multiple variables can be viewed as extensions of these. Therefore, it is vital that you understand them and all introductory statistics books stress them.

The final two points are less often stressed. Many introductory statistics books wait until later chapters to talk about transformations or leave discussion of them out altogether. We decided to bring this topic up in Chapter 2 because transformations are an important tool for statistics and they help to introduce the idea of measurement. As far as units, we are surprised that psychologists seems less concerned about units than other scientists, particularly as many of the scientific concepts in which we are interested present many measurement issues. If you are doing physics, for example, the importance of reporting the correct units will likely be stressed from your first lecture (Tipler & Mosca, 2007: Ch. 1). Reporting the correct units keeps the reader aware of the meaning of any numbers that you present. Omitting the units will leave the numbers as dry uninformative numbers, which is why perhaps statistics courses often seem detached from the exciting discipline of what James (1890) described as 'the science of mental life, both of its phenomena and of their conditions'.

EXERCISES

2.1 Why is it important to report the units of measurement?

2.2 Can two values be added together if they are in different units? Give an example (not from the text) where they can, and an example (not from the text) where they cannot.

2.3 Can two values be added/multiplied together if they are in different units? Illustrate your answer with an example (not from the text).

2.4 Find an example in a recent newspaper of a mean people reported. Try not to use the sports section.

2.5 The median is to the IQR as the mean is to the _____ . Which statistic from this chapter fits best here and why? If you think two fit equally well, think why one may be better.

2.6 The DNA exoneration example from Chapter 1 showed 163 people who had been convicted of, and imprisoned for, horrendous crimes they did not commit. In total, they spent 2095 years in prison. What was the mean time each of these innocent people spent in prison?

2.7 Using the response time data presented earlier in this chapter, calculate the variance for the older group's response times. How does this compare with the variance of the younger group (see Table 2.2)? Which set of scores is more spread out? Why might this be the case?

2.8 Reeve and Aggleton (1998) were interested in people's memories for *The Archers*, a popular UK radio soap opera. Participants ($n = 48$, 12 in each of four conditions) were given one of two made-up scripts. One depicted a typical day, a visit to a livestock market. The other was of an atypical event (for the Archers), a visit to a boat show. Participants were either Archer novices or experts and were asked 22 questions about the script they were given. The

(Cont'd)

means and standard deviations for the experts were 15.08 (*sd* = 4.17) for the livestock market, 8.42 (*sd* = 2.11) for the boat show, and were 9.50 (*sd* = 4.48) and 8.42 (*sd* = 3.23), respectively, for the novices. Make an appropriate graph to display these results and comment on what they show.

2.9 Here are rainfall statistics for two cities:

	Sun	Mon	Tue	Wed	Thur	Fri	Sat
Toledo	0	0	1	6	0	0	0
Brighton	1	1	1	1	1	1	1

What are the means, the standard deviations, and variances of the rainfall for each of these two places? What do these tell you about the climates?

2.10 The noon temperatures in Toledo and Brighton for one week are listed below. Because the Toledo we refer to is the one in the US, and the Brighton is the one in the UK, they use degrees Fahrenheit and Celsius respectively.

	Sun	Mon	Tue	Wed	Thur	Fri	Sat	
Toledo	43	40	38	38	42	59	65	in °F
Brighton	8	10	10	14	8	9	11	in °C

Which place has the higher mean temperature? The following may be useful:

°C = 5/9 (°F − 32)

°F = 9/5 °C + 32

2.11 Schkade et al. (2000) collected data from jurors on 15 different cases. They ask for ratings of severity of the crime, on a 0 (no punishment) to 8 (extremely severe punishment) before jury deliberation and after jury deliberation. The values for each case are as given in Table 2.4.

Find the standard deviation and variances of these values. Speculate why any difference in standard deviation between before and after deliberation ratings might have occurred.

2.12 At the beginning of this book it was stated that 'it takes *about* 20 minutes to cook rice' is a statistical phrase. Suppose that you were hired to come up with the time to write on the side of the containers for spicy cheese bread and a vegetable stir-fry. With various different cooking arrangements in different climates and at different altitudes, you cooked these products to perfection. Here are the times, in minutes:

Table 2.4 *Severity ratings for 15 cases*

Case	Before severity	After severity
Reynolds	5.5	0.0
Glover	5.0	5.0
Lawson	4.3	4.5
Williams	5.0	5.0
Smith	5.5	6.0
Nelson	5.0	5.0
Hughes	5.0	5.0
West	4.5	5.0
Douglas	4.0	4.0
Crandall	4.0	4.0
Sanders	3.5	3.0
Windsor	3.0	2.0
Stanley	1.0	1.5
Stanley	1.0	1.5
Newton	0.0	0.0
Means	3.71	3.73

Spicy cheese bread:	8	15	12	16	11	8	14	9	12	15
Veggie stir-fry:	11	14	10	12	12	13	11	13	13	11

Which dish would you give the longer time to, and why? Think about the purpose of the estimate before giving your answer. Think about this both as a statistician and as a cook. The correct answer is not that they should have the same cooking time printed on the side of the box.

FURTHER READING

The graphing references from the last chapter are all applicable here.

Douglas Altman and Martin Bland have written many clear and focused (i.e., short) articles to help medical researchers understand statistics and these have appeared over the last decade in the *British Medical Journal* (your university computer may have access on www.bmj.com, but are also on Professor Bland's webpage, http://www-sers.york. ac.uk/~mb55/pubs/pbstnote.htm). For example:

Bland, J.M., & Altman, D.G. (1996). Transformations, means, and confidence intervals. *British Medical Journal, 312*, 1079.

Measurement is a difficult topic and one which is related to statistics. To be a scientist you have to have some measurement theory about your objects of investigation. We assume that most of you have either taken a methodology course where some of these issues are covered or are concurrently taking one. Your textbook for this course will provide an introduction to measurement. Therefore we suggest an excellent book on measurement, but one aimed at students who already have some grasp of the basics.

Hand, D.J. (2004). *Measurement Theory and Practice: The World Through Quantification.* London: Arnold.

3

Univariate Statistics 3: Proportions and Bar Charts

The first two chapters introduced you to statistical and graphical techniques which are appropriate when the variables are measuring something that has a scale, like years spent in prison or income. The focus of this chapter is on what are called categorical variables. These are variables which do not have some underlying scale. We introduce two examples of categorical data to show how to calculate proportions and odds. There is much discussion about *levels of measurement* in psychology and we examine two ways in which this framework can be used. The final part of this chapter describes the bar chart, which is a popular and useful method for graphing categorical data, and we also show some examples of bad graphs.

CALCULATING PROPORTIONS: WITCHES AND SCIENCE

What Type of Woman is Accused of Being a Witch?

Witchcraft is studied within many disciplines and seems like it should be of great interest within psychology. During certain historical periods people (mostly women) were accused of witchcraft and sentenced by hoards of people believing their crimes. Parallels can be drawn to present-day cultures where often the populace jumps on bandwagons to point their fingers of guilt towards people without evaluating the evidence or being against some scientific findings because your campaign financers do not like the answer.

Carol Karlsen's (1987) *The Devil in the Shape of a Woman* is a detailed look at the hysteria surrounding witches in colonial New England. The most famous of these were the Salem outbreaks, but there were others in New England (and in others places, including some still occurring).[1] Karlsen recorded the marital status of those accused (from her Table 9): 51 single, 38 widowed, 4 divorced/deserted and 148 married. Marital status is a categorical variable. People can be placed in one of the categories and it is difficult to think of a scale that underlies this variable. That is, we can count up the number of people falling into each category but we cannot assign numerical values to the different categories (e.g., that single is more than widowed which is more than divorced, etc.).

An appropriate univariate statistic for categorical data are the proportions in each of the categories. A proportion is the number of people in that category divided by the total number of people in the whole sample. The total number of people in the sample, usually labelled *n*, is: 51 + 38 + 4 + 148 = 241. The proportions for these categories are:

Single:	51/241	0.21
Widowed:	38/241	0.16
Divorced:	4/241	0.02
Married:	148/241	0.61

---

1 A disturbing experience of contemporary humanity is walking into the Salem Witch Museum and seeing their shop of gifts and souvenirs (see http://secure.salemwitchmuseum.com/shop/). Human beings were hanged by other humans for being witches. Killing 'witches' is a grotesque and repeated stain on human history and yet it is trivialized to such an extent by our ultra-consumerism that you can buy shot glasses commemorating it. Maybe we are being overly sensitive, but imagine if the museum curators of Dachau, Auschwitz, Hiroshima etc. took such an approach (for comparison, see http://www.kz-gedenkstaette-dachau.de/englisch/content/index.htm, http://www.auschwitz.org.pl/ and http://www.pcf.city.hiroshima.jp/top_e.html).

The total of all the proportions should add up to 1, so $0.21 + 0.16 + 0.02 + 0.61 = 1.00$, although sometimes the sum is slightly different because of rounding, so if you get 1.01 or 0.99 do not worry. The category with the largest proportion is called the *mode*. Here the mode is for married women, and is 0.61. This means the most frequently occurring category of marital status in these accused witches was married.

Proportions are related to probabilities. Proportions are the observed values, so 148 of the 241 in the sample, or 0.61 or 61%, are married. Probabilities refer to some underlying values in the whole population. The demographic data for the general population of colonial New England are not as accurate as modern data from the census, but from Karlsen (1987) we estimate that about 75% of all the adult women were married. Therefore, if we knew nothing about an adult colonial woman, picked at random from the entire population, we would say the probability of her being married was about 75%. If we sampled a large number of women who we expected to be typical with respect to marital status then we would predict to observe a proportion of about 75% in that sample. This is the basis of much of the statistics covered in this book, and is talked about in detail in the next chapter and in the remaining chapters. Here, the observed proportion was only 61% which suggests that unmarried women stand a higher probability of being accused of witchcraft than married women (and this imbalance exists for men also).

It is worth noting that sometimes proportions are written as .61, 0.61 (which is more common in the UK), and 61%. The important thing is that you remain consistent within any single assignment so that you do not confuse your readers.

An alternative statistic to proportions is the odds. The observed *odds* of a response are the number of people with that response divided by all the people without that response. Thus, there were 51 married women and in total 241 women, and therefore $241-251 = 190$ unmarried women. The odds of being married is $51/190 = 0.27$. If the proportion is 0.50, the odds will be 1.00, and if the proportion is greater than 0.50 the odds will be greater than 1.00. The odds of being married in this sample is 1.59. Here are the odds for each category:

	Odds	
Single:	51/190 = 0.27	A proportion of 0.50 equates
Widowed:	38/203 = 0.19	with an odds of 1.00
Divorced:	4/237 = 0.02	
Married:	148/93 = 1.59	

A couple of aspects of the odds need to be considered. First, although odds may seem a less intuitive statistic than proportion, it has better statistical properties than proportions and therefore more advanced statistics for categorical data tend to build on the odds rather than the proportion. Second, the word 'odds' is used both for the observed value in the sample, and for the population estimate. This is different from the proportion which can be differentiated from the population probability.

Table 3.1   *What comes to mind when science is mentioned data (Gaskell et al., 1993) (n = 2099)*

	Frequency	Proportions	Odds
Physical science	774	0.37	0.58
Life science	625	0.30	0.42
Technology	302	0.14	0.17
Environmental science	222	0.11	0.12
Social science	80	0.04	0.04
Other/Don't know	96	0.05	0.05

What Comes to Mind when Science is Mentioned?

Gaskell and colleagues (1993) asked $n = 2099$ people in the UK 'what comes to mind when science is mentioned?' and these are listed in Table 3.1. Here 774 people said something to do with the physical sciences came to mind. This is the highest frequency and therefore 'physical science' is the mode. This is the most common response, but it does not mean that most of the people said it. It only means that more people said this than any of the other responses. The proportion that gave this response is $774/2099 = 0.37$. When reporting the mode it is almost always advisable also to report the proportion for that modal value. The odds is $774/(2099-2774) = 0.58$. The other proportions and odds are calculated in the same way as above.

LEVELS OF MEASUREMENT (LoM)

Levels of Measurement (LoM) is a controversial topic. While there exists a real debate among methodologists about the importance of LoM, none of the experts agrees with the Draconian approach often advocated in textbooks. The traditional textbook approach, which is derived from work by mathematical psychologists, describes how LoM underpins which statistical tests are *meaningful* in different situations. *Meaningful* as it is used here is a statistical word and basically means consistent with some assumptions of the data and the rules of measurement. The standard textbook description is more inflexible than most mathematical psychologists support. We present it in an extreme form, but one which is common in textbooks. The second approach to LoM, which we label as pragmatic, is more often argued by statisticians and is what most researchers implicitly use. According to this view while it is important to think about the meaning of the data (and most of these people would agree that LoM is a good framework for doing this), the scientist should not be prevented from using some statistical test if they believe it may help to uncover interesting patterns in the data. The two approaches agree on one thing, hence the identical sentences to start these sections.

The Traditional Textbook Approach

Stevens (1946) introduced the notion of levels of measurement (LoM) over 60 years ago and it has become the cornerstone of the way most psychologists are taught statistics. LoM is a simple framework that helps tell people which statistical procedures 'can legitimately be applied to empirical data' (p. 677). Stevens (1968) described several levels but the three that are the focus of most psychology statistics textbooks are interval, ordinal and categorical (or nominal). Through detailed application of axioms of measurement theory, Stevens showed that statistics like the mean require that the variable has certain qualities. Suppose you asked somebody: 'How much do you despise Manchester United [replace "Manchester United" with "the Yankees" if that makes more sense]?' and gave them a scale like this:

   1   2   3   4   5   6   7

Only a little   Immensely

Stevens showed that in order for the mean to have appropriate measurement properties, the distance between 2 and 3 must be the same as between 3 and 4. Basically, any difference of size 1 needs to have the same psychological meaning anywhere on the scale. If a variable has this property then it is *interval*.

Every psychology statistics book gives some sort of definition like this, and every psychology methods book points out that it is very unlikely that the psychological distances between these points are actually equal. The methods books note that circling 4 means more hatred than 3, which means more than 2, but that it is difficult to say how much more hatred, and therefore it is not possible to say that these distances are exactly the same. Many describe different types of scaling that people have devised to try to meet these properties (e.g., Coombs et al., 1970: Ch. 2, but also in most psychology methods books), but these are much less common than simple rating scales like the one shown above. If all we can say about the points on the scale is that 4 is higher than 3 (and that all the others are in order too), then we have *ordinal* data. Stevens showed that the median is an appropriate statistic in these circumstances. Curiously, although most of the methods books state how we should be cautious treating any psychological variable as interval, most of the statistics books describe mostly techniques that require, according to this framework, interval data and spend little time on those appropriate for ordinal data. This discrepancy is why we describe an alternative approach of using LoM below and also why we present more statistical tests based on the median than most textbooks.

Some variables, like marital status and types of science from previous examples in this chapter, do not have any underlying scale on which we can compare. In most senses it is not possible to say being single is higher than being widowed or that social science is higher than technology. In these cases neither the mean nor the median should be used.

The textbooks say that the researcher is limited to reporting proportions, odds and statistics based on these variables. They are called either categorical or nominal.

In summary:

> interval data $\rightarrow$ mean
>
> ordinal data $\rightarrow$ median
>
> categorical $\rightarrow$ proportions

For interval data, you can also calculate the median and the proportions of certain values. For ordinal data, you can also calculate the proportions of certain values. People often talk about interval data as being a higher level of measurement than categorical, with ordinal data in between. If data are at a higher level, statistics appropriate for lower levels can be used, but the opposite is not true. According to the LoM framework you should not use statistics designed for higher levels. What we dislike about this approach is that it is often taught as inflexible. The poor researcher, knowing that the data are not truly interval, is filled with guilt as he or she calculates the mean, fearful that the LoM Police may swoop down.

An important aspect of this framework (and the univariate statistics that are appropriate for each of these levels) is that more complex statistics have been developed based on the mean, median and proportion, and so the LoM has to be considered when conducting any statistical procedure. Most of these procedures have been developed for the mean and proportion, not the median. This brings us back to the dilemma that the methods textbooks suggest that few variables are truly interval, but the statistics textbooks focus on statistics for interval data. While Stevens did discuss levels between ordinal and interval, as Abelson and Tukey (1959) noted, most variables are probably between these levels. An alternative way to approach the measurement of variables is now described.

A Pragmatic Approach to Measurement

Stevens (1946) introduced the notion of levels of measurement (LoM) over 60 years ago and it has become the cornerstone of the way most psychologists are taught statistics. It is an easy way to structure courses and textbooks. However, since its introduction it has been criticized by many statisticians and methodologists (e.g., Velleman & Wilkinson, 1993). The mathematics in Stevens's framework is sound and even anticipated future mathematical developments (Hand, 2004). It is necessary, however, to avoid the rigidity of the textbook approach. We should look to LoM to guide rather than dictate the statistics we use. Tukey described this best: LoM does 'not control which statistics may "sensibly" be used, but only which ones may "puristically" be used' (1986: 244). If the purpose of statistics is about discovering patterns in data, then it seems wrong to be restricted on which statistics can be used. That said, we should be guided by measurement considerations.

The pragmatist asks how the choice of tests may affect the results. The choice between the mean and the median, described in the first two chapters, provides a good example. The traditional textbook approach is that the mean is only appropriate for interval data, but that the median can be used for interval or ordinal data. A pragmatist would ask how each statistical test may be influenced by the measurement. For example, many variables have extreme values. If you are doing a survey of people's incomes, a very high income will have a large impact on the mean but a much smaller impact on the median. While in some situations researchers want extreme points to be highly influential, at other times they do not and would therefore use the median.

Mean   highly influenced by extreme points

Median   not highly influenced by extreme points

Extreme points are usually fairly rare. Therefore, the mean is more influenced by these rare occurrences than is the median. We say the median is *robust* because these rare occurrences do not alter its value as much. Several more robust statistics are discussed in later chapters.

Pragmatism does not mean anything goes. All researchers agree that there is a fundamental distinction between variables that have some underlying mapping onto a scale (so, the typical attitude scale) and variables that do not (categorical variables, like, what is your favourite brand of coffee?).

In summary, the pragmatic view asks if treating the variable in a certain way can be informative in understanding relationships in the data. However, it is important that any researcher does not perform (or at least report) tests that are either uninformative or mis-informative. Rather than using LoM as something that restricts what is mathematically acceptable, LoM can be used to guide what is likely to be most informative. The LoM debate has at times been hostile, so it is worth stressing that those who advocate a more purist application of LoM still do not support the rigid textbook approach. For example:

> for this 'illegal' statisticalizing there can be invoked a kind of pragmatic sanction: In numerous instances it leads to fruitful results ... we should proceed cautiously with our statistics, and especially with the conclusions we draw from them. (Stevens, 1946: 679)[2]

Most methodologists would be happy with the statistician's use of means in Box 3.1 because, although the actual numbers have not changed, the meaning imposed on them has changed and hence their level of measurement has changed. To make conclusions 'meaningful', at least to some extent, the researcher needs to argue that the variable can be conceived of at the level of data appropriate for the statistics conducted. This of course is a risky strategy, because others can argue against you. But, if you have found interesting patterns in your data, then those will exist regardless of the level of measurement.

---

2 It would be historically inaccurate to paint Stevens as somebody making it harder for psychologists to conduct statistics legitimately. Prior to Stevens much of the theory of measurement was by physicists, many of whom did not feel psychological variables could be measured. Stevens' framework shows how they can fit within a measurement theory.

Box 3.1   The Level of Measurement depends on the Situation

Frederic Lord did some of the most important work on what is now called *item response theory*. In English, this is how to construct standardized tests and how to use people's responses to calculate scores. He also wrote about some catalysts to different student uprisings in his university. Lord (1953) described two fetishes Professor X had with numbers (think which professor in your department seems most like Prof. X?). First, she sold 'football numbers' to students (the students may have been odd also). The football numbers on the backs of players' shirts are usually thought of as just categorical, not forming a scale, and in fact this was the first example Stevens (1946) provided for categorical data. Professor X's second fetish was to collect ordinal data, but then calculate means on these data. While she performed her first fetish in public, much to the delight of her students, she hid in a darkened room, behind locked doors away from the LoM Police (would Fox be interested in 'LoM Police: Miami'?), to perform the unsightful (though strangely gratifying) task of calculating means on ordinal data.

Then her worlds collided. She sold her numbers to both first- and second-year students. Second-year students mocked their younger colleagues for having smaller numbers, and the freshers began a campaign of civil unrest. Professor X told the local press that the number sales were random. Could she be wrong, and how could she tell? She went to a statistician friend who promptly calculated the means by adding the numbers and dividing by the number of numbers. Professor X exclaimed 'You can't add them', to which the statistician retorted 'Oh, can't I? I just did.' Professor X, now furious at the statistician's behaviour, yelled, 'Why, they aren't even ordinal scores.' To justify his apparently anti-social behaviour the statistician said, 'The numbers don't know that [they are categorical] … since the numbers don't remember where they came from, they always behave just the same way, regardless.' After much introspection and playing with her numbers, Professor X unlocked her door and accepted the statistician's explanation.

The moral of this story is not that if you get too involved with statistics you develop strange fetishes (we have better stories to show this). The moral is the choice of using, for example, a mean versus a median, depends not just on the data, but on the research question posed. When the first- and second-year students began quibbling about who had higher scores, a fairly legitimate way to answer this question is which group had the higher mean. This was despite 'football numbers' being a common textbook example for a categorical-level variable. The attribute of interest had changed, and with it the LoM.

MAKING BAR CHARTS

Note: This section should be read in conjunction with the paper *Producing Bad Results Sections,* which is reprinted as an appendix. That paper describes the philosophy of producing clear graphs. In this section we describe how to produce these.

Bar charts are one of the main graphical techniques to display categorical data in both the scientific literature and popular magazines. In this section we describe how to make one properly and then show how a good chart can be ruined by technology. We draw directly on Wainer (1984), Wright and Williams (2003) and on the writing of Tufte (see www.edwardtufte.com).

The following data come from the UK on the first destination of employment of psychology graduate students (see Wright & Williams, 2003, for details).

Teaching/lecturing	3.8%
Psychologist	4.9%
Marketing, sales, retail	13.5%
Administration/management	18.0%
Social, welfare, health	24.2%
Clerical, secretarial	24.6%
Other	10.7%

Bar charts look similar to histograms, but for categorical data. The first choice is whether to have a vertical or a horizontal one. Examples of these are shown in Figures 3.1 and 3.2. We will go through in detail how to make 3.1 by hand and then describe it.

Making a Bar Chart

1   Order the values from lowest to highest (or highest to lowest), with any odd categories like 'other' and 'don't know' at the end.
2   Draw a horizontal line at the bottom of the graph and mark off enough bins for all the values. There are seven values for this variable, so these have been marked off and we have put the first letter of each below where the bar will be. Label the axis with the variable's name (here, 'Job Destinations'). We are doing this in Word, but it can be done with pen, paper, and also a ruler.
3   Add a vertical axis. It should start at zero and go higher than the highest observed percentage. The highest observed percentage for this variable is 24.6%, so we will go to 30%. Label enough of the values to make it easy for the reader (we label, 0%, 10%, 20% and 30%). Because the values are in percentages, write 'Percentages' as a label for this axis. A variation of this is to use the observed frequencies rather than percentages.
4   Create bars up to the height of the observed value for each category. Here we have placed an X for every two percentage points, so this involves rounding the observed values to: 4%, 4%, 14%, 18%, 24%, 24% and 10%. An alternative is drawing a line at the appropriate height and making a box.

Figure 3.1 is not particularly pleasing to the eye nor is it as useful as it could be. While very nice diagrams can be drawn by hand (Playfair, 2005 [1801]) or using expensive publishing software, most statistics packages allow publication-quality graphics to be produced. The two main problems with Figure 3.1 are that you have to look up what the value labels mean,

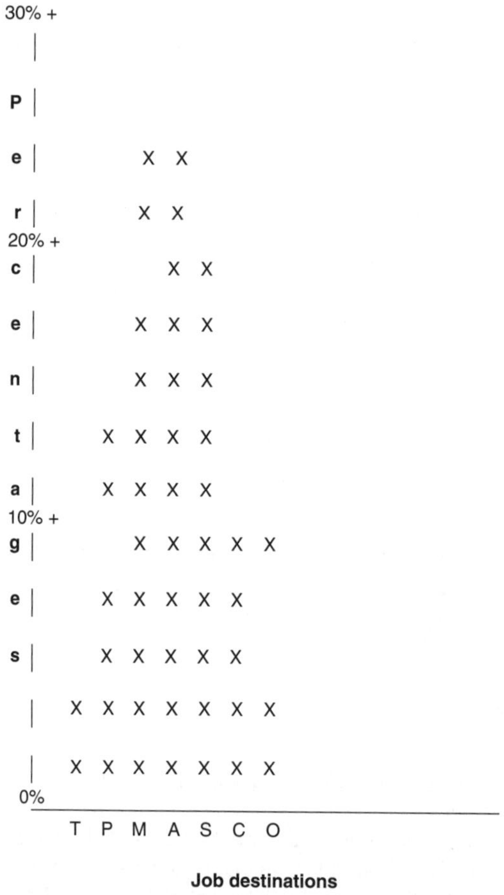

```
30% +
     |

P |

e |            X   X

r |            X   X
20% +
c |                X   X

e |            X   X   X

n |            X   X   X

t |        X   X   X   X

a |        X   X   X   X
10% +
g |            X   X   X   X   X

e |        X   X   X   X   X

s |        X   X   X   X   X

  |    X   X   X   X   X   X   X

  |    X   X   X   X   X   X   X
0%
       T   P   M   A   S   C   O
```

Job destinations

Figure 3.1   A bar chart showing the destinations of psychology studies. The procedure to make this by hand is described in the text. This particular graph was made in Word. Statistical packages have procedures to make these look better

and having to round to every 2% may mean that useful information is lost. Figure 3.2 addresses these. We feel this provides ample information for the reader. This is made with the statistics package SYSTAT, but all statistics packages have bar chart procedures. However, the default graphs made with most statistics packages are not good. So it is important that you are prepared to make changes to these so that they are clear and accurate.

Let us go through one more example, for the science data (Gaskell et al., 1993). Figures 3.3 and 3.4 show two versions of this. Often bar charts are done with frequencies rather than percentages. The point of showing these is to stress the problem of pressing the 3D button on your graphics package. The same information is shown in these two figures, but in Figure 3.4 worthless information has been added: a false

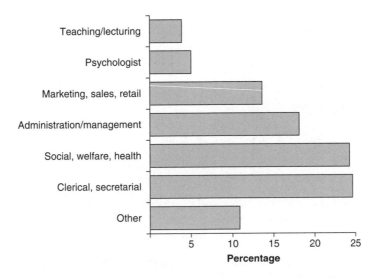

Figure 3.2   A bar chart made with a statistics computing package (SYSTAT) showing the destination of psychology students. The bar chart is horizontal which allows value labels to be easily included within the graph

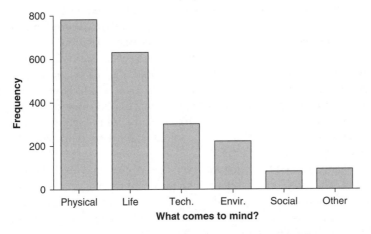

Figure 3.3   A bar chart of the numbers of people responding to different categories for 'What comes to mind' when science is mentioned. The data were calculated from Gaskell et al. (1993)

third dimension. This is at best a waste of ink and is likely to make the graph more difficult to read. Many graphics packages include this repulsive option. Wallgren and colleagues (1996: 71) suggest this is included because it 'symbolize[s] the triumph of data technology' over thought. We think it was included because some deranged

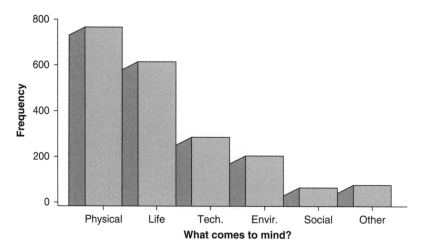

Figure 3.4 A heinous graph. A 'false' third dimension, which adds no further information, has been added to the graph in Figure 3.3. This third dimension can easily confuse the reader

computer scientist wanted to impress his boss with the marvels of computer science rather than for any scientific purpose. When we politely criticize people for adding a false dimension to a graph, they often tell us it looks 'pretty'. 'Pretty' does not count. Information, clarity and accuracy count. 'Pretty' is fine providing these other three are fulfilled, but this and all false 3D graphs are not even 'pretty'. They are repugnant. If we were not so polite, we would ask, at the end of a talk by one of these 'pretty' people, what the third dimension represents. The person would have to admit that it meant nothing and that they were just trying to impress you that they can press the 3D button on the computer package. Yeah, like we'd be impressed. A lot of you probably are not as polite as us, so go and ask people this question. This will improve how the person makes graphs in the future.

You have probably noticed that we have several pet peeves, and one is false 3D graphs. There are lots of other ways that graphs can be made uninformative, unclear and inaccurate. Wainer (1984) and Wright and Williams (2003) described many of these. In general, look at your graphs and ask yourself: 'Is this the best way to communicate the information clearly and accurately?' Make sure that all the information you want to display is displayed, and that no part of the graph is uninformative.

In summary, graphs can be used both to explore data (*exploratory data analysis* or EDA) and to display information to others (*data display*). The steadfast goal for both of these is:

> *Graphs are for presenting information/data as clearly and as*
> *accurately as possible. Their purpose is not to be artistic,*
> *though a good graph has its artistic appeal.*

SUMMARY

The first two chapters described some univariate statistics and graphs that are appropriate when your variable measures some kind of scale. Here, univariate statistics (proportions, odds and the mode) and a graph (the bar chart) were presented when your variable is categorical. The proportion is the number of cases with that value divided by the total number of cases. The odds is the number of cases with that value divided by the number of cases that do not have that value. The mode is the category with the most cases. A bar chart is the main graphical technique used with categorical data.

We also described one framework for distinguishing types of data: the levels of measurement (LoM). This is a controversial framework. Part of the reason for this controversy is that people differ on how they define key words like data, meaningful and measurement. LoM was developed with precise definitions of these, and if the meanings of these key phrases are changed, this use of the framework also changes. We think the greater cause of disagreement about LoM is, however, due to the rigid way in which it is described in some textbooks. We describe a more flexible way of using LoM.

EXERCISES

3.1 What is the difference between proportions and odds, and when might you use each?

3.2 What is the mode? Does the mode need to have more than 50% of the data?

3.3 According to LoM, what levels of measurement are most associated with the following statistics: the mean, the median, the IQR, the mode, proportions and standard deviations? Not all of these were mentioned in the text, so you will have to think about some of these.

3.4 What is the difference between a bar chart and a histogram?

3.5 The town we grew up in had a small sandwich shop with five choices: cheese, chicken, roast vegetables, ham and egg. One lunchtime we sat there doing *participant observation*. This involved eating sandwiches (and ice-cream) for two hours straight so not to look conspicuous and recording what other people were ordering. Not including our own food, here are the sandwiches that people ordered:

13 people had cheese

23 people had chicken

 8 people had roast vegetables

 4 people had ham

14 people had egg

(Cont'd)

What statistic or statistics would you use to describe these data? What are their values?

3.6 Make a bar chart of the data in Exercise 3.5.

3.7 According to the FBI, there were 7163 reported hate crimes in 2005 in the United States (http://www.fbi.gov/ucr/hc2005/table1.htm). Three had multiple biases. Of the remaining 7160, there were 3919 motivated by race, 1227 motivated by religion, 1017 motivated by sexual orientation, 944 motivated by ethnicity/nationality, and 53 motivated by disability. Create a bar chart based on these data. What proportion of the hate crimes were motivated by religion? What are the odds of a hate crime being religiously motivated?

3.8 From the FBI webpage (http://www.fbi.gov/ucr/ucr.htm#cius) find a table with categorical data. Create a bar chart for these data.

3.9 Go to a parking lot, and record the colour of the first 100 cars. What is the most common colour of car of these 100? What is its proportion and odds?

📖 FURTHER READING

The references from Chapter 1 on graphing also apply here, as does Hand (2004).

Levels of measurement papers include:

Stevens, S.S. (1946). On the theory of scales of measurement. *Science*, *103*, 677–680.
A poor photocopy is on http://www.murraystate.edu/polcrylst/Stevens.pdf. This provides background to LoM and explains it fairly well.

Velleman, P.F., & Wilkinson, L. (1993). Nominal, ordinal, interval, and ratio typologies are misleading. *American Statistician*, *47*, 65–72.
Available on http://www.spss.com/research/wilkinson/Publications/Stevens.pdf. Velleman and Wilkinson argue against using LoM.

Reese, R. CA. (2007). Bah! Bar charts. *Significance*, *4*, 41–44. Allen Reese has a number of nice short papers in the journal *Significance*.
This is a journal of the Royal Statistical Society, but the papers are readable for a general audience (see www.rss.org.uk).

4

Sampling and Allocation

The previous three chapters dealt with what are often called *descriptive* statistics. Included in these are the measures of central tendency and variability which are important in describing the distribution of a variable. In addition, the importance of graphing the data to provide more information about the distributions was stressed. In short, descriptive statistics and graphs tell us about the shape, average and spread of the data. These procedures provide the core for doing most of the statistics in this book. From Chapter 5 onward these statistics will be used to *build inferential* statistics. Inferential statistics are used when you are trying to infer something about the entire population of interest from just the sample used in your study. These are the two main branches of statistics: descriptive and inferential. Descriptive statistics summarize the findings observed in our sample. Inferential statistics allow us to use these descriptive statistics to infer (hence inferential) characteristics about an entire population. Sampling and allocations are the key concepts for bridging these two branches of statistics.

Because this is a statistics book, rather than a methodology book, the focus is mostly on statistical techniques. However, two topics usually covered in methodology books are so vital for statistics that we are going to take a quick detour from purely statistical issues and look at these methodology topics: sampling participants and allocating them to conditions. We describe methods for good samples and good allocation, and also describe the possible consequences when these procedures are not used. We have written this chapter in a more 'methods style' than a 'statistical style'. This means it focuses more on conceptual issues and – we hope that none of you mind – there are no equations. After three chapters with several equations, and even more to follow in later chapters, most of you will not mind a break.

GOLD STANDARDS

A few preliminary definitions are worth making here (some are repeated from Chapter 1). First, a *population* is the entire set of people or items (or anything) for which the researcher wants her/his study to be applicable. When you investigate a research question, you have in mind a population for which your results should hold. Sometimes you would want your results to hold for all humans or all inhabitants of a country, but sometimes the population is smaller. For example, you might only be interested in people with Korsakoff's syndrome or members of a particular street gang.

Sampling is the process by which cases are chosen from a population. In social sciences, usually it is assumed that people are the cases being sampled, but other types of cases are possible. Below we sample pizza toppings. The *sample* is the resulting set of people chosen, the outcome of the sampling procedure. *Allocation* (sometimes called *assignment*) is the process by which people in the sample are assigned to conditions. Sampling and allocating are the processes; the sample and the conditions are the outcomes.

The hope is usually that the sample is *representative* of the population and that the people in each condition are representative of the sample. Representative means that the characteristics of the sample are similar to those of the population. Thus, you would not want your sampling procedure to produce a sample of people all over 6 feet (1.82m) tall if the mean height in the population of interest was 5 feet 6 inches (1.68m). Similarly, if your sample was about half males and half females, you would not want one of the conditions to be all of one gender. Good sampling and allocation procedures increase the likelihood that the sample is representative of the population and that the conditions are representative of the sample.

To illustrate the importance of sampling and allocation, let us suppose that we are health psychologists interested in alcohol consumption on college campuses. In order to get information on how we should target alcohol awareness classes, we decide to examine whether drinking behaviour differs in males and females. To sample, we decide to give an alcohol survey to females enrolled in an upper-level 8:00am nursing class. Then we give our

Process		Sampling	Allocation
Outcome	Population $\longrightarrow$	Sample $\longrightarrow$	Conditions

Figure 4.1   Sampling is done to select a subset of the population to be in the sample. In experimental research this sample is then allocated conditions

survey to males at 11:00am who are sitting in the food court area of the university. We find our female sample reported drinking far less alcohol compared to our male group. Can you think of other factors that might have driven these findings besides simply the person's gender?

Most methodology and statistics books lay down firm rules on exactly how sampling and random allocation should be carried out. Statistical tests assume that these are done in particular ways. While we describe these 'gold standards' of sampling and allocation, we also note they are often not used even in very good research. We will discuss when certain aspects of these rules are critical and when they become less critical.

Besides assisting in your own endeavours, a good knowledge of sampling and allocation issues is a great asset for evaluating the work of others. Often people describe their research as if they have used the 'gold standard' when in fact they have not. This allows the astute reader to question whether the deficiencies are detrimental to the study or not.

Sampling and allocation can be divided into two stages in the typical study (see Figure 4.1): first, deciding on a sample from the population and then, if appropriate, allocating people from this sample to the different conditions. For example, if we compared weight gain among girls hospitalized with anorexia who received Treatment 1 versus Treatment 2, the experimental conditions are Treatments 1 and 2. Our population is all girls hospitalized for anorexia. Our sample is the particular group we selected and then allocated to receive either Treatment 1 or Treatment 2. In non-experimental or correlational studies, the allocation step is not used. We will discuss these stages separately and refer to the first as *sampling* and the second as *allocation*.

SAMPLING

The 'Gold Standard' for Sampling

The 'gold standard' is that the participants are sampled at *random* from the population. The word 'random' is critical here. The English dictionary definition of 'random' is usually something like 'without aim or purpose or principle' (Allen, 1985: 613). In any science, certain terms that have perfectly adequate definitions for everyday life are given more precise

Table 4.1 *Pizza combinations. The first column shows all possible pizza combinations. The second is where all toppings have an equal probability of being picked, but random sampling from these pizzas will not be a simple random sample of the toppings. The third column shows the possible samples for a vegetarian (there would be only three toppings in the population). The final column lists the possible samples from a quota sample where one of the toppings has to be meat. It is worth noting that the order of the toppings is irrelevant: mushrooms & pepper is the same as pepper & mushrooms*

All possible combinations (equally possible with SRS)	All toppings equally likely	Vegetarian samples	One meat quota samples
Mushrooms & pepper	Mushrooms & peppers	Mushrooms & pepper	Mushrooms & pepperoni
Mushrooms & olives	Peppers & olives	Mushrooms & olives	Mushrooms & sausage
Mushrooms & pepperoni	Olives & pepperoni	Pepper & olives	Pepper & pepperoni
Mushrooms & sausage	Pepperoni & sausage		Pepper & sausage
Pepper & olives	Sausage & mushrooms		Olives & pepperoni
Pepper & pepperoni			Olives & sausage
Pepper & sausage			
Olives & pepperoni			
Olives & sausage			
Pepperoni & sausage			

meanings. In statistics and methodology, 'random' means that each possible sample is equally likely to be chosen. Sometimes this is referred to as a *simple random sample* (SRS). As most statistical techniques assume that this has been done, we will describe exactly what it is, why it is an important assumption for the statistical techniques used in behavioural sciences, what alternatives exist, and what possible problems there are with the alternatives.

First, we will describe in more detail what an SRS is and what it is not. It will be easiest to do this by using an example with a small population, say five items. These items might be your siblings, your professors, or many other things.

We grew up together in the southern Italian town of Salerno and our local pizza outlet had five possible toppings: mushrooms, peppers, olives, sausage and pepperoni. So, the population is the five toppings. It also had a special price for large pizzas with any two toppings and even as young methodologists we were frugal. We carefully calculated that this was a good deal and always got it. We need to decide which two toppings to order. Stated another way, our sampling procedure involves choosing two toppings from a population of five. If we were going to take an SRS then any of the 10 combinations shown in the first column of Table 4.1 would be equally likely to be chosen. Since there are 10 possible combinations, each has a probability of 1 in 10, or a 10% chance, of being chosen if we sampled at random.

The word *probability* is tricky. There are entire books written about what it means and even experts disagree. Here it means that in the long run, after hundreds or thousands of trials (yum-yum!), each one of those 10 possible combinations would be ordered approximately one-tenth of the time. This is referred to as the frequentist meaning of probability (Dienes, 2008).

The important aspect of an SRS is that it tells us some likely characteristics about the samples. We would expect mushrooms to be on the pizza about 40% of the time. Also, we would expect a vegetarian pizza about 30% of the time. This is because, of the 10 possible pizzas, four have mushrooms and three are suitable for vegetarians (assuming vegetarian cheese is used). The word *about* is also important. If 1000 pizzas with two toppings were ordered (i.e., if 1000 SRS samples of size 2 were taken), we would not expect exactly 300 (30%) to be vegetarian pizzas. Statistics work because we know how unlikely it is, assuming an SRS is used, that the sample will have certain characteristics. For example, if more than 500 of the pizzas were vegetarian, then it would be very unlikely that an SRS was being used. We would conclude that there was a non-random process in the sampling, like one of us (KL) occasionally toying with vegetarianism as a teenager.

There are some common misconceptions about what constitutes an SRS. The most common one is still using the dictionary definition of the word random, meaning that the toppings were chosen in some haphazard manner. Another common misconception is that having some chance element in the sampling makes it an SRS. In the pizza example, suppose a coin was flipped to determine whether to have mushrooms or not and then the choice was random. This is not an SRS because there will be a 50% probability of having a mushroom pizza, and we know that it should only be about 40% with a simple random sample. Finally, some people think that the SRS is defined by each element (i.e., topping) having an equal chance of being chosen. As there are five toppings and two toppings picked, having equal probability would mean each topping was chosen about 40% of the time. The SRS has this characteristic, but so do lots of other forms of sampling. In the second column of Table 4.1 are five pizzas. If we randomly sampled from this group of five, each topping would be chosen about 40% of the time. However, not all combinations are possible and this can make some differences. For example, the probability of a vegetarian pizza is only 20% if taking a random sample from this group, while it is only 30% from an SRS.

In practice, using an SRS is very time-consuming and expensive and hence not often used. For example, when a psychiatrist is interested in whether some new medicine helps with depression, she is interested in the entire population of depressed individuals. In order to conduct an SRS, every single individual with depression would need an equal chance of being selected into her study. In practice, she probably would randomly assign half her new patients to receive the old medicine and half the patients to receive the new medicine. While she is interested in all depressed individuals, it would be nearly impossible to sample from the population of all depressed individuals in the world (or even in her country or state). The reader of such a study would need to evaluate how representative her sample is of all depressed patients. For example, does her sample have more severely depressed individuals? Perhaps her clientele is primarily females with high education and income levels. Readers should be critical when reading all such studies. Limitations in research design such as the sampling are why studies must be repeated: if the results of a study do generalize to larger populations, then researchers should find the results can be replicated across many different types of samples.

While an SRS is rare, there are a few very well-known examples of it. One of these is the UK's National Lottery (and most lotteries in the United States and other countries). In the UK version the population is 49 balls with the numbers 1 to 49, and six are sampled. Any possible combination of the six balls is possible. There are about 14 million possible combinations so the probability of winning the jackpot with one lottery ticket is about 1 in 14 million. While the lottery is random (though see Box 4.1), we can calculate the probability of the sample of six balls having certain characteristics. For example, it is known that having all six balls with even numbers on them should happen slightly less than 1% of the time.[1]

Box 4.1   When Random Sampling Isn't

In most research small deviations from random sampling are unlikely to be important. But what if it could cost you your life?

At several points throughout US history young men have been conscripted into the military based on a lottery system. Fienberg (1971), in an excellent article describing what 'random' means, discussed some of the problems with the 1970 lottery which determined if men were sent to Vietnam. The lottery system was based on people's birth dates: 366 capsules, one for each possible birth date, were placed in a box. The January capsules were put in and pushed over to one side. Next the February capsules were put in, and pushed up next to the January ones. This continued for the other months, and resulted in capsules for dates early in the year (i.e., January, February, etc.) being predominantly on one side and capsules for later dates on the other. The box was shaken, carried around a bit, and then its contents were poured into a bowl. This resulted in the early months' capsules being towards the bottom of the bowl, and the late months capsules being towards the top. The capsules were then picked. According to Fienberg's sources, they were generally picked from the top of the bowl. The result was that people were much more likely to have the ball with their birthday on it picked first if they were born in the late months and therefore be drafted first. The draft was done differently the following year.

Alternatives to an SRS

There are several alternatives to an SRS. We will describe three of them: cluster sampling, quota sampling and convenience sampling.

A *cluster sample* is where the researcher first samples large clusters of people, like whole neighbourhoods or districts, and then samples people within these clusters. If doing a face-to-face survey, this means the interviewer can go to one designated location and

---

1 Here is a tricky question. The probability of having all six balls with odd numbers on them is slightly *greater* than 1%. Why the difference? (Don't try working out the numbers. If you think you know the reason you are probably right.)

Stage 1   **Stage 2**

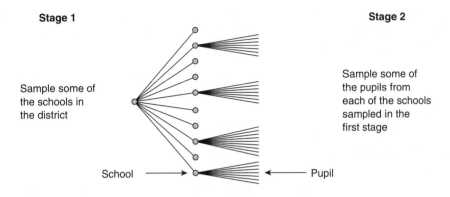

Sample some of
the schools in
the district

Sample some of
the pupils from
each of the schools
sampled in the
first stage

School ⟶   ⟵ Pupil

Figure 4.2   A two-stage cluster sample of schools and pupils

sample several people from there, and then move on to another. An example that could be used in educational research is shown in Figure 4.2. The population may be all pupils in schools in the United Kingdom. If an SRS sample was taken, the researcher might have to travel to several different schools to test only one or two pupils in each. This would be a waste of effort and money. Instead, the researcher might take an SRS of schools. A handful of schools would be sampled, and then within these schools (or clusters) individual pupils could be sampled. Figure 4.2 is described as a two-stage cluster sample, sampling schools in the first stage and then sampling pupils. In general the estimates are less accurate than you get with an SRS. However, the cost savings are often quite large. Although there are methods to analyse clustered data, these are beyond the scope of this book (see Wright & London, 2009).

Quota samples are very popular in social science. In quota sampling the interviewers or researchers choose the sample so that there are specific percentages of various groups. An example might be that they want their sample to be half women and half men. In some cases the researcher may purposefully choose the sample to be non-representative of the whole population. With the pizza topping example, suppose we wanted one meat topping and one vegetable topping (see Table 4.1, fourth column). This is a type of quota sample but it over-represents the meat toppings (both meat toppings have a 50% chance of being sampled while each vegetable has a 33% chance). Consider another example. If a researcher was comparing left- and right-handed people, she or he would probably want approximately equal numbers of people in these groups, even though about 90% of humans are right handed. Thus, while an SRS would probably produce a sample that was about 90% right handed, a researcher using a quota sample could specify that she or he wanted left-handed people to be oversampled.

The final technique produces what is called a *convenience sample*. As the name suggests, this sample is the easiest to attain. This is the most common sample in psychology and in many cases it is justified. Convenience samples, which are sometimes called opportunity samples, include where you just go around and ask the first 20 people you can find in the school cafeteria, or use the first group of people who sign up for your study. The problem with convenience samples is that it is difficult to justify generalizing your findings to the population at large.

ALLOCATION

The 'Gold Standard' for Allocation

As with sampling, there is a 'gold standard' for allocating people from these samples to the experimental conditions. This is called *random allocation* and means each person is randomly allocated to a condition. For example, if there were two conditions, you could flip a coin for each person to determine which condition the person is in. While no coin is perfectly balanced, most are close enough. Random allocation is much easier to do than an SRS, and so it is often used. There are some slight variations from it. For example, some people will put the first person into condition 1, the second into condition 2, the third into condition 1, etc. This is not random allocation, but it is not a bad approach and ensures there is approximately the same number of people in each condition. What would be bad, for example, is if the people sampled in the morning tended to be in one group, but those sampled in the afternoon tended to be in another. This would introduce a *bias* into the allocation. It might mean that only people who wake up early are in the first group. Another bias would be choosing people whose names are at the beginning of the alphabet to be in one group and those with names at the end to be in the other. It could happen that there are systematic differences between these groups. Box 4.2 describes biased allocation in a large-scale study.

Box 4.2   When Random Allocation Isn't

In 1930 an experiment with 20,000 children was carried out in Lanarkshire, Scotland, to test how giving children milk every day affected height and weight. Children's height and weight were measured at both the beginning and end of the experiment. William Gossett, who went by the pseudonym 'Student' (1931) and who you will hear more about in Chapter 6, described a variety of problems with the design of this study. Here we describe just one: that the allocation of students to conditions was made by the teachers. The teachers were supposed to allocate children randomly to the control group, who received no milk, and to the experimental group, who received milk.

According to a report 'Student' quotes from, teachers were allowed to substitute well-fed or ill-nourished children if the control and experimental groups in their

---

classrooms did not appear equally nourished. This allowed the teachers to bias the allocation. 'Student' states:

it would seem probable that the teachers, swayed by the very human feeling that the poorer children needed the milk more than the comparatively well to do, must have unconsciously made too large a substitution of the ill-nourished among the 'feeders' and too few among the 'controls'. (1931: 399)

When the initial heights and weights were compared the 'control' children were taller and weighed more (see his Diagrams 1–4). It is likely, therefore, that the controls differed in several other ways, including general health and socio-economic status. 'Student' summarized this expensive (£7500 in 1930, which is over £300,000 or $600,000 now, from http://eh.net/hmit/ppowerbp/) study:

though planned on the grand scale, organised in a thoroughly business-like manner and carried through with the devoted assistance of a large team of teachers, nurses and doctors, [it] failed to produce a valid estimate of the advantage of giving milk to children. ('Student', 1931: 406)

Random allocation is extremely important in interpreting experimental results (Wright, 2006). Figure 4.3 shows a typical experiment. In this experiment there is a population from which a sample is chosen, and then people in this sample are allocated to one of two conditions. The conditions are treated differently. Let's say the experiment is on whether people dislike English or Australian soap operas more. The first group was forced to watch 10 hours of an English soap opera and then physiological instruments rated their despair. The second group had the same measures taken, but after watching 10 hours of an Australian soap. The researcher would probably take the mean despair rating for each group and see which is larger. Now people differ in how much they dislike soaps. If the two samples differ greatly on this, then any difference on the final despair measure could reflect this.

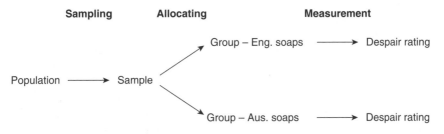

Figure 4.3   An example experiment comparing viewers' reactions to English and Australian soap operas

Therefore, in an ideal circumstance, the two conditions would be exactly the same on over-all soap dislike prior to the study. While random allocation does not guarantee this, as with random sampling, we do know how unlikely it is to have two groups which differ greatly. Although we know individuals are bound to differ on many different characteristics (e.g., IQ, level of depression etc.), by using random assignment, individuals stand an equal chance of being assigned to each group. Therefore, these individual differences should be approximately equal in the different groups.

It is easier to allocate people randomly to conditions than to have an SRS of a large pop-ulation. There are several ways to do random allocation and it is (usually) not any more expensive than other methods. Because of this it is expected that random allocation is used in experiments.

SUMMARY

The most elegant statistics, the most informative graphs, and the clearest of writing styles are all for naught if the design of the study is poor. Depending on the purpose of the study, if poor sampling or poor allocation is used, then the results from the study may be worthless. When trying to estimate the value of some variable for a population, the sample must be representative of the population. If not, whatever oddities exist in the sample may be errantly inferred to exist in the population. When doing experi-ments, the critical aspect is how people in the sample are allocated to conditions. In our earlier alcohol example, we might conclude that males drink more than females so males should be targeted more in alcohol awareness efforts. However, our findings might have been driven by our sampling method. We sampled studious females in an 8:00 am class versus our males from the food area at 11:00 am. Before the manipula-tion, the people in the different conditions should be as similar to each other as possi-ble. If they are markedly different, then this difference may lead to incorrect inferences about the effect of any manipulation.

The gold standards of sampling and allocation are simple random sampling and ran-dom allocation. These standards are assumed in most statistical tests. Yet, particularly with reference to sampling, often in the real world, other methods are used. While gross violations, like that described in Box 4.1, are unacceptable, small variations are usually acceptable. What this usually means is that your statistics are not as precise as they should be. Many statistics textbooks take a hard, and unproductive, line. They state that all variations are unacceptable and that the data should be either thrown out or analysed in much more complex ways. This is not helpful. Much useful data do exist where these standards are not met and sometimes complex analyses serve only to limit the potential audience. The main point we stress is that the gold standards are what you should aim for, but if you fall short then the sample should be as representative of the population as possible, and the conditions as similar (pre-manipulation) to each other as possible. In practice, when the gold standards are not met, the statistics calculated are less precise than they appear, so you should be extra cautious. We can trust the findings more once they have been replicated in other samples.

Throughout the rest of this book, we present statistical techniques and move away from the issues of sampling and allocation. Readers should keep in mind that, when conducting their own research or reading that of others, the statistical methods are meaningful and valid only if proper methods were used.

EXERCISES

These exercises are not statistics exercises, but methods questions. Ask your instructor for the appropriate length for your answers. For questions 4.1 to 4.5, describe the population, the sample, and any experimental conditions. For each also assume that you are on a limited budget.

4.1   Design a study to investigate the effects of television violence and children's aggressive behaviour.

4.2   An environmental scientist feels that people's attitudes towards the problems with the rapidly increasing global population are changing. Design a study to help to answer this question.

4.3   A marketing firm has just thought up a new advertising campaign to use for its toothpaste. Design a study to evaluate this campaign.

4.4   Around half of the time that someone is falsely convicted of crime, the main evidence against them is errant eyewitness testimony. A psycho-legal researcher wondered if having witnesses first try to draw the person helped them in later attempts to identify the culprit in an identification parade (i.e., a line-up). How would you go about testing this hypothesis?

4.5   In the United Kingdom, the party in government can call when it wants to have an election. Obviously it only wants to call an election when it thinks that it will win. Suppose that you were asked by the party leader to design a study to see whether she or he should call an election. How would you do this?

4.6   What is a simple random sample?

4.7   We want to do a study examining whether playing classical music to newborns leads to smarter toddlers. We randomly allocate half the newborns to receive classical music and half not to receive classical music. How does random allocation help us control for the fact the different newborns would be expected to be at different intelligence levels before they are assigned to conditions?

4.8   Define 'probability'.

📖 FURTHER READING

Cook, T.D., & Campbell, D.T. (1979). *Quasi-Experimentation: Design & Analysis Issues for Field Settings.* London: Houghton Mifflin.
This is one of the best books ever on social science methods. Chapter 1 provides an excellent discussion on causation.

Fienberg, S.E. (1971). Randomization and social affairs: the 1970 draft lottery. *Science, 171*, 255–261.
People were sent to war and died because of biased sampling. Great paper on sampling and probability!

Gossett, W., writing as 'Student' (1931). The Lanarkshire milk experiment. *Biometrika, 23*, 398–406.
This is an interesting paper to read because the style of older papers is sometimes different. Nowadays we would say his style is 'direct'.

Wright, D.B. (2006). Causal and associative hypotheses in psychology: examples from eyewitness testimony research. *Psychology, Public Policy, and Law, 12*, 190–213.
Available from the APA website from many university websites through PsychLit. The main points of this paper are that it is important to use good allocation procedures if you want to draw causal conclusions and good sampling procedures if you want to describe associations. The topics are drawn from eyewitness testimony. This paper is for both psychologists and lawyers, so does not require much statistics knowledge.

5

Inference and Confidence Intervals

One of the most important uses of statistics is to take information about a sample to infer something about the population from which the sample was drawn. This is called *inference*. It involves using characteristics of the sample to make some best guesses for characteristics of the population. In this chapter we describe how this is done for the mean of a variable, for the difference between two means. We also examine the median, which is less affected by extreme values. You will learn what confidence intervals are and how to construct them.

INFERRING A POPULATION MEAN: CONSTRUCTING CONFIDENCE INTERVALS

In one sense, the inference from a sample mean to a population is simple. If we have used a simple random sample (SRS), then a sensible guess for the population mean is just the sample mean. If an SRS of 100 people found the mean number of cigarettes smoked per day was 6.2 cigarettes, then this is a good estimate for the population mean. The lower case Greek letter µ (pronounced *mu*) is used to refer to the population mean. We never know exactly what the population mean is, unless we sample the entire population. The purpose of statistics is to get the best estimate. Statisticians call this the *plug-in principle*, that in many cases we can use a sample statistic, like the sample mean, to estimate a population parameter, like the population mean.

While it is useful knowing that a good single-point estimate for a population mean is the sample mean, in most cases you want to give an interval which you feel is likely to contain the population mean. This is more complicated. When a newspaper article states that the average person consumes 42 ± 2 grams of broccoli a year (the ± means 'plus or minus'), it means that, based on some survey, they have some level of confidence that the population mean for grams of broccoli eaten in a year is between 40 and 44 grams per person. The width of a confidence interval tells you how precise your estimate is. If the newspaper reported the amount was 42 ± 30 grams, then you would only be confident that the population mean was somewhere between 12 and 72 grams. This latter interval is not very informative because it is so imprecise.

To calculate a confidence interval of a mean you need to know the number of people in the sample, the sample mean and the sample standard deviation, and decide on what confidence level you want to use. You also need to make a couple of assumptions. The main assumption to consider is that the variable is sampled from a population that is normally distributed. You can then use something called a *t* table (see Appendix C). We will go through an example to show how confidence intervals are made.

Newton (1998) was interested in hostility levels on arrival and at discharge from Grendon prison in the United Kingdom. She gave a sample of 94 people the *Hostility and Direction of Hostility Questionnaire* (HDHQ) at both time points. This questionnaire produces a total hostility score (high scores mean more hostility). According to Caine et al. (1967) the mean in the general population is about 13.0. The mean score on arrival for the 94 prisoners was 28.3 with a standard deviation of 8.0. Both of these are in units defined by the *Hostility* scale. We will assume that they are from normally distributed population.

The equation for the 95% confidence interval is:

$$CI_{95\%} = \bar{x} \pm t_{0.05} \frac{sd}{\sqrt{n}}$$

There is a symbol here that you have not encountered.[1] It relates to the *t* distribution which is located in Appendix C. It is fairly complex to calculate the value of $t_{0.05}$ but it is usually around 2 (Appendix C gives further details on how to use the table). The letters *df* in the table stand for *degrees of freedom*. When calculating the confidence interval for the mean of a single variable the degrees of freedom are *n* − 1. With 94 prisoners in Newton's data set, *df* = 93. In Appendix C you should go to the row with 93 in the *df* column and look for the value in the $t_{0.05}$ column. However, there is no row corresponding to *df* = 93. You should go to the closest row, here *df* = 90. The value is 1.99. The '0.05' in $t_{0.05}$ is due to the 95% in '95% confidence interval'. It is because 100% − 95% is 5%, which is 0.05. The reason why 5% is printed in the table instead of 95% will become clear when discussing hypothesis testing in Chapter 6. Inserting these values into the equation yields:

$$CI_{95\%} = 28.3 \pm 1.99 \frac{8.0}{\sqrt{94}} = 28.3 \pm 1.6$$

Sometimes the 1.6 is added to and subtracted from the mean and the confidence interval is written as (26.7, 29.9). These are in the same units as the original variable. This interval is a lot higher than the value for the general population.

So what does having $CI_{95\%}$ of 28.3 ± 1.6 mean? We expect that about 95% of the time when a confidence interval is made that the population mean (μ) will be within the interval created. This allows us to be fairly confident that the confidence interval we calculate contains the population mean (see Box 5.1).

Box 5.1   Confidence Intervals and Dead Cats

The view of most methodologists is that if you have just found a 95% confidence interval, it does not mean that there is a 95% probability that the true mean lies in that interval. They argue that the population mean, which is denoted with the Greek letter *μ* (mu), either is or is not in the observed interval.

This situation is similar to a famous physics experiment called Schrödinger's cat experiment (Schrödinger, 1983, originally published 1935). This experiment was prompted by some disagreements in quantum physics and Schrödinger wanted to convince people that some aspects of probability states in the microscopic world of quantum physics do not manifest themselves in our macroscopic world. Schrödinger placed a cat in a

(Cont'd)

---

1 Those symbols which you have already encountered are for the mean ($\bar{x}$), the standard deviation (*sd*) and the sample size (*n*).

box, with a radioactive substance, a Geiger counter, a hammer and a flask of poison. There is some probability associated with an atom of the substance decaying. For argument's sake, let's say that the probability is 95% that an atom will decay in an hour. If it does, this will be measured with the Geiger counter, which triggers the hammer to smash the flask, releasing the poison and killing the cat. There is no way to look into the box. The question is: if you cannot look into the box, what is the cat's condition after being in this box for one hour?

One interpretation is that, at least at the microscopic level of quantum physics, the cat can be both alive and dead. One might say that, without looking in the box, the cat was 95% dead. When the box is opened, the cat either makes an immediate and miraculous recovery, or instantly dies. However, for most people when considering the macroscopic level of cats, the cat is either alive or dead. This was what Schrödinger was trying to show, that quantum 'weirdness' does not manifest itself in the macroscopic world, and many people agreed. Einstein, for example, stated that 'nobody really doubts that the presence or absence of the cat is something independent of the act of observation' (Przibram, 1967: 39).

In the same way, when you calculate a 95% confidence interval, this particular interval either includes the population mean, or it does not. We do not know which because we do not know the true mean; we cannot open the box. What we can say is that if you repeat the procedure, over and over, calculating hundreds of confidence intervals on new samples of data, then approximately 95% of the time this procedure will produce an interval that will include the population mean. But the mean is either inside or outside of any individual interval, it is not part inside and part outside. Similarly, if the cat experiment were repeated over and over, 95% of the time the cat would die.

Now because this sounds pretty close to '95% probability that *the* confidence interval includes the population mean', it is generally agreed that people are allowed to say that they are 'confident that *the* confidence interval includes the population mean'. This is not an ideal solution, but it has become a convention. It is simply because the word 'confident' carries less philosophical baggage than 'probability', but it also carries less meaning. For example, we cannot say '95% confident', because that does not mean anything unless you incorrectly translate 'confident' as a probability. Further, confidence is a statement about a person's belief, while probability is usually about an event. This distinction is at the heart of much contemporary debate about the word 'probability' (Dienes, 2008).

We should probably add that the Schrödinger cat experiment was a *thought experiment*. If it had been a real experiment there would have been ethical considerations. A more detailed version of this box, delving more into some of the philosophical issues, is on this chapter's web page.

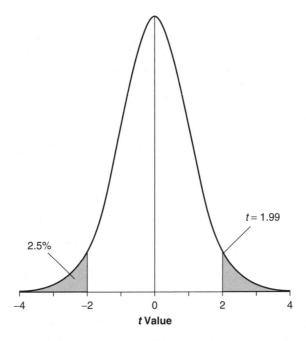

Figure 5.1   A *t* distribution with 93 degrees of freedom: 2.5% of the curve lies above *t* = 1.99 and 2.5% lies below *t* = −1.99. These areas are shaded. This curve looks very similar to the normal distribution (which is a special case of the *t* distribution with an infinite number of degrees of freedom)

Figure 5.1 shows the *t* distribution with 93 degrees of freedom (*df* = 93). The area underneath the curve can be thought of as the total probability of some event. If we want to include 95% of this probability in our confidence interval, this means we exclude 2.5% at each extreme. The shaded areas in Figure 5.1 contain, in total, 5% of the total area under the curve. Statisticians say that there is 2.5% in each *tail*. The place on this graph that separates 5% into the shaded area is $t_{0.05}$. Here it is 1.99, but this number varies with the degrees of freedom, as can be seen from the table in Appendix C.

If we wanted a 99% confidence interval we would want to exclude a total of 1% of the area under the curve. This means only 0.5% of the total area under the curve would be in each tail. Here are the numbers for Newton's 'at arrival' data for a 99% confidence interval:

$$CI_{99\%} = \bar{x} \pm t_{0.01} \frac{sd}{\sqrt{n}} = 28.3 \pm 2.63 \frac{8.0}{\sqrt{94}} = 28.3 \pm 2.2$$

Notice that this new confidence interval is larger, going from 26.1 to 30.5, than the 95% confidence interval. By increasing the confidence from 95% to 99%, the interval becomes larger and includes the population mean. It is a tradeoff between confidence and precision. The most common confidence intervals are the 95% and 99% intervals and usually the 95% confidence interval is used. It is fairly arbitrary that this particular level is used, but because it has become a convention it will be used here.

When constructing and interpreting a confidence interval, three assumptions are made. The first is that simple random sampling (SRS) was used. In this case we would probably assume the population was all the prisoners who might be in a unit like Grendon. Newton (1998) describes the sampling and notes that some prisoners who are only there a short time could not be part of the sample. Thus, it is important to make sure that the inference is not made to all people or even all prisoners.

The second assumption is that the data points are independent. This means that having one person sampled should not determine whether someone else is chosen. It also means that the responses of one person should not influence what someone else says. So, for example, with a hostility questionnaire it would be bad to test people in groups because if there is an extremely hostile person present, this might affect everybody's scores.

Finally, the distribution in the population is assumed to be normally distributed. The normal distribution is an important concept in statistics. In Chapter 1 we made histograms, and the shape of the histogram is often called its distribution. A normal distribution is very similar to Figure 5.1. In fact, if we had printed a normal distribution on top of that curve, they would have been so similar that you would not have been able to tell the difference. The critical place for the shaded areas would have been 1.96 rather than 1.99. A t distribution with an infinite number of degrees of freedom *is* the normal distribution. For many of the statistical procedures that are discussed in this book we assume the data follow a normal distribution. Since researchers seldom have data from the entire population, they usually look at the sample distribution and see if it looks roughly normally distributed (another example of the plug-in principle). If it does, then this assumption is usually made. If you do not wish to make this assumption, there are alternatives. Often when the data are not normally distributed people use the median, which is described later this chapter, instead of the mean.

Because the 95% confidence interval is in the same units as the original variable it is common practice to graph confidence intervals onto graphs. This is usually done for graphs showing means, but can also be done for histograms. Figure 5.2 shows the DNA data from Table 1.1 and Figure 1.1, years spent in prison before exoneration, with both plus/minus a standard deviation and the 95% confidence interval. There is often confusion between these. The standard deviation shows how spread out the data are. The confidence interval shows how precise the estimate of the mean is. As you increase the sample size the measurement of the mean gets more precise and therefore the confidence interval gets smaller. As the sample size increases, the standard deviation does not have this tendency.

In summary, confidence intervals are very useful: they provide information about an estimate of the population mean and also how precise the estimate is.

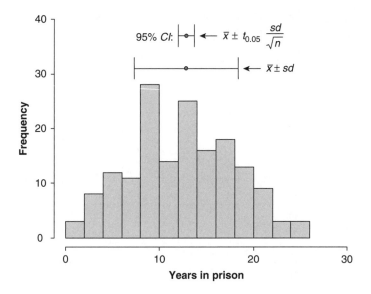

Figure 5.2   A histogram of years spent in prison before exoneration. The 95% confidence interval is shown along with the interval ± the standard deviation. The confidence interval shows the precision of the estimate and, providing $n > 5$, it will be smaller than the standard deviation interval

EXAMINING THE DIFFERENCE BETWEEN TWO MEANS FOR THE SAME PERSON

Social scientists often differentiate 'between-subjects' and 'within-subject' studies. Between-subjects studies are where you are comparing different groups of people. Within-subject studies are where you are comparing one group of people in different situations. In between-subjects studies each person is in only one condition, while in within-subject studies each person is in multiple conditions. In this section we will describe a simple within-subject design, where there are only two conditions and each person takes part in both conditions. We will first describe an example on coffee preference with a small number of participants for illustrative purposes, and then examine Newton's (1998) data set, comparing the prisoners' hostility levels when they arrived at Grendon with when they were discharged.

The basic equation for within-subject confidence interval is:

$$CI_{95\%} = \overline{x1_i - x2_i} \pm t_{0.05} \frac{sd_{diff}}{\sqrt{n}} = \overline{diff} \pm t_{0.05} \frac{sd_{diff}}{\sqrt{n}}$$

Table 5.1 *Data from 10 participants comparing how much they like two different types of coffee*

	$FRESH_i$	$INSTANT_i$	$DIFF_i$	$DIFF_i - \bar{x}$	$(DIFF_i - \bar{x})^2$
	5	3	2	1	1
	4	3	1	0	0
	6	5	1	0	0
	3	4	−1	−2	4
	4	4	0	−1	1
	5	3	2	1	1
	6	3	3	2	4
	3	3	0	−1	1
	5	3	2	1	1
	4	4	0	−1	1
Sum	45	35	10	0	14
Mean	4.5	3.5	1.0	0	1.56*

* This 1.56 is not the actual mean. It is the variance of the variable $DIFF_i$, the sum of squares divided by the number of cases minus one (14/9). We calculated it this way because it can be used in later calculations.

This first part is the mean of the differences (subtract each $x2_i$ from the corresponding $x1_i$ and find the mean of this difference). This will be the same as the difference between the means for each condition. sd_{diff} means the standard deviation of the differences. The first example goes through these calculations.

Suppose 10 regular coffee drinkers were asked to taste two cups of coffee and to rate them for enjoyment on a 1 to 7 scale. The data are shown in Table 5.1. The first coffee they tasted was a freshly ground coffee from *Brewed Awakenings* on West Central Ave, Toledo, where part of this book was written. The second was instant coffee bought at the mini-market across the road. Not surprisingly most people liked the fresh coffee more.

The first two columns give the scores people gave for the different coffees, $FRESH_i$ for the freshly ground coffee and $INSTANT_i$ for the instant coffee. $DIFF_i$ is simply $FRESH_i$ minus $INSTANT_i$, being careful to make sure that if the person liked the instant coffee more that they have a negative difference (only the fourth person liked instant coffee more, 3–4 = −1). The next step should be to find the 95% confidence interval for this variable, $DIFF_i$, in the same way as was done with the hostility scores in the last section. The next two columns are used to help calculate the standard deviation of the difference which is used in the confidence interval equation.

The final column of Table 5.1 gives the values for $(DIFF_i - \bar{x})^2$. Recall from Chapter 2 that the variance is $\Sigma(x_i - \bar{x})^2/(n-1)$. This is the number in Table 5.1 marked with the asterisk. If we take the square root of it we get the standard deviation: $sd = 1.25$. We already know the mean of $DIFF_i$ (1.0) and the sample size ($n = 10$). With $n = 10$, there are nine degrees of freedom. If we go to Appendix C and look up $t_{0.05}$ for $df = 9$ we find $t_{0.05} = 2.26$. Putting all these into the confidence interval equation yields:

$$CI_{95\%} = 1.0 \pm 2.26 \frac{1.25}{\sqrt{10}} = 1.0 \pm 0.89$$

So the 95% confidence interval goes from just a little above zero (0.11) to about two (1.89) for the difference on the seven-point scales. Therefore, we would have some confidence that people do like the fresh coffee better, but with only 10 people in the sample we cannot be very precise about how much more people like freshly brewed coffee.

Let's consider Newton's research on the differences in hostility between when inmates entered Grendon prison and when they were discharged. At discharge the HDHQ was also administered (the mean was 21.6 with a standard deviation of 9.2), and Newton compared these with the earlier scores. She subtracted the scores for each person and found the mean of this difference was −6.6 with a standard deviation of 9.0. We can then find the 95% confidence interval for this difference variable in the same way as we did with the coffee example.

$$CI_{95\%} = -6.6 \pm 1.99 \frac{9.0}{\sqrt{94}} = -6.6 \pm 1.8$$

The confidence interval runs from −8.4 to −4.8. As this confidence interval does not overlap with zero we can say that we are confident the scores on the *Hostility* scale were lower at discharge. A 99% confidence interval is −6.6 ± 2.4, which also does not overlap with zero. This interval is larger, so is less precise, but we have more confidence that the 99% interval will contain the true value than we did with the 95% interval procedure.

The width of a 95% confidence interval is dependent on two things: the sample size and the standard deviation. As the sample size increases, the measurement becomes more precise and therefore the interval becomes smaller. As the standard deviation increases the interval also increases.

CONFIDENCE INTERVALS FOR THE DIFFERENCE BETWEEN GROUPS

Tatar (1998) sampled 295 Israeli secondary school students and asked them to rate (on a 1 to 5 scale with 5 being high) how much several descriptions characterize, in their opinions, a 'significant' teacher. One of the descriptions was 'makes me learn willingly'. In this sample, 166 were girls and 129 were boys. The mean for girls was 3.51 with a standard deviation of 0.99. The mean for boys was 3.26 with a standard deviation of 1.05. Tatar was interested in

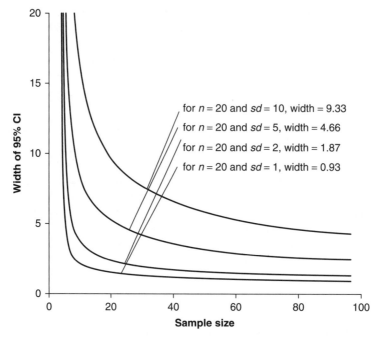

Figure 5.3   The width of the confidence interval by the sample size and the standard deviation. To have a small confidence interval (which you want), you should have a large sample and small standard deviation

this gender difference. One approach would be to calculate the 95% confidence intervals for each gender individually. The calculations for the confidence intervals are:

$$\text{For girls}: \quad 95\% \text{ CI} = 3.51 \pm 1.98\frac{0.99}{\sqrt{166}} = 3.51 \pm 0.15$$

$$\text{For boys}: \quad 95\% \text{ CI} = 3.26 \pm 1.98\frac{1.05}{\sqrt{129}} = 3.26 \pm 0.18$$

The degrees of freedom are 165 and 128 for the girls and the boys, respectively. When the degrees of freedom are above 100 you should use the row for $df =100$ in Appendix C; 1.98 is found in the row for $df = 100$ and in the 0.05 column. So we can say with some confidence that the population mean for girls is between 3.36 and 3.66 and that the population mean for boys is between 3.08 and 3.44. The two confidence intervals overlap. If they did not then we could be fairly sure that the population mean for girls was higher than for boys.

If the confidence intervals do not overlap then you can be confident that the means of the populations from which these two samples were drawn are different from each other. However, if the confidence intervals do overlap, this does not provide a test of whether the means in their populations are different. In order to examine if there is a gender difference, we need to find the confidence interval for the difference. When you are comparing two variables for the same person, as in the coffee example, you can simply calculate a difference variable for each person. Here we want to compare two groups. This is a between-subjects design and is more complicated. Recall the formula for the 95% confidence interval when a within-subject design was used:

$$CI_{95\%} = \overline{x1_i - x2_i} \pm t_{0.05} \frac{sd_{diff}}{\sqrt{n}} = \overline{diff} \pm t_{0.05} \frac{sd_{diff}}{\sqrt{n}}$$

where $x1_i$ and $x2_i$ are the two variables, the bar above denoting that this is the mean of this difference, and sd is the standard deviation of the difference. The formula for the between-subjects situation is conceptually similar. It is the difference between the two means $\pm t_{0.05}$ multiplied by the standard deviation divided by a function of the number of people. The tricky part is calculating the appropriate standard deviation and the number of people. It will be easier to work with the variances (recall squaring a standard deviation produces a variance). The variances for the groups, call them var1 and var2, are combined into what is called the *pooled variance*:

$$pooled\ var = \frac{(n1 - 1)var1 + (n2 - 1)var2}{(n1 - 1) + (n2 - 1)}$$

where $n1$ and $n2$ are the sample sizes. If girls are group 1 and boys are group 2, and remembering to square the standard deviations to turn them into variances, you get:

$$pooled\ var = \frac{(166 - 1)\ 0.98 + (129 - 1)\ 1.10}{(166 - 1) + (129 - 1)} = \frac{161.7 + 140.8}{165 + 128} = 1.03$$

This is a weighted mean of the two variances. If you get a pooled variance that is not somewhere between the variances of the two groups, then something has gone wrong.

The formula for the 95% confidence interval for the difference in means for a between-subjects design is:

$$CI_{95\%} = \overline{x1} - \overline{x2} \pm t_{0.05} \sqrt{pooled\ var\left(\frac{1}{n1} + \frac{1}{n2}\right)}$$

The new degrees of freedom are $n1 + n2 - 2$, or here $166 + 129 - 2 = 293$. The t table does not go up this high. For values above 100 it is best to use $t_{0.05} = 1.98$. For Tatar's (1998) data, this is:

$$CI_{95\%} = 3.51 - 3.26 \pm 1.98 \sqrt{1.03 \left(\frac{1}{166} + \frac{1}{n2} \right)} = 0.25 \pm 1.98 \sqrt{0.014} = 0.25 \pm 0.24$$

The 95% confidence interval goes from 0.01 to 0.49. Since all of the interval is positive, we can be confident that the mean for girls, in the population, is higher than for boys. If a 99% confidence interval ($t_{0.01} = 2.63$) was used the confidence interval is:

$$CI_{99\%} = 3.51 - 3.26 \pm 2.63 \sqrt{1.03 \left(\frac{1}{166} + \frac{1}{n2} \right)} = 0.25 \pm 2.63 \sqrt{0.014} = 0.25 \pm 0.31$$

or from –0.06 to 0.56. The interval now includes negative values. Therefore, at this level of confidence we cannot say that the mean for the girls in the population is higher than the mean for the boys.

CONFIDENCE INTERVALS FOR MEDIANS

Medians were introduced in Chapter 1. A median is the middle point of a variable's distribution and is found by sorting the data in ascending (or descending) order and finding the value in the middle. The median is less affected by extreme points; it represents the centre of a distribution better than the mean. There are different ways to calculate confidence intervals for medians and the different methods sometimes produce different results. Sometimes it surprises people that there is not a single agreed-upon way of calculating things like a confidence interval for something as basic as the median. The reason is that the different methods make different assumptions and are better, or worse, in different situations. Similarly, although we introduced the confidence interval equation for the mean as if it were the only option, using it requires certain assumptions, and if those assumptions are not met then other methods should be used. We will keep with some of the simpler methods for calculating confidence intervals for the median.

Consider the Scottish witch data (Goodare et al., 2004) introduced in Chapter 3. Suppose we are interested in the age when a person was convicted of witchcraft during this period (1563–1736). Goodare and colleagues could only discover the age of 166 of the 3219 accused, but this is enough for our purposes. These ages, in years and in ascending order are (these data are on the chapter's web page, so you do not need to retype them):

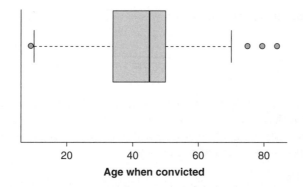

Figure 5.4   Boxplot of the age when 166 witches were convicted (Goodare et al., 2004)

$wyear_i$ = 9, 10, 10, 12, 14, 14, 14, 15, 15, 16, 16, 17, 23, 25, 25, 25, 25, 25, 25, 25, 27, 27, 28, 28, 29, 29, 30, 30, 30, 30, 30, 31, 31, 31, 32, 32, 32, 32, 33, 33, 34, 34, 34, 35, 35, 35, 35, 36, 36, 36, 36, 36, 37, 37, 37, 37, 38, 39, 39, 39, 39, 39, 39, 40, 40, 40, 40, 41, 41, 41, 41, 41, 42, 43, 43, 43, 43, 43, 44, 45, 45, 45, 45, 45, 45, 45, 45, 45, 45, 45, 45, 46, 47, 47, 47, 48, 48, 49, 49, 50, 50, 50, 50, 50, 50, 50, 50, 50, 50, 50, 50, 50, 50, 50, 50, 50, 50, 50, 50, 50, 50, 50, 50, 50, 50, 50, 50, 50, 50, 50, 50, 50, 50, 50, 51, 51, 53, 53, 53, 55, 55, 55, 55, 55, 55, 55, 56, 56, 57, 60, 60, 60, 60, 60, 60, 61, 63, 63, 64, 65, 70, 75, 75, 80, 84

Using the procedures of earlier chapters, we begin by finding the minimum (9 years), maximum (84 years), median (45 years), and lower and upper quartiles (34 and 50 years, respectively). These can be used to make a boxplot, as in Figure 5.4. We might also calculate the mean (42.58 years), and using the procedures described earlier in this chapter find that the 95% confidence interval for the mean is 40.48 to 44.69 years.

If you are interested in the precision of the median estimate, you need to calculate the standard error of this estimate. While there are different methods to estimate this, the one suggested by Wilcox (2005: 64–65, 133) is one of the simplest. First, calculate a number k which is:

$$k = \frac{n+1}{2} - 2.576\sqrt{\frac{n}{4}}$$

so for these data this is:

$$k = \frac{166+1}{2} - 2.576\sqrt{\frac{166}{4}} = 66.91$$

You then round this number to the nearest whole number, so let k be 67. In general, the standard error is:

$$se = \frac{X_{(n-k+1)} - X_k}{5.152}$$

where X_i means the value of X for the ith case once the variable's values have been placed in ascending order. Here, $n-k+1$ is $166-67+1 = 100$. Once the variable is sorted, the 100th value is 50 and the value for the 67th is 40. The difference between these divided by 5.152 is 1.94. To calculate the 95% confidence interval:

$$95\% \; CI = median \pm z_{0.05} \; se = 45 \pm 1.96 \cdot 1.94 = 45 \pm 3.80$$

where $z_{0.05}$ is the z value beyond which only 2.5% of the population lie (so 5% in both tails); it is 1.96. This is a number worth remembering; it is also the value for $t_{0.05}$ when the degrees of freedom is very large because the t distribution with an infinite number of degrees of freedom is the normal (z) distribution. This produces an interval of (41.20, 48.80). This allows us to say that we are confident that the population median lies somewhere between 41 and 49 years old. If you want the 99% confidence interval, use $z_{0.01}$, which is 2.576 and you get an interval from 40 to 50 years old. As said, there are other algorithms for calculating this interval, but some of these are mathematically complex. An alternative which relies on computing power rather than mathematics, called *bootstrapping*, is described in Box 5.2.

The second situation we will describe, comparing two medians, involves sex. Aah, got your attention. In most surveys that ask people about the number of opposite-sex partners, the mean for male participants is higher than the mean for female participants. The difference is gigantic; often males have two to four times more sexual partners. Logically, this should not happen because when a male gets a new partner, so does a female.[2] There are several explanations for this: differential morbidity (maybe that over-sexed males live longer than over-sexed females), sampling bias (for example, female prostitutes are under-represented in most sample surveys), and measurement error. Measurement error looks the most likely source for this discrepancy. Some of the difference appears due to males and females providing socially desirable responses (Alexander & Fisher, 2003), and some due to males using response strategies that tend to over-estimate frequencies (like just trying to guess the approximate number) and females use strategies that tend to under-estimate frequencies (like trying to count all their partners) (Brown & Sinclair, 1999).

Suppose we are not interested whether the means for the two genders are the same, but whether the typical male has about the same number of sexual partners as the typical

---

2 Look around your class. The mean number of sexual partners for the males is probably similar to the mean number for females. Makes you think, doesn't it!

female. So, we are not interested in the modern-day Don Juans. We would be interested in differences between the medians rather than differences between the means. To calculate the confidence interval for the difference between two medians we use the estimate for the standard error for each group's median as calculated above, and apply the same methods as used for calculating the difference between two means. This is one method for doing this. Our choice is based in part on computational ease, and it will provide a good estimate of the confidence interval. Other methods exist and readers should consider using a bootstrap method (Box 5.2; the web page for this chapter shows using a bootstrap estimate for this example using the BCA method, produced a 95% CI from −1.0 to 2.5 partners different between the medians). The 95% confidence interval for the median is:

$$95\% \ CI = median_{males} - median_{females} \pm z_{0.05} \ se_p$$

where se_p is the pooled standard error associated with the estimates:

$$se_p = \sqrt{\frac{n_1 \ se_1^2 + n_2 \ se_2^2}{n_1 + n_2}}$$

Figure 5.5 shows a back-to-back histogram of the number of opposite-sex partners from 100 males and 200 females, as well as some descriptive statistics (the five-point summary). We created these data ourselves so that we know what they should look like. All the females were drawn from a population with a mean and standard deviation of 10. Eighty of the males were drawn from this population, but 20 males were drawn from a population with a mean and standard deviation of 20. If we assume that the females are accurate, and one of the authors says this is a valid assumption, then we could assume that 80% of males are accurate, but that 20% over-estimate the number of sexual partners that they have had. Male researchers (Brown & Sinclair, 1999), have data suggesting this is due to using a different response strategy; female researchers (Alexander & Fisher, 2003), have data suggesting this is due to lying.[3] The means are 12.04 partners for males and 9.94 partners for females. The 95% CI for this difference is from 0.90 to 3.30 partners. Because it does not overlap with zero we can be confident that the mean is higher for males than females.

The question here is whether the typical male differs from the typical female, or in statistical terms, whether the medians differ. The median for males is 10.5 partners and for females it is 10.0 partners. Their standard errors, using the method described above, are 0.58 and 0.39. It is not surprising that the males have the larger standard error because there are fewer males in the sample. The pooled standard error is 0.46. Plugging these numbers into the equation gives us: 0.5 ± 1.96·0.46 = 0.5 ± 0.90, or −0.4 to 1.4 years different. As this

---

3 Sadly, Michele Alexander died in late 2003 in an automobile accident. In recognition of her work, the Society for the Psychological Study of Social Issues now awards the Michele Alexander Early Career Award for Scholarship and Service.

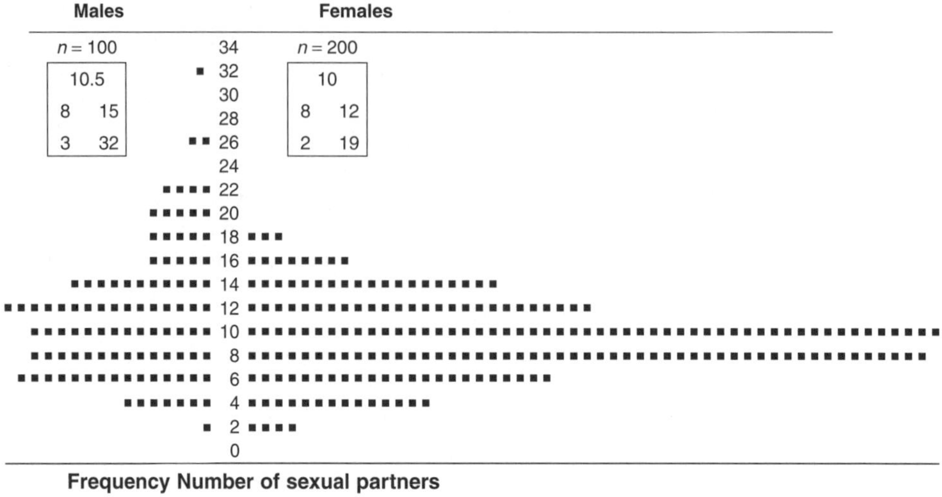

```
         Males                    Females

      n = 100          34       n = 200
     ┌────────┐        ■ 32    ┌────────┐
     │  10.5  │          30    │   10   │
     │ 8   15 │          28    │ 8   12 │
     │ 3   32 │      ■ ■ 26    │ 2   19 │
     └────────┘          24    └────────┘
                 ■ ■ ■ ■ 22
               ■ ■ ■ ■ ■ 20
             ■ ■ ■ ■ ■ 18 ■ ■ ■
             ■ ■ ■ ■ ■ 16 ■ ■ ■ ■ ■ ■ ■
       ■ ■ ■ ■ ■ ■ ■ ■ ■ 14 ■ ■ ■ ■ ■ ■ ■ ■ ■ ■ ■ ■ ■
■ ■ ■ ■ ■ ■ ■ ■ ■ ■ ■ ■ ■ ■ 12 ■ ■ ■ ■ ■ ■ ■ ■ ■ ■ ■ ■ ■ ■ ■ ■ ■ ■
   ■ ■ ■ ■ ■ ■ ■ ■ ■ ■ ■ ■ ■ 10 ■ ■ ■ ■ ■ ■ ■ ■ ■ ■ ■ ■ ■ ■ ■ ■ ■ ■ ■ ■ ■ ■ ■ ■ ■ ■ ■ ■ ■ ■ ■
     ■ ■ ■ ■ ■ ■ ■ ■ ■ ■ ■ ■ 8 ■ ■ ■ ■ ■ ■ ■ ■ ■ ■ ■ ■ ■ ■ ■ ■ ■ ■ ■ ■ ■ ■ ■ ■ ■ ■ ■ ■ ■
   ■ ■ ■ ■ ■ ■ ■ ■ ■ ■ ■ ■ ■ 6 ■ ■ ■ ■ ■ ■ ■ ■ ■ ■ ■ ■ ■ ■ ■ ■ ■
       ■ ■ ■ ■ ■ ■ ■ ■ 4 ■ ■ ■ ■ ■ ■ ■ ■ ■
             ■ 2 ■ ■ ■ ■
                   0
```

Frequency Number of sexual partners

Figure 5.5   Back-to-back histogram of the number of opposite-sex partners for males and females. The numbers in the figure are the five-point summaries (the median, the lower and upper quartiles, and the minimum and maximum). The data are based on actual studies, but were created for this example (see web page). This figure was made in Word

interval overlaps with zero it means that we cannot be confident that the medians are not the same. Because this is a fairly large sample it suggests that the typical male and the typical female report having about the same number of sexual partners.

Box 5.2   Optional: Bootstrapping Confidence Intervals

Bootstrapping is a computationally intensive procedure and thus it has to be done by computer (or by very bored people). Different statistical programs have different built-in procedures. In SPSS 14 it is available through a syntax applied to some specific procedures, like regression. In R/S-Plus, there are also specific bootstrap functions applied to specific procedures, but there are also more general procedures that allow you to put in any function. We will illustrate this procedure with the Scottish witch example (the sex data are explored on the web page). Suppose the data listed above for *wyear_i* represented the entire population of interest. If we sampled one suspected witch from that sample of 168, that would be like sampling one from the population. If we repeatedly did this, each time returning the datum to the set of 168, it would be like collecting a sample from the population. This is called a bootstrap sample of wyear. Given that the original sample size was 168, let's take a bootstrap sample of 168, one-by-one, from the original sample of 168. We can find the median and mean, and any other statistic for this new bootstrap sample. Because we are interested in medians in this example, we can find the median of this sample. Because computers are fast with simple tasks, we could tell the computer to do this 1000 times or more. We would get 1000 bootstrap samples, each with its own median.

Using the package boot (Canty & Ripley, 2008; based on Davison & Hinckley, 1997), which runs in R and is described on the web page, the following command creates a variable for medians of 1000 bootstrap samples of *wyear*:

```
yearboot <- boot(wyear,function(x,i) median(x[i]), R=1000)
```

This is a very general procedure; we could have calculated any statistic of *wyear* where it says median. We could then look at the histogram of the medians of the bootstrap samples. We can also calculate a 95% confidence interval which is the interval that includes the middle 95% of this distribution. The command

```
quantile(yearboot$t,c(.025,.975))
```

produced, when we first ran it, a 95% confidence interval from 41 to 48 years. We ran it again, and it produced an interval from 41 to 47.5 years. Because we are randomly sampling values for each bootstrap sample, the resulting numbers will often be a little different from each other. That there is a shift of an entire half year is a little worrying, but that is because the data are discrete and this is a relatively simple type of bootstrap confidence interval. During the past 20 years there have been several modifications of this procedure. Probably BCa, which stands for Bias Corrected and Accelerated, intervals are currently the most popular. BCa produces an interval from about 40 to 45 years (the exact interval varying for different bootstraps). Calculating these intervals is more complex.

Bradley Efron (e.g., Efron & Gong, 1983) has been one of the principal architects of the bootstrap method. These computationally intensive methods represent one of the most active areas of statistics research. Because bootstrapping can be applied to any statistic, it is a very general approach. Further, it assumes only that the sample data are representative of the population of interest. It is an extreme example of applying the plug-in principle. While some assumptions are made when constructing some of the confidence intervals, these methods are less reliant on assumptions about the distribution than traditional methods. Currently bootstrap techniques tend to only be used when traditional methods are not available, but it is possible that in the future bootstrapping may be used instead of traditional methods for all statistics.

SUMMARY

At the core of any scientific endeavour is inference, the ability to estimate population characteristics from observations of only a sample of this population. This can be done poorly or well, depending on how well the sampling and allocation are done (see Chapter 4). When giving an estimate it is important not just to give a single point, but to convey information about the precision of the estimate. This is what confidence intervals are for. They allow you to say that you are confident, to a certain degree, that the population mean lies somewhere within the interval.

Ten years ago confidence intervals rarely were reported. Usually there would be enough information (i.e., the mean, standard deviation and sample size) so that the reader could calculate the confidence interval. During the past decade many journal editors have stressed that confidence intervals should *always* be reported. This has affected practice and will continue to do so (Cumming et al., 2007). Both the American Psychological Association (Wilkinson et al., 1999) and the British Psychological Society (Wright, 2003) have endorsed the use of confidence intervals.

After reading this chapter you should have a conceptual grasp of why confidence intervals are used and be able to explain to other people what they mean when reported in newspapers. Further, you should be able to calculate the confidence interval for a mean, for the difference in means between two variables, for the difference in means between two groups, for the median, and for the difference in medians between two groups.

EXERCISES

5.1 Look in a newspaper to find(a) where a confidence interval is used and describe what it means, *and* (b) where an estimate is produced without a confidence interval, and describe what additional information the confidence interval would have provided.

5.2 For the coffee preference example from earlier in this chapter, calculate the 99% confidence interval for the difference between the means. What conclusions do you make? Are the conclusions different from those made with the 95% confidence interval, and if so why?

5.3 Thirty-six female undergraduates were given a 15-minute math test in groups of three (Inzlicht & Ben-Zeev, 2000). Half were in a group with two other females. Their mean was 70% correct. Half took the test in a room with two male confederates. Their mean was 55% correct. For both the standard deviation was about 20%. Calculate the 95% confidence intervals for these two groups, and for the difference between the two. What would you conclude from this study?

5.4 Cuc and Hirst (2001) asked Conservatives and Liberals in Romania if they could remember the prices of several common items (e.g., bread, butter, a national newspaper) from 1975 and 1985. The 1970s were a fairly prosperous period in Romania. This contrasts with the 1980s where the economic situation was dire. Price estimates from 48 Conservatives and 49 Liberals were compared with the true prices. They gave each person a price estimate score where 0 means accurate, positive scores mean overestimating the price, and negative scores mean underestimating the price. These, with the associated standard deviations, are given in Table 5.2. Calculate the 95% confidence intervals for each of these and display them in a graph. What would you conclude?

Table 5.2 *Price estimation of common goods in Romania (Cuc & Hirst, 2001)*

	1975		1985		
	Mean	sd	Mean	sd	n
Liberal	0.00	0.26	0.27	0.62	49
Conservative	−0.17	0.22	0.10	0.24	48

5.5 Soon after Einstein proposed general relativity, nature presented science with an excellent opportunity to test it; a total eclipse where light from a group of bright stars would pass near the Sun. There are three main hypotheses about how light will travel when near massive objects like the Sun. First, it could be that light will not be affected, that its direction will not bend. The second is based on special relativity and the prediction is that it will bend 0.87″ as it passes the edge of the Sun. The third is based on general relativity and predicts the bend is 1.75″. Dyson et al. (1920; see Eddington, 1920, for a less technical account and one available in many university libraries) measured the bending of the light in two separate locations. The estimates for the bending of the light at the edge of the Sun were 1.98 ± 0.24″ in Brazil and 1.61 ± 0.60″ in West Africa.[4] What conclusions should the researchers have drawn?

5.6 Maccallum and colleagues (2000) took 24 highly hypnotizable participants, hypnotized them, and then told them to be sad, neutral or happy. They also had

(Cont'd)

4 These are not 95% confidence intervals. They are based on 'probable accidental errors' and these were what was often used back then. As with standard errors, the conventional 'margin of safety [is] about twice the probable error on either side' (Eddington, 1920: 118). Therefore, for present purposes these can be treated as 95% confidence intervals.

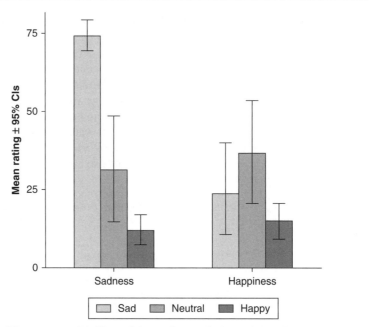

Figure 5.6 The mean and 95% confidence intervals for ratings of sadness and happiness

them go through a sad, a neutral or a happy story. Participants were then asked how happy they were and how sad they were (both on 0 (not at all) to 100 (extremely) scales). Figure 5.6 shows the means and 95% confidence intervals for these data. Discuss what this graph shows. Does it show that the manipulation works?

5.7 Eyewitnesses took part in an identification parade (i.e., a line-up) and identified one of the people. Before being told whether they chose the suspect or one of the other people, they were asked using a 1–10 scale how easy the task was (Wright & Skagerberg, 2007). The data for the 35 people who chose the suspect are:

10, 2, 10, 10, 3, 6, 3, 10, 9, 10, 10, 3, 10, 10, 7, 10, 5, 10, 5, 8, 7, 10, 10, 10, 7, 10, 9, 6, 10, 8, 2, 10, 8, 3, 10

The data for the 16 people who chose someone else (called a filler or a foil) are:

1, 5, 3, 1, 5, 6, 3, 5, 3, 2, 5, 7, 10, 7, 5, 10

(a) Find the median and confidence intervals for these for each group.
(b) What is the confidence interval for the difference between these two medians?
(c) Why might researchers choose a median in this situation?

📖 FURTHER READING

Smithson, M.J. (2003). *Confidence Intervals*. Thousand Oaks, CA: Sage.
This brief book and the associated web page (http://psychology.anu.edu.au/people/ smithson/details/CIstuff/CI.html) are useful references on confidence intervals. A simpler web page that calculates some confidence intervals is: http://glass.ed.asu.edu/stats/analysis/.

Wilkinson, L. and the Task Force on Statistical Inference, APA Board of Scientific Affairs (1999). Statistical methods in psychology journals: guidelines and explanations. *American Psychologist, 54*, 594–604.
This is an excellent report which stresses the value of confidence intervals, as well as other techniques.

6

Hypothesis Testing: *t* Tests and Alternatives

Chapter 5 described how to compute confidence intervals for means, medians, and differences between means and medians. These allow you to create a band within which you are confident that the population values (for the mean, median, and differences between means and medians) lie. In some situations there are values that are of specific interest. In these cases scientists might wish to test whether the observed data are likely to have arisen if the population mean (or median or difference) was this value. An example is if the difference between two means is zero. In this chapter you are taught two *t* tests, devised by 'Student', who you were introduced to in Box 4.2. The first of these is that there is no difference between the means of two variables for a group of people. It is called the *paired t test*. The second is that there is no difference in the means of a variable for two groups. This is called the *group t test*. We also discuss alternative procedures which have fewer assumptions than these *t* tests.

THE PAIRED *t* TEST: INTRODUCING NULL HYPOTHESIS SIGNIFICANCE TESTING

In the coffee preference example from Chapter 5 there is a special interest in the value zero for the difference. If the mean in the population were zero this would mean that overall both coffees are preferred equally. Some people may prefer the fresh coffee from *Brewed Awakenings* more, but others will prefer the instant coffee from the mini-mart. One way to explore the coffee data is to assume that the population mean for the difference is zero and to test how likely it would be to observe data as extreme as observed. This general approach is called *null hypothesis significance testing* (NHST). You hypothesize a certain value for the population, usually that a difference is zero, and then you see whether the observed data look too extreme to have arisen from this hypothesized population. The particular test used in this situation is a *paired t test* (also called related *t* test, matched *t* test and within-subject *t* test). This was the first significance test devised by 'Student'/Gossett in 1908. Since then significance testing has become the most common approach in the social and behavioural sciences, although it is controversial (see Box 6.1). We will go through the coffee data to show how this is done.

The first step in NHST is deciding what the null hypothesis is. For the coffee example we would state that the null hypothesis is that there is no difference between the means for the two types of drink. Researchers often write: H0: mean difference equals zero. H0 is used to denote the null hypothesis. It is important to realize that the null hypothesis is about population values, not the sample values. If the two coffees are equally liked in the population and 10 people were asked to rate the two coffees, sometimes the mean difference in the sample would be above zero (fresh coffee better) and sometimes below zero (instant coffee better). Sometimes the mean would be *a lot* higher or lower than zero, but providing simple random sampling is used this is fairly rare when the null hypothesis is true. Significance testing quantifies how rare this is.

Significance testing is closely related to confidence interval construction. It involves finding the *t* value that would make the confidence interval just touch the hypothesized value, here zero. The equation for the observed *t* value is:

$$t = \frac{\overline{DIFF_i}}{se} = \frac{\overline{DIFF_i}}{sd/\sqrt{n}} = \frac{1.0}{1.25/\sqrt{10}} = 2.53$$

It is the mean of differences divided by *standard error*, here denoted *se*. The standard error for a mean is the standard deviation divided by the square root of *n*. Standard errors are related to the precision of the estimate. The confidence interval was the mean plus and minus approximately two times the standard error. The *t* value is the mean difference measured in units of standard errors.

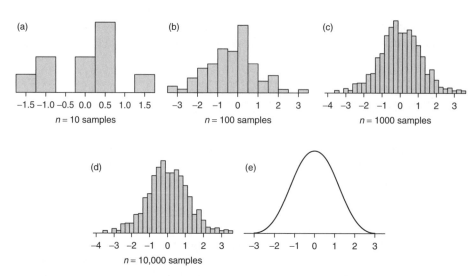

Figure 6.1(a–e)   Samples of size 10. As the number of samples increases the distribution gets more and more similar to the mathematical distribution shown in (e)

The next step is to find the probability associated with this t value. This is the probability of observing a t value as large in magnitude as observed, or larger, assuming that the null hypothesis is true. It is necessary to make some assumptions. The first assumption is that the data are independent, meaning the answers for one person are not dependent on the answers for another person. In the coffee-drinking example, this would mean you should not test people in groups where one of them could spontaneously break into a 'its rich dark aroma' food critic mode, influencing other people's judgements. While there are methods to analyse clustered data (Goldstein, 2003; Hox, 2002; Kreft & de Leeuw, 1998), they are beyond the scope of this book. The second assumption is that the distribution of the differences in the population is normally distributed. You were introduced to the normal distribution in Chapter 5. Usually if the sample distribution looks roughly 'bell shaped' then this assumption is accepted. If this assumption is not met, then the Wilcoxon, the Mann–Whitney–Wilcoxon, and the median tests, which are discussed later in this chapter, can be used.

Suppose that the mean difference in coffee preference is zero in the population (and the data are independent and normally distributed). If we take a sample of 10 people, we can find the t value. Sometimes the t value will be very small, other times it will be very large. Because random sampling is used, sometimes you will get a sample of primarily instant coffee lovers and sometimes you will get a sample of primarily fresh coffee lovers, even though the population mean difference is zero. It is because of random sampling that it is possible to quantify how likely each of these is.

To make Figure 6.1 we created a population where the mean difference was exactly zero and that was normally distributed. We took samples of size 10 from these. In Figure 6.1(a), we have taken 10 samples of 10 people, and graphed their *t* values in a histogram. As can be seen, some are above zero, some below. If there was no difference in the population, and you ran 10 different studies, these are the sort of *t* values you might expect. Figure 6.1(b) shows what happened when we took 100 samples of size 10. As can be seen a general pattern is emerging. There are some fairly high scores, some low scores, and most near zero. As we move through 1000 and 10,000 samples, it is clear we are getting something that looks like a bell-shaped curve. It is not quite the normal distribution, but is very close. It is called the *t* distribution with nine degrees of freedom. The nine degrees of freedom, or 9 *df*, is because for the paired *t* test $df = n-1$. The mathematical form of it is in Figure 6.1(e). It is this *t* distribution listed in Appendix C and it is from this that the associated probability, or *p* value, is found. The *p* value is the probability of observing data as extreme as observed (or more), assuming the null hypothesis is true.

As was true with confidence intervals, where 95% is used as the convention, there is a convention for the critical *p* value. 'Critical' means that the *p* value has to be smaller than this to be felt so unlikely (assuming the null hypothesis is true) that the researcher would want to conclude that the null hypothesis is not true. If the *p* value is less than 5%, or 0.05, people tend to say it is 'significant'. This is an unfortunate choice of word because it does not have the same meaning as its English definition of 'significant', but sadly it has stuck. It does not mean that the size of the difference is of any practical significance, only that if there were no difference in the population, then getting a result like the one observed is unlikely. A lot of people misinterpret the *p* value. A better word than 'significant' would be to say an effect was 'detected', if the *p* value was less than 5%, but this still does not perfectly convey the concept. Box 6.1 describes what *p* is and what it is not in more detail.

Figure 6.2 shows a *t* distribution with nine degrees of freedom. The tails on each side are shaded. Each tail contains 2.5% of the total area under the curve. In total, 5% of the area under the curve is included in these tails. This corresponds approximately to $t = 2.26$ and $t = 2.26$ for nine degrees of freedom. If the observed value is either less than 2.26 or greater than 2.26 the null hypothesis is rejected at the 5% level.

An obvious question is: how well does this work? In the group of 10,000 samples in Figure 6.1(d), 257 had a *t* value below 2.26 and 232 had a *t* value above 2.26. Thus, for 4.89% (489 of the 10,000) of the samples we rejected the null hypothesis (even though it was true). This is known as a Type I error, falsely rejecting the null hypothesis. While it is best to avoid any errors, this result is actually about what we expect. By using a 5% level, we would expect that when the null hypothesis is true, it will be falsely rejected about 5% of the time (and 4.89% is close to 5%). If 5% were too high (i.e., if there were grave consequences of falsely rejecting the null hypothesis), then a more stringent level could be set, like a critical *p* value of 1% or 0.01. For the *t* distribution with nine degrees of freedom, the critical points for 1% are below 3.25 and above 3.25 for $p = 0.01$. In total, there are 101 of the 10,000 samples (1.01%) outside these points. Using the 1% level lowers the chance of a Type I error, but as we will see later it increases the chance of another type of error, creatively called a Type II error. This is where there is an effect, but the *p* value is non-significant, and we fail to detect the effect.

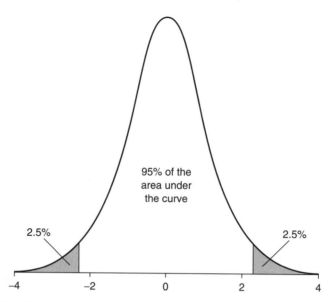

Figure 6.2   The *t* distribution with nine degrees of freedom

Taking lots of samples (as is done in Figure 6.1) illustrates the concept of a frequentist probability: that in the long run we should make about the right number of Type I errors when the null hypothesis is true. However, in most circumstances there is just a single trial, and the *t* table is used. Appendix C shows what the observed *t* values must exceed in order to reject the null hypothesis at the *p* values of 5% and 1%. If the observed value either exceeds the critical value or does so when ignoring the minus sign then you know that the associated probability value, referred to as *p* value, is lower than 5% and/or 1%. Here we see that 2.53 is larger than 2.26 (the degrees of freedom are still nine), so that the probability level is less than 5%. However, the observed *t* is smaller than 3.25, so the probability is not smaller than 1%. You would report $p < 0.05$. Appendix C does not allow you to be more precise.

To get a more precise *p* value you have to use a computer (or a more detailed table). Most statistical packages will compute precise *p* values from an observed *t* and the degrees of freedom. The more precise *p* value for this example is 0.032. This is what you should report (usually with two digits, so $p = 0.03$) when available as it provides more information than simply saying $p < 0.05$ (see Wright, 2003, for more details).

Because of the way we have described how to use the *p*, a good question is why we should be interested in the more precise values of *p*. There are several different philosophies for statistical inference and, according to one (based on work by Neyman, Pearson and Wald), you should decide your critical significance level before the study depending on the cost of different types of errors. If you adopt this approach then you should simply report if *p* is higher or lower than the critical value. Very few people use this extreme approach. The norm is to accept that different values of *p* provide different levels of evidence against the null hypothesis. Trawling through the most important book in the history of statistics, Fisher (1925), where much of the groundwork for statistical inference is laid down, we find:

0.1 to 0.9	'certainly no reason to suspect the hypothesis tested' (p. 79);
0.02 to 0.05	'judge significant, though barely so … these data do not, however, demonstrate the point beyond possibility of doubt' (p. 122);
below 0.02	'strongly indicated that the hypothesis fails to account for the whole of the facts' (p. 79);
below 0.01	'no practical importance whether P is .01 or .000001' (p. 89).

Similar verbal phrases are used in what is arguably the most important statistics book of the last 20 years (Efron & Tibshirani, 1993: 204):

< 0.10	borderline evidence against H0
< 0.05	reasonably strong evidence against H0
< 0.025	strong evidence against H0
< 0.01	very strong evidence against H0

Fisher's approach means that you should report the precise *p* value. Any *p* value above about 0.1 should be treated equivalently (little or no evidence against H0) and any *p* value below about 0.01 should be treated equivalently (strong evidence against H0). It is important to realize, however, that each of these philosophies (and there are others) stresses that the *p* value is only a small part of how you should interpret your data. For an entertaining comparison of these approaches see Gigerenzer (1993). He stresses that modern statistics has taken what it likes from different schools of statistical inference and that the resulting approach is somewhat muddled. Efron (1998) does a similar comparison which includes many of the new approaches to statistical inference (see his Figure 8), but at a more advanced level. For more detailed discussion of these philosophies in a textbook aimed at psychology students see Dienes (2008).

Box 6.1   What is *p*?

Almost every science journal is filled with *p* values. Significance testing is taught in most courses as if it is uncontroversial, straightforward and conceptually simple. However, *p* is a difficult concept. People are often taught a watered-down incorrect meaning of *p* and this leads to much misinterpretation and in the end increases confusion.

(Cont'd)

After taking statistics courses many students (and some professors) think the *p* value is the probability that the null hypothesis (that there is no difference in the population) is true. Another popular definition is the opposite: that *p* is the probability that the null hypothesis is false. Neither of these is the correct definition. In fact the null hypothesis is always false. In the entire population the chance of the mean difference in coffee preference, for example, being *exactly* zero is zero. To quote one of our favourite statisticians (yes, we have favourite statisticians), 'the null hypothesis ... is always false in the real world' (Cohen, 1990: 1308).

p is not a probability about any hypothesis. It is the probability about the data, assuming that the null hypothesis is true. In the examples in this chapter you first draw (or at least think about) the *t* distribution that would arise if the null hypothesis were true. You are assuming the hypothesis is true. Then you look for the probability of observing a mean of data as extreme as observed. We are repeating ourselves, but this message is important. The *p* value is the probability of data, as extreme as observed (or more extreme), assuming that the null hypothesis is true. It can, however, provide evidence against the null hypothesis, because if the null hypothesis were true, we would expect the data to have certain characteristics.

This is a very difficult concept. Most people who think that they understand the concept of *p* will confidently give an incorrect answer when asked what *p* is the probability of. If people knew (and understood) the correct meaning of *p* they would probably use confidence intervals more and *p* values less. They would probably also use more graphs and be more careful to report means, standard deviations and other descriptive statistics. Among methodologists, there is agreement that *p* values are over-used. This is nicely summarized by one of the more vocal and well-respected critics: 'the almost universal reliance on merely refuting the null hypothesis is a terrible mistake, is basically unsound, poor scientific strategy, and one of the worst things that ever happened in the history of psychology' (Meehl, 1978: 817). Yet, it is the dominant approach.

The use of *p* values is hotly debated. The American Psychological Association's Task Force on Statistical Inference (Wilkinson et al., 1999) makes clear that there are lots of ways to look at data. Good statistical practice is best summarized by a statement made in an interview with one of the co-chairs of that Task Force, Robert Rosenthal, that researchers should 'make friends with their data' (Wright, 2003).

Let's consider another example from Chapter 5. The main purpose of Newton's research was to examine differences in hostility between when the 94 inmates entered Grendon prison and when they were discharged. At discharge the HDHQ was also administered (the mean was 21.6 with a standard deviation of 9.2), and Newton compared these with the earlier scores. She subtracted the scores for each person and found the mean of this difference was 6.6 with a standard deviation of 9.0. To do a *t* test you simply plug these numbers into the *t* test equation:

$$t = \frac{\overline{DIFF_i}}{sd/\sqrt{n}} = \frac{-6.6}{9.0/\sqrt{94}} = -7.11$$

The *t* value is negative, but remember that you look at the magnitude of the *t* value, so you can treat -7.11 as if it were 7.11.[1] With a *t* value of 7.11, and 93 degrees of freedom (for *n*-1), it surpasses the critical values for *p* of 5% and 1%. The actual *p* value is very close to zero, though still slightly above zero. Many statistical packages print *p* = 0.000. Instead of writing this, it is better to write $p < 0.001$ so that the reader knows that you know it is still above zero. If you write $p < 0.0000$ your friends will ridicule you because this would mean the probability was negative, which is not possible. Thus, observing a *t* value this large in magnitude is extremely unlikely if the null hypothesis were true (thus, according to Efron and Tibshirani, 1993, provides very strong evidence against H0), but theoretically it is still possible to get a *t* this large when the null hypothesis is true. However, because it is so unlikely, we reject the null hypothesis that the population difference is zero, and say that hostility decreased.

COMPARING TWO GROUPS (ASSUMING EQUAL VARIANCES)

Tatar (1998) had a sample of Israeli secondary school students, 166 girls and 129 boys, rate on a 1 to 5 scale (with 5 being high) how much 'makes me learn willingly' characterizes a 'significant' teacher. The mean for girls was 3.51 with a standard deviation of 0.99. The mean for boys was 3.26 with a standard deviation of 1.05.

The question often asked is: 'Are girls' and boys' attitudes the same or does one gender feel that "makes me learn willingly" is a more important attribute for a "significant" teacher?' The way that this is usually evaluated is with a group *t* test (sometimes called a between-subjects *t* test). Conceptually, it has a very similar format to the paired *t* test and computationally it has similarities to constructing a confidence interval for mean group differences in Chapter 5. It is the difference between the means of the two groups divided by the standard error of this difference. However, the way that the standard error is calculated is different from the paired *t* test. There are a few ways to do a group *t* test depending on which assumptions you are willing to make.

First, we will assume that the standard deviations (or the variances) are the same in the populations from which the two samples are drawn (i.e., Israeli boys and girls). It is easier to work with variances because it makes the calculations slightly simpler (recall that squaring the standard deviation results in the variance). As with Chapter 5, let var1 and var2 be the variances of the two groups and let *n*1 and *n*2 be their respective sample sizes. Then, as with Chapter 5, the 'pooled variance' is:

$$pooled\ var = \frac{(n1-1)\,var1 + (n2-1)\,var2}{n1+n2-2}$$

---

1 For those of you who have encountered the distinction between one- and two-tailed tests, this is a two-tailed test. We discuss this distinction later in this chapter.

This is a weighted mean of the two sample variances. If one sample is larger, it is given more weight. If the two sample sizes are equal (i.e., $n1 = n2$), then it is simply the mean of the two variances. This is then put into an equation for t:

$$t = \frac{\overline{x1} - \overline{x2}}{\sqrt{pooled\ var(1/n1 + 1/n2)}}$$

From Chapter 5 we know that pooled variance is 1.03 for Tatar's data. Putting this, the means, and the group sizes into the t test equation yields:

$$t = \frac{3.51 - 3.26}{\sqrt{1.03\,(1/166 + 1/129)}} = \frac{0.25}{\sqrt{0.014}} = \frac{0.25}{0.12} = 2.08$$

The next step is to see whether this is statistically significant. The t table is used (Appendix C). The t table requires knowing the degrees of freedom (df). The degrees of freedom for a group t test, when equal variances is assumed, are

$$df = n1 + n2 - 2$$

So for this example $df = 293$.[2] Being conservative we can use the $df = 100$ row and we see that the value exceeds 1.98 and therefore we can say that the difference is significant at a critical p of 5%. However, it does not exceed the value for 1%. While statistically significant (at 5%) it is important to think about the size of the effect. A difference of 0.25 on a five-point attitude scale is not large regardless of any statistical significance. With large samples trivial effects may become statistically significant. It is important to look at the confidence intervals, as discussed in Chapter 5, and think about what your data are like.

The equations shown in this section are suitable when the standard deviations, or variances, of the two groups are approximately the same.

NOT ASSUMING EQUAL VARIANCES: ACUPUNCTURE

There is much debate about the therapeutic value of acupuncture. Numerous theories have been put forward for *why* acupuncture may work, but this does not mean that it *does* work. As scientists we need data to help to judge the therapeutic value of sticking needles into your body. Given the popularity of acupuncture, there has been surprisingly little empirical research

---

2 For the paired t test $df = n-1$ because we were calculating only one mean. For the group t test we calculate two means, so it is $df = n - 2$, where n is the total sample size.

using proper scientific methods to assess its value. An exception is by Allen et al. (1998). Their sample was composed of depressed women who were randomly assigned either to an acupuncture condition ($n1 = 12$) or put on a waiting list ($n2 = 11$). This is a common 'control' group in such studies, though it raises some ethical issues.[3]

Participants were given a scale for measuring depression both when they arrived and after eight weeks. The authors calculated a change score where negative scores mean that the person became less depressed (i.e., negative scores are good). The mean and standard deviation for the acupuncture group were 11.7 and 7.3. The equivalent scores for the waiting list group were 6.1 and 10.9. While the standard deviations in the students' attitudes example were fairly close, the standard deviations in this example are different. A rough rule of thumb is that if the ratio of the larger variance to the smaller variance is greater than 2 then you should be concerned. Here, $10.9^2 - 7.3^2 = 118.853.3 = 2.23$. The procedures in the previous section assumed that the variances were equal. Here we describe a procedure that can be used when this assumption is not made.

Again, it is best first to calculate the confidence intervals and to graph these. The confidence intervals are:

$$\text{For acupuncture}: \text{CI}_{95\%} = -11.7 \pm 2.20\frac{7.3}{\sqrt{12}} = -11.7 \pm 4.6$$

$$\text{For waiting}: \text{CI}_{95\%} = -6.1 \pm 2.23\frac{10.9}{\sqrt{11}} = -6.1 \pm 7.3$$

The improvement was better (i.e., the depression scores dropped more) for the acupuncture sample compared with the waiting list sample, but the difference appears small. A group *t* test can be used to see if the difference is statistically significant. There are two popular approaches to running a *t* test when the variances are different: one to use when you are doing the calculations yourself and the other when a computer is doing the calculations. Here only the 'by hand' approach will be discussed. You calculate *t* as follows:

$$t = \frac{\overline{x1} - \overline{x2}}{\sqrt{\text{var}1/n1 + \text{var}2/n2}}$$

$$t = \frac{-11.7 - -6.1}{\sqrt{53.3/12 + 118.8/11}} = \frac{-5.6}{3.90} = -1.44$$

Next, you have to calculate the degrees of freedom. The 'by hand' method is to take the smaller of ($n1-1$) and ($n2-1$) because here $n2 = n1$, we use $df = 11-1 = 10$. Next, go to the *t* table. In the 10th row it shows that the critical value *p* at 5% is $t = 2.23$. As the observed value does not exceed this value we fail to reject the hypothesis that the values of the treatments are identical. This is a conservative method, meaning that it is less likely that the value will be statistically significant than the computer approach. The approach used by

---

3 There was a third group given a non-specific treatment. Despite random allocation this group had a much lower initial mean than the other groups. Therefore, this group will not be considered here.

many computer programs calculates the degrees of freedom in a more complex way. It is best to use those values if available. Do not worry that the number of degrees of freedom is not a whole number.

There were a lot of new equations in Chapter 5, so we did not include a 95% confidence interval for the difference between the means of two groups when the variances are not assumed to be equal. The equation is:

$$CI_{95\%} = (\overline{x1} - \overline{x2}) \pm t_{0.05}\sqrt{\frac{\text{var1}}{n1} + \frac{\text{var2}}{n2}}$$

which here yields

$$CI_{95\%} = -5.6 \pm 2.23(3.9) = -5.6 \pm 8.70$$

which includes zero, the population mean assumed for the null hypothesis.

Box 6.2   Two- Versus One-Tailed Tests

When we explained null hypothesis significance testing (NHST), we said that the null hypothesis was usually something like the means for each group were the same in population. As discussed in Box 6.1, this means *exactly* the same, which is one of the problems with NHST. The alternative hypothesis is usually thought of as whatever the null hypothesis is not. So, this would be that there would be some difference between the means. Technically, if you reject the null hypothesis you can say that there is a difference, but the significance does not tell you which group has the larger mean. For this you have to look at the means, or whichever statistics you are comparing. The statistical test is sensitive to finding either the first mean being bigger than the second, or the second mean being bigger than the first. When we look at the *t* distribution (Figure 6.2) this means that we shade 2.5% of distribution's left tail and of its right tail. For this reason it is called a two-tailed test.

There is an alternative that some people prefer. It is to specify a direction in the alternative hypothesis. Instead of saying that the alternative hypothesis is that the two groups will be different, we would say, for example, that the acupuncture group will be better. When testing the significance you have all 5% of the shaded area on the side that you are predicting. This means that a lower *t* value is necessary to reach significance. Instead of requiring $t = 2.23$ for $df = 10$, it only requires $t = 1.81$. So, if the difference is in the direction that you predict it is easier to get a significant result. This is called a one-tailed test because all the shaded area is on one tail of the *t* distribution.

At first glance this seems like an attractive option, but we discourage it for three reasons. First, ideally your null hypothesis, what you are testing, should be something that you believe might be true. Meehl (1967) describes one of the problems with the way psychologists often use NHST is that they do not believe their null hypothesis. If people actually believed their null hypotheses, then it is likely they would be interested if the difference was in either direction. The second reason is related to this. If you do a one-tailed test and you find a huge effect in the opposite direction as predicted, then you simply have to report that the test was non-significant and pretend like you did not observe this effect. This might mean you miss some groundbreaking finding. As the prolific science fiction writer, Isaac Asimov (see http://www.asimovonline.com/) said: 'The most exciting phrase to hear in science, the one that heralds the most discoveries, is not "Eureka!" (I found it!) but "That's funny"'. This is particularly important as often psychological and medical therapies could be tested which actually cause harm (Lilienfeld, 2007, stresses the first priority should be 'to do no harm', but that some treatments appear harmful). If one-tailed tests were done on these then damaging therapies might not be as easily detected. Third, it would be very easy for someone to have an effect that just fails to reach significance with a two-tailed test so they pretend that they planned to do a one-tailed test all along.

For these reasons we urge people not to do one-tailed tests, but to always do two-tailed tests, report the precise p value (unless $p < 0.001$, where saying this is fine), and say whether the observed differences show the predicted pattern. This advice is shared by many, and in fact this approach is required for many journals, including the *New England Journal of Medicine*, considered by many the top science journal. For these reasons we do not cover one-tailed tests in this book.

Finally, the phrase one- versus two-tailed refers to the tails on distributions like the *t* distribution. Here, the word 'tail' makes sense. For some other distributions that we encounter later in this book you would always be looking at one end of the distribution even if your hypothesis was directional. This makes this phrase confusing (which is another reason to avoid it).

WILCOXON AND MANN–WHITNEY–WILCOXON TESTS AS DISTRIBUTION-FREE ALTERNATIVES

For the *t* tests to be accurate the researcher has to make assumptions about the distributions of the variables. In the 1940s and 1950s Frank Wilcoxon and others devised several tests that do not make these distributional assumptions. These tests involve ranking the data. They still make some assumptions, but not as many as the *t* tests and they are less influenced by outliers, so in statistical jargon they are more robust. Much as Gossett has two tests to his *nom de plume* ('Student'), in his landmark 1945 paper Wilcoxon described two alternatives to these *t* tests, and each bears his name. The first test is called the Wilcoxon signed ranks test and it is an appropriate alternative to the paired *t* test. The second is often called the Wilcoxon rank sum test and it is an appropriate alternative to the group *t* test. At about the same time as Wilcoxon described this test, Henry Mann and D. Ransom Whitney described an equivalent test often called the Mann–Whitney *U*. To avoid confusion we will call the first test the Wilcoxon test and the second test the Mann–Whitney–Wilcoxon or MWW test.

Two caveats are worth mentioning before describing these tests. First, sometimes people describe how these tests can be used when you do not make any assumptions about the data. This is simply wrong. It is just that they do not require the normal distribution assumption of the *t* tests. The second caveat is that these tests are not used very often. There are at least four reasons for this. One is a myth that you are much less likely to find significant results with these than with *t* tests. In fact, when there are a lot of outliers the opposite is true. The second is that if you use tests like this in part of a paper, it suggests that you should also use this type of test for other parts, and there are not as many rank-based procedures available as those that have developed out of the *t* test. The third reason is that there are modern and more complex methods that have many of the advantages of these tests (i.e., they are less influenced by outliers than the *t* test), but do not require losing information about the distance between points. The final reason is that when ranking the data this can make it difficult to describe the hypotheses in concrete easily understood ways.

The Wilcoxon Signed Ranks Test: An Alternative to the Paired *t* Test

The Wilcoxon signed ranks test is an alternative for the paired *t* test either when you do not want large differences to have a large effect (which they do with the *t* test) or when the distribution of these differences is not normally distributed. This test requires ranking the data, so it is worth briefly reminding you how to rank data. If you have the following 10 scores:

| 4 | 7 | 3 | 9 | 14 | 5 | 8 | 10 | 22 | 2 |

the ranks of these are:

| 3 | 5 | 2 | 7 | 9 | 4 | 6 | 8 | 10 | 1 |

Because 2 is the lowest value, it gets rank 1. The second lowest value is 3 so gets rank 2, and so on until 22, which is the highest value, and gets rank 10. If the data had been:

| 3 | 7 | 3 | 9 | 14 | 5 | 8 | 10 | 22 | 2 |

these would get the ranks:

| 2.5 | 5 | 2.5 | 7 | 9 | 4 | 6 | 8 | 10 | 1 |

Because two scores have the value 3, the ranking is slightly more complicated. The lowest value is still 2 so it has rank 1. The next lowest value is 3. There are two scores with this value. We could arbitrarily give one rank 2 and one rank 3. Instead of doing this we give them the mean of the ranks that we would have arbitrarily assigned to the pair. The mean of 2 and 3 is 2.5. This is called assigning the *mid-rank* of the values. If there were three scores with the value 3, the mid-rank of 2, 3 and 4 would be 3. It is easiest to rank data if you have sorted them in order.

The *t* tests make assumptions about the distribution of the variables. The Wilcoxon does not. Because of this it is often called a *distribution-free test*. Many textbooks state that the Wilcoxon does not assume that the variables have an interval level of measurement (see Chapter 3). This is wrong. The Wilcoxon works in a very similar way to the paired *t* test, and it begins like the paired *t* test comparing differences between values, which is only meaningful for interval data. This will be illustrated through an example.

A total of 25 people were asked to retrieve a memory of a happy occasion and of a sad occasion. The response times, in seconds, are shown in the second and third columns of Table 6.1. Response times often are not distributed like the normal distribution because they tend to have a few very large times. They are usually positively skewed. Therefore, more robust statistics are often used with response times.

The first step for conducting a Wilcoxon test is the same as when doing a paired *t* test: subtract the scores of one variable from the other. Here we took $HAPPY_i - SAD_i$ to make $DIFF_i$. Most of these scores are negative, which corresponds to slower retrieval times for sad memories than for happy memories. There is one zero difference. People who have the same scores for the two variables, like participant 23, are excluded from the analysis making the effective sample size $n = 24$. These people are excluded because they provide no information about which set of reaction times is faster. Next, rank the remaining differences by their magnitude, at first *ignoring* whether they are negative or positive. The smallest difference is 0.1 seconds so this is given rank 1. The next smallest is 0.4 which is given rank 2. Some of the ranks are tied. For example, participant 2 has a difference of positive 2.9 and participant 9 has a difference of negative 2.9. They are tied at the sixth lowest. As there are two of them they could be ranked 6 and 7 if no ties were allowed. The mid-rank of these is 6.5. The ranks are in the fifth column of Table 6.1.

The next step is to separate the ranks for the people who had positive differences from those who had negative differences. We have denoted the positive ranks as $T+_i$ and the negative ranks as $T-_i$. We have included the subscript *i* to make clear that people can have different values on this variable. Next, add up all the $T+_i$ and all the $T-_i$ to get 66.5 and

Table 6.1 *Hypothetical data comparing reaction times, in seconds, for retrieving a happy memory and a sad memory*

Participant	HAPPY$_i$	SAD$_i$	DIFF$_i$	RANK$_i$	T+$_i$	T−$_i$
1	3.9	10.4	−6.5	16	−	16
2	10.0	7.1	2.9	6.5	6.5	−
3	7.1	12.1	−5.0	14	−	14
4	9.7	6.3	3.4	8.5	8.5	−
5	10.0	8.8	1.2	4	4	−
6	9.9	5.1	4.8	13	13	−
7	6.1	14.9	−8.8	21	−	21
8	18.9	6.6	12.3	22	22	−
9	5.9	8.8	−2.9	6.5	−	6.5
10	2.8	11.0	−8.2	19.5	−	19.5
11	3.8	20.4	−16.6	23	−	23
12	5.7	11.4	−5.7	15	−	15
13	8.5	7.7	0.8	3	3	−
14	5.4	9.0	−3.6	10	−	10
15	6.2	14.4	−8.2	19.5	−	19.5
16	6.0	6.4	−0.4	2	−	2
17	6.4	14.5	−8.1	18	−	18
18	9.2	9.1	0.1	1	1	−
19	2.3	9.5	−7.2	17	−	17
20	7.0	30.6	−23.6	24	−	24
21	10.1	14.4	−4.3	12	−	12
22	6.1	9.8	−3.7	11	−	11
23	7.4	7.4	0.0	−	−	−
24	8.7	5.3	3.4	8.5	8.5	−
25	5.2	8.1	−2.9	5	−	5
					$\sum T+_i = 66.5$	$\sum T−_i = 233.5$

233.5, respectively. Either of these can be used in the next equation, but it is usually easier to use the smaller of these, 66.5, and to denote it as just plain T. It is then placed into the rather frightening equation:[4]

$$z = \frac{T - n(n-1)/4}{\sqrt{n(n+1)(2n+1)/24}}$$

---

4 We are actually simplifying this procedure a bit. There is a special adjustment that is made when there are many ties (like participants 2 and 9), but usually it does not make a large difference. Also, for small samples there is a special table that can be used (see Siegel & Castellan, 1988, for more details).

Inserting $T = 66.5$ and $n = 24$ (since one participant is excluded) yields:

$$z = \frac{66.5 - 24(23)/4}{\sqrt{24(25)(49)/24}} = -2.39$$

If we had used $T = 233.5$ we would have found $z = 2.39$, which produces the same p value for a two-tailed test (see Box 6.2).

This z value can be looked up on a table of the normal distribution. However, if you are just interested in whether this value is statistically significant at the 5% level, then all you need to know is that the observed z must be greater than 1.96 (or less than −1.96). Appendix B is used to find the more precise p value associated with the observed z value. The values in the z columns are the z values. Positive and negative values are treated the same so to find the p value associated with z of −2.39 go to 2.39 in the z column. Then go the column labelled p. The p value is $p = 0.016$. We would write '$z = 2.39, p = 0.02$'. Since this is less than 0.05 we can say that z of 2.39 is statistically significant. If a z value is greater than 1.96 then it is statistically significant at the 5% level. For the 1% level a z value of 2.58 or greater is necessary for statistical significance. Therefore these data are not significant at the 1% level.

MANN–WHITNEY–WILCOXON TEST: AN ALTERNATIVE TO THE BETWEEN-SUBJECTS *t* TEST

The Mann–Whitney–Wilcoxon test (also called the Mann–Whitney U, the Wilcoxon–Mann–Whitney, and the Wilcoxon rank sum test) is an alternative to the between-subjects, or groups, t test. Here we will abbreviate it as the MWW test. It involves ranking all the data, ignoring which group the person was in, and then comparing the ranks for the two groups.

Helsen and Starkes (1999) ran several very clever studies comparing expert football (soccer) players with novices on a number of tasks. In one of their studies participants watched 30 re-enactments of plays from European and World Cup games on a life-size screen. These were filmed from the vantage point of one of the players, whose part the participant was supposed to play. The participant had a football in front of her/him and at a particular point in the film the participant had to shoot, dribble around the goalkeeper, or pass to a team-mate. For each of these options there was a correct option. Data based on their study are shown in Table 6.2. Here there are 16 novices and 14 experts.

Before calculating any statistics it is worth graphing these data. One option is a boxplot (see Chapter 1), as is done in Figure 6.3. Two outliers are clear from this figure. There are two novices who perform very poorly. While these could be very influential for a t test, the MWW test is less influenced by these points.

Table 6.2 *The number of correct plays out of 30; data based on Helsen and Starkes (1999). The ranks are done for the entire sample, from 1 to 30*

Novices		Experts	
Number correct	Rank	Number correct	Rank
8	1.0	22	5.5
9	2.0	23	9.0
17	3.0	23	9.0
20	4.0	24	14.0
22	5.5	25	17.0
23	9.0	26	19.0
23	9.0	26	19.0
23	9.0	27	23.0
24	14.0	27	23.0
24	14.0	27	23.0
24	14.0	28	27.0
24	14.0	28	27.0
26	19.0	29	29.5
27	23.0	29	29.5
27	23.0		
28	27.0		
Sum of ranks = 190.5		Sum of ranks = 274.5.	

The first step in conducting an MWW test is to rank the variable. Table 6.2 shows the ranks for these data. The lowest number of correct choices was 8, so this value receives rank 1. The second lowest was 9, so it receives rank 2. The third lowest was 17 so it receives rank 3, 20 receives rank 4, etc. There were several ties. There were two participants who got 22 correct, one novice and one expert. These are dealt with by giving the mean of the ranks if the values had been arbitrarily differentiated (i.e., the mid-rank). The most important thing to remember is to do the ranking for the entire sample.

Next, the ranks within each group are added together. Here the sums are 190.5 and 274.5 for the novice and experts, respectively. For notational ease, we will refer to novices as group 1 and experts as group 2, and therefore $n1$ will be the number of novices (16), and $n2$ the number of experts (14), $T1$ is the total sum of ranks for novices (190.5), and $T2$ the total sum of ranks for experts (274.5). The test statistic for MWW, called the Mann–Whitney U, is the smaller of:

$$\left(n1\ n2 + \frac{n1(n1+1)}{2} - T1 \right) \quad and \quad \left(n1\ n2 + \frac{n2(n2+1)}{2} - T2 \right)$$

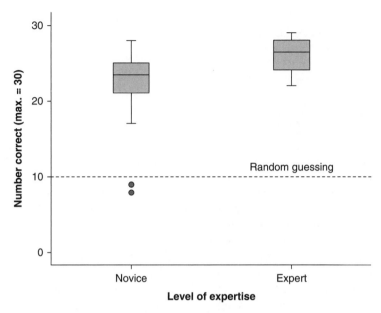

Figure 6.3 Boxplots of the number of correct football decisions for novices and experts. As there are 30 trials and three possible choices, the two outliers depicted by dots in the novice group are near chance levels. These data are based on Helsen and Starkes (1999)

For these data these values are:

$$(16)(14) + \frac{16(16+1)}{2} - 190.5 = 169.5$$

and

$$(16)(14) + \frac{14(14+1)}{2} - 274.5 = 54.5$$

Because 54.5 is smaller, $U = 54.5$. As with the Wilcoxon test this value can be changed into a z value. Here the equation is:

$$z = \frac{n1\,n2/2 - U}{\sqrt{(n1\,n2/12)(n1 + n2 + 1)}}$$

which results in:

$$z = \frac{(16)(14)/2 - 54.5}{\sqrt{((16)(14)/12)(16 + 14 + 1)}} = \frac{57.5}{24.06} = 2.39$$

This can be looked up in the z table and the null hypothesis can be rejected at the 5% level. As with the Wilcoxon test, there is a complex correction for ties (see Siegel & Castellan, 1988). Most computer packages make these adjustments, so if using a computer package your results may be slightly different.[5]

TESTS FOR MEDIANS

The Wilcoxon and the MWW each rank the data and therefore the resulting hypotheses are about the ranked data. This is one reason that many people do not use them, because telling somebody that the ranks of one variable tend to be higher than another does not convey as much concrete information as saying the means differ. The Wilcoxon and MWW each use the values of the ranks during their calculations. An alternative is to see whether the medians are different for the two variables or the two conditions. Most people have a more concrete definition of what it means to have two different medians than to talk about the differences between the two sets of ranks.

There are three different questions that you can ask about comparing medians for two variables. The first two relate to paired data and will be discussed first. The first is that the medians for the two conditions are different. The second is the median of the differences between the two conditions is zero. When the hypotheses were about means, these were the same; the difference between two means is equal to the mean of the differences. This is not true for medians; the difference between two medians is not generally equal to the median of the differences. The computations for a test comparing two medians are complex, so we leave interested readers to consult more advanced textbooks (like Wilcox, 2005: sec. 5.9.3).

The second hypothesis, being interested in whether the median of the differences is zero, is much more common. There are several approaches you could take to test this hypothesis. One approach would be to take the differences, find the median and calculate the standard error using the techniques described in Chapter 5. Consider the difference data from Table 6.1, in ascending order.

First 12:   −23.6, −16.6, −8.8, −8.2, −8.2, −8.1, −7.2, −6.5, −5.7, −5.0, −4.3, −3.7

Median: −3.6

Last 12:   −2.9, −2.9, −.4, 0.0, 0.1, 0.8, 1.2, 2.9, 3.4, 3.4, 4.8, 12.3

---

5 The differences when using a computer are slight for this and for the Wilcoxon. So, using SPSS 14.0, we find $U = 54.5$ and $z = 2.41$. The default in R 2.14 produces $z = 2.39$, but if one of the corrections it uses is turned off you get $z = 2.41$. The fact that two major statistical programs have defaults that reach different answers is quite common (it also happens between these two programs for the t test). The differences are almost always small.

If you calculate the standard error you get 1.55 (first find that $k = 7$). The median divided by its standard error is: $z = -3.6/1.55 = -2.32$. As this is greater in magnitude than 1.96 it is statistically significant. However, this is a rough approximation and not recommended. There is a more popular way to test this hypothesis.

The standard method is called a *sign test*. Testing whether the median is different from zero is the same as saying whether there are more positive values than negative values, or vice versa. Therefore, all you need to do is count the number of positive values (8) and compare this with the number of negative values (16). The one case with a zero difference is excluded. The question now becomes the same as if you had a fair coin and flipped it 24 times: what is the probability of finding one of the two results happening 16 times or more? For small samples this probability can be calculated directly, and when conducting these tests by computer, the computer will use this approach. We do not recommend this approach by hand because the number of computations becomes fairly large, and with lots of computations the chance of arithmetic and rounding errors is large. Instead, when doing a sign test by hand we recommend using the following (from Siegel & Castellan, 1988):

$$z = \frac{2x - 1 - n}{\sqrt{n}}$$

where x is the larger of the two sets of values, so here it is 16 since 16 is greater than 8, and n is the sample size minus any zero differences, so here 24. The resulting $z = 1.42$ which is not significant at 5% since it is less than 1.96. The p value is 0.156. If we let a computer use more exact methods, we find $p = 0.152$. With very small numbers the difference can be larger, but for most purposes this approach works well.

The third comparison of medians in which people are often interested is comparing the medians of two groups. As with the last example, similar methods to those used in Chapter 5 can be used. When calculating the confidence interval of the difference between medians the standard error of this difference was calculated. For the gender and sex example the median for males was 10.5 partners and for females was 10 partners, a difference of 0.5 partners. The pooled standard error was 0.46, so an estimate for the z value is $0.50/0.46 = 1.09$, which is less than 1.96 so we know that $p > 0.05$ (and using a more precise table $p = 0.28$). Therefore, we fail to reject the hypothesis that the medians are different.

There is also something called a *median test* that is discussed in Siegel and Castellan (1988), which is often used. You find the median of the entire sample (10 partners) and find how many males are below (37) and above (50) this median, and do the same for females (92 and 83, respectively), and see if these ratios differ by gender. This relies on using a test (the χ^2 [chi-square] test) which is covered in later chapters so will not be discussed here, but the resulting p value is 0.15, so fairly similar.

It is worth stressing that these tests are comparing the medians, so they are not sensitive to differences between groups at either end of their distributions. With these data we expected the medians to be the same because we created the data ourselves and we created

80% of the males to be like the females, and just 20% of males to be claiming large numbers of sex partners. If we wanted to look for differences throughout the distribution, we could have used the MWW and we would have found a statistically significant difference ($p = 0.01$) and if we were interested in difference in means, which are not just sensitive to differences at the extremes, but highly influenced by them, we would have also found a statistically significant difference ($p < 0.001$). These procedures are all testing different hypotheses, so it is important to carefully consider what you want to test before you actually do your statistics.

Often people are interested in the median, and in the introductory chapters of most psychology statistics books they stress this. They spend several pages describing the median, make you do exercises finding the median, and then do not mention them again. One result of this is that the tests involving medians are much less common than others. We present these tests because when we were students we believed those introductory chapters. After our first lecture where the professor discussed the merits of the median, we went off for our usual helpless-frolicking sessions and toasted the median with our equally enamoured classmates. The next morning we scoured the pages for any further mention of medians in vain; we were sad. We do not want you to have to go through what we had to!

SUMMARY

In this chapter you were introduced to null hypothesis significance testing. We also introduced you to several tests. The most popular of these are the two t tests: the paired and the group t tests. The paired t test is used when you are comparing the mean of two variables. The group t test is used when you want to compare the means of two separate groups of people. It is important before you do either of these that you look carefully at your data (i.e., make friends with your data). It is worth graphing the variables' distributions (Chapter 1) and constructing confidence intervals (Chapter 5). Too often people leap into a statistical test simply wanting to see if it is statistically significant. As discussed in Box 6.1, finding a significant p value is not as important as some social scientists believe.

We also presented some alternatives. The first two, the Wilcoxon and the Mann–Whitney–Wilcoxon, are appropriate alternatives to the paired and group t tests when you do not think the data are normally distributed. They involve ranking the data. They are still sensitive to differences anywhere in the distributions, but they are less influenced by extreme points than are the t tests. The final set of alternatives involved tests of medians. These are often not used in psychology, but one of the main reasons, we believe, is that they are not well publicized. Therefore, we presented them here in the hope that people consider more tests of medians.

EXERCISES

6.1   Fisher and Geiselman (1992) developed what is called the *cognitive interview*. It is a method for interviewing eyewitnesses that has been shown to elicit more accurate information compared with the standard police interview. In a hypothetical study, suppose 10 people were trained in the cognitive interview and 10 other people were trained in the standard police interview. Twenty participants were shown individually a video of a bank robbery. The first 10 participants were interviewed by the 10 cognitive interviewers. The numbers of accurate details recalled were

20,   22,   17,   32,   16,   9,   18,   19,   23,   24

The second 10 were interviewed by those trained in the standard police interview. The numbers of accurate details recalled were

17,   11,   21,   9,   14,   23,   10,   14,   20,   11

What is the evidence for there being a difference between the two interview techniques?

6.2   A sports psychologist was interested in UK and USA people's attitudes towards football/soccer. Suppose that 20 people in each country were asked, 'Do you think that football/soccer is a fun sport to watch?' using a 1 to 7 scale where 1 is boring and 7 is exciting. The mean in the United Kingdom was 5.2 with a standard deviation of 3.0, while the USA had a mean of 2.2 with a standard deviation of 2.0. Are means of these samples sufficiently different to reject the hypothesis that the UK and USA people have the same attitude towards the 'beautiful game' (Pelé & Fish, 2007)?

6.3   (a) Find a student from the social, behavioural or physical sciences who has done statistics (probably avoid maths and stats students) and who has used *p*-values. Ask the student what she/he thinks *p* is the probability of. Write down what the student said and say whether she/he is right or wrong.
(b) Find a student who has taken no statistics. Explain to this student what a *p*-value is and why you use it. Write down the problems you had explaining it to the student.

6.4   From the data in Table 5.1, test the hypothesis that instant and fresh coffee are equally well liked, but instead of using the *t* test, as done in the text, use a test that does not assume the differences are normally distributed.

6.5   Give the ranks for the following set of data:

−4   12   4   0   2   2   2   8   −1   1

(Cont'd)

6.6 A drug company has created a drug that it feels can increase people's memory. The company randomly allocated a group of 20 people into two groups. One group of 10 people received a pill containing the drug while the other group received a pill without the drug (what is sometimes called a *placebo*). Participants were then given a memory test, scored from 0 to 10 where higher scores stand for having better memory scores. The data are:

Placebo group:	2	5	4	4	1	3	4	10	4	4
Drug group:		5	8	10	3	5	1	1	9	8	8

What are the means for the two groups? Does one group have a higher mean than the other?

6.7 Suppose for the data in Exercise 6.6 that you were not willing to assume that they were from a normal distribution. Conduct a statistical test of whether the drug is making a difference.

6.8 Suppose one of your fellow students wrote in a laboratory report: '$t(58) = 6.44$, $p < 0.0000$'. Would they still be your friend? If not, why?

6.9 Rothblum and Factor (2001) were interested in differences between lesbians and their heterosexual sisters on a number of characteristics. They had 173 lesbian–heterosexual pairs of sisters fill out the Rosenberg Self-Esteem Scale. In this study they compared the sisters using a within-subject design versus a between-subjects design. The mean for lesbians was 33.9 with a standard deviation of 4.55. The mean for the heterosexuals was 32.0 with a standard deviation of 5.04. Conduct a between-subjects t test using these means and standard deviations.

Rothblum and Factor realized that self-esteem might relate to both genetic and environmental factors. They felt that taking pairs of lesbian–heterosexual sisters and subtracting the scores for each pair (the pair is now the unit of analysis) would help to control for some of these additional factors.[6] If you subtract the heterosexual sister's score from the lesbian sister's score, you get a mean of 1.9 with a standard deviation of 7.00. Calculate the within-pair t test for this mean and standard deviation.

---

6 This is the same conclusion 'Student' (1931) comes to in his criticism of the Lanarkshire milk study (see Box 4.2). He said how it would have been much more effective to use siblings; he actually suggests monozygotic twins as participants. Here it appears that the genetic and sibling environmental effects were not large as the effects are of a similar size.

6.10   Wright and Hall (2007) were interested in whether the instruction given to jurors could affect their ratings of guilt of the defendant. They had two conditions. A control condition ($n = 86$) was given the standard instruction which said they should only convict if they believed in guilt 'beyond a reasonable doubt'. The experimental condition ($n = 86$) had the further definition that even if they could imagine a scenario in which the defendant was guilty, this need not surpass the reasonable doubt threshold. Wright and Hall felt this might prompt participants to contemplate the innocence of the defendant and lower their belief in guilt. The data are negatively skewed and therefore a *t* test on these data is not appropriate. An alternative is to do the MWW test. The variable was ranked, and the sum of the ranks for the control group was 8077. The sum for the experimental group was 6801. Conduct an MWW test. What conclusions would you reach?

6.11   Brown and Cline (2001) examined all motor vehicle accidents in part of North Carolina over a couple of years to assess the importance of wearing a seatbelt, and found that wearing a seatbelt greatly reduced the severity of injuries. Suppose injury severity is measured on a 0 to 10 scale where 0 is no injury and 10 is fatal. The data are not normally distributed. The following could be data from 20 vehicle occupants:

Wearing seatbelt:	4	0	0	1	2	0	7	1	1	2	3	9
Not wearing seatbelt:	0	8	9	1	0	0	6	10				

What can you conclude from these data regarding seatbelt use?

6.12   Students from the University of California at Santa Cruz and at Berkeley were questioned about experiencing the Loma Prieta earthquake and hearing the news that the Bay Bridge had collapsed (Neisser et al., 1996). A year and a half later they were questioned about these events to see how consistent these reports were with their initial reports. Neisser and colleagues created an accuracy scale that could range from 0 to 100. Most of the students had very consistent memories. The scores were negatively skewed. The researchers found that memories were significantly more accurate for experiencing the earthquake than for hearing about the bridge. They also found that the memories were better for the Santa Cruz students than for the Berkeley students. They used two of the statistical tests described in this chapter. Which ones did they use (and for which comparison) and why?

6.13   There are a lot medications that say they can make you happier. Fifteen people were asked on a 0–100 scale how happy they were and then given seven

(Cont'd)

placebos to take one a day. One week later they were asked the same question. What is the median of the differences? Is it significantly different than zero?

Person	Time 1	Time 2
1	10	70
2	15	95
3	15	90
4	20	70
5	25	60
6	40	80
7	45	45
8	50	45
9	50	50
10	50	45
11	60	50
12	70	60
13	70	65
14	80	70
15	95	90

FURTHER READING

Further information of distribution-free tests:

Siegel, S., & Castellan, N.J. Jr. (1988). *Nonparametric Statistics for the Behavioral Sciences* (2nd ed.) London: McGraw-Hill.
This is one of the most used textbooks for distribution-free statistics. It goes through several tests and shows how to solve each of them with an example. The book follows more of a step-by-step recipe approach than many textbooks.

There are dozens of good articles talking about what NHST is and is not. Our favourite is:

Cohen, J. (1990). Things I have learned (so far). *American Psychologist, 45,* 1304–1312.
This is a great article. It is informative and well written, elegantly presenting wisdom gained through years of research.

7

Comparing More than Two Groups or More than Two Variables

In Chapter 6 you were shown how to compare the means of two groups of people for a single variable and of two variables for a single group of people using null hypothesis significance testing (NHST). Sometimes you want to compare the means of more than two groups or more than two variables. While this can be done using a series of t tests or Wilcoxons, there is a special procedure, called analysis of variance or ANOVA, which has been designed for this purpose. There is a version for between-subjects designs (where you are comparing the values of one variable for several groups) and a version for the within-subject designs (where you are comparing the values of several variables for one group). The assumptions, like normality and having similar variances, are basically the same as with the *t* tests. As with the *t* tests, we will also describe alternatives which do not make all of these assumptions.

The ANOVA procedure is important because it is easily extended to more complex designs. It is a very popular procedure that is reported in many journal articles. In this chapter you will learn how to do what is sometimes called a *one-way between-subjects* and *repeated measures ANOVA,* and popular distribution-free alternatives, the Kruskal–Wallis and Friedman tests. These are the simplest types of ANOVA. Some extensions are presented in Chapter 9.

AN EXAMPLE: COGNITIVE DISSONANCE

In one of the classic studies of social psychology, Festinger and Carlsmith (1959) had participants spend about an hour putting spools onto a tray and turning square pegs a quarter rotation. It was designed to be boring and succeeded. After participants finished this tedious task, the experimenter pretended as if the study was over and gave them a pretend debriefing. Participants were told that there were two groups in the study and that they were in the control group who had received no information before the study. They were told that people in the other group spoke with a confederate (someone working for the experimenter but pretending to have just taken part in the study as a participant) who told them that the experiment was enjoyable. At this point, the real study was just beginning.

There were three groups in Festinger and Carlsmith's study. There was a control group who after the fake 'debriefing' were ushered into a waiting-room. There were two experimental groups. For both of these the experimenter explained that the usually reliable confederate had phoned saying that he could not make it. The experimenter asked if the participant would help out and tell a female participant who was waiting in the next room that the experiment was enjoyable. One group was paid $1 and the other was paid $20.[1] Most complied, although a few said they were suspicious and their data were discarded.[2] After the participant either waited in an empty room (control group) or told the confederate that the boring task was enjoyable, they thought they were done. On leaving the building, they were informed that the department monitors all experiments and asked if they would fill out a questionnaire. This in fact was an integral part of the study. It included a question asking them, on a −5 to +5 scale,

---

1 All were asked for this money back at the end of the real experiment. Festinger and Carlsmith (1959: 207) said all 'were quite willing' to do this. It would be nice to think that this aspect of the study would replicate.

2 Another participant's data were discarded because he asked for the female's phone number and said 'he would call her and explain things' (p. 207) and wanted to stay around until she was done with the experiment so they could talk, presumably wanting to 'debrief' the young lady (who was the actual confederate). After the actual experiment, participants were debriefed with the female confederate present. The participant slept alone that night.

Table 7.1   *Data created to match very closely Festinger and Carlsmith's (1959) classic study of cognitive dissonance*

	Condition				
Control (mean = –0.45)		$1 (mean = 1.35)		$20 (mean = –0.05)	
x_{i1}	$(x_{i1} - \bar{x}_{\cdot 1})^2$	x_{i2}	$(x_{i2} - \bar{x}_{\cdot 2})^2$	x_{i3}	$(x_{i3} - \bar{x}_{\cdot 3})^2$
0	0.20	3	2.72	1	1.10
–3	6.50	1	0.12	2	4.20
3	11.90	1	0.12	3	9.30
2	6.00	3	2.72	0	0.00
–2	2.40	2	0.42	1	1.10
–1	0.30	3	2.72	3	9.30
2	6.00	3	2.72	0	0.00
3	11.90	2	0.42	–2	3.80
–3	6.50	2	0.42	2	4.20
–5	20.70	2	0.42	1	1.10
2	6.00	2	0.42	0	0.00
–3	6.50	2	0.42	0	0.00
3	11.90	–4	28.62	–1	0.90
0	0.20	4	7.02	–2	3.80
–2	2.40	0	1.82	–1	0.90
–2	2.40	–3	18.92	–4	15.60
–2	2.40	4	7.02	–3	8.70
–2	2.40	1	0.12	–1	0.90
–1	0.30	1	0.12	0	0.00
2	6.00	–2	11.22	0	0.00
SS = 112.95		SS = 88.55		SS = 64.95	
var = 5.94		var = 4.66		var = 3.42	
df = 19		df = 19		df = 19	

how interesting and enjoyable the study (the boring spools and pegs tasks) was. The prediction from Festinger's cognitive dissonance theory is that those paid only $1 would be more likely to say the task was enjoyable compared with the other groups.

Festinger and Carlsmith had 20 people in each condition. We have recreated these data so they closely resemble their original data. Table 7.1 gives the data and some calculations. The first step in analysing these data would be to look at the distributions, perhaps doing a boxplot and some histograms (see Chapter 1). After this you would probably want to find the 95% confidence intervals and plot these, as is shown in Figure 7.1. It shows that the highest level of enjoyment was for those given only $1 (enjoyment ratings were taken before they were asked to return the money). Overall, the mean of the entire sample was 0.28 units. This is called the grand mean or GM. The means for the individual conditions are Control = –0.45, $1 Group = 1.35, and $20 Group = –0.05. We label these with the subscripts 1, 2 and 3, so the means are $\bar{x}_{\cdot 1}$, $\bar{x}_{\cdot 2}$, and $\bar{x}_{\cdot 3}$, respectively, for the three groups: We

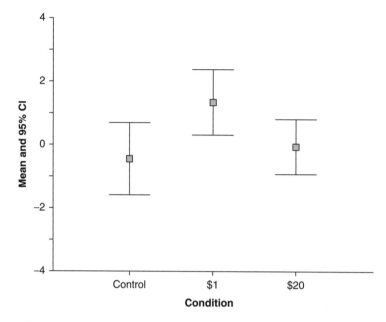

Figure 7.1 The means and 95% confidence intervals for Festinger and Carismith's (1959) classic demonstration of cognition dissonance

have added a dot in front for the group number to show that the mean is for all those people in each of the groups. This is helpful notation for more complex designs.

ANOVA is used to examine differences among means. The null hypothesis is that the means are the same in the population for each of the three groups. Conceptually it works by dividing the total variation among all the data points into variation within each condition and variation between the conditions.

$$\text{Total variation} = \text{within-group variation} + \text{between-groups variation}$$

The 'total variation' is found by subtracting the grand mean (0.28 for the data in Table 7.1) from each score, squaring these differences, and summing all these. It is often called the *total sum of squares* and is 302.18. If you divided by n−1 (59 here) you get the variance. The number 59 is also the degrees of freedom of the total variation.

The next step is calculating the within-group sum of squares. This is done in Table 7.1. The columns marked x_{i1}, x_{i2} and x_{i3}, give the value for each person in each group. $(x_{i1} - \bar{x}_{\cdot 1})^2$ gives the squared deviations from the mean within the first group. In the bottom row the sums of these deviations are reported. Adding these three values together produces the within-group variation:

$$\text{Within-group variation} = 112.95 + 88.55 + 64.95 = 266.45$$

There is also the number of degrees of freedom associated with this sum of squares; it is $n-k$ where n is the total sample size (60) and k is the number of conditions (3).

Next, the between-groups variation is calculated. This can be done in two ways. First, because the total variation comprises the within-group variation and the between-groups variation,

$$\text{Between-groups variation} = \text{total variation} - \text{within-group variation}$$

$$35.73 = 302.18 - 266.45$$

The second way is for each group to subtract the overall mean (GM, or it could be labelled $\bar{x}_{\bullet\bullet}$) from the group's mean, square the difference, multiply this by the number of people in the group and sum up these three values. This is a more complicated procedure, but it is necessary to use for the ANOVAs done in Chapter 9. Using the notation introduced above, and letting j stand for the groups (so $j = 1, 2, 3$) the between-groups variation (labelled SS_b for between groups sums of squares) is:

$$SS_b = \sum_{j=1}^{3} n_j \left(\overline{x_{\bullet j}} - GM \right)^2$$

This looks scary, but we will walk through it. We have added the limits on the summation signs (the $\sum$) to avoid any ambiguities. The n_j are the sample sizes for the j groups, so here $n_1 = n_2 = n_3 = 20$. The means are all listed above. So, for $j = 1$, it is $20(-0.45 - 0.28)^2 = 10.658$. The value for group 2 is 22.898 and for group 3 is 2.178. Add these together and you get: 35.73.

The between-groups variation is that attributable to variation, or differences, among the group means. The larger this difference the more variation among means. It is useful to calculate the percentage of total variation that is within-group variation and the total that is between-groups variation. Here, the within-group variation is 266.45/302.18, which is 88% of the variation. That leaves 12% of the total variation. Thus, we can say that 12% of the total variation is accounted for by differences among the means of the conditions. We refer to this as η^2 (eta squared), although it is also often referred to as R^2 or r^2 for reasons that will become clear in Chapter 8. Sometimes people refer to it as η_p^2 which stands for partial eta squared. This is a different statistic, which discussed in Chapter 9, and it happens to be the same as η_p^2 in this situation, but not in general.

People often say '12% of the variation is explained' by the difference among groups. Avoid the word 'explained' because no statistical test 'explains' a finding – that is up to the researcher. It is important to realize what statistics can and cannot do, and people should be careful in the way they describe their results.

You could stop here. Finding that 12% of the variation is accounted for by between-groups variation is important.[3] However, often researchers want to know if there is a statistically

---

[3] While we have stressed the importance of constructing confidence intervals, so ideally we would provide a simple formula for the confidence interval for η^2, there is no simple formula. Smithson (2003) provides a complex formula which is recommended for interested readers.

significant difference among the conditions. As with the t test, the first step is to assume that in the population the means of each group are the same. If we let μ_1, μ_2 and μ_3 stand for the population means in these three groups, H0 is $\mu_1 = \mu_2 = \mu_3$. When people are allocated to the different groups, by chance there is likely some differences among the means. If the means in the population are the same, then hypothesis testing allows us to say how unlikely it is to have large differences in the sample means (assuming the means are all the same in the population).

Dividing the within-group variation by the associated degrees of freedom provides an estimate for the variance *if* there are no group differences. The degrees of freedom for this variation are the total number of cases, minus the number of groups. Here that is 60–3 or 57. This estimate is called *MSe*, which stands for mean sums of squares error. By error it means variation within the groups:

$$MSe = \frac{within-group\ variation}{df_e} = \frac{266.45}{57} = 4.67$$

Similarly, if the means in the population are equal, then another estimate for the variance is the mean sums of squares between conditions (*MSb*). Here the degrees of freedom are the number of groups minus one (3–1 = 2). The within-group df_e plus the between-groups df_b equal the total df_{total}: $(n-k) + (k-1) = (n-1)$.

$$MSb = \frac{between-groups\ variation}{df_b} = \frac{35.73}{2} = 17.87$$

If the null hypothesis, that the means in the population are the same, is true, then these two should be estimating the same thing. If they are estimating the same thing, then the ratio of one to the other should be about one. If the differences among the groups are larger than would be expected, then *MSb* will be larger than *MSe*. Therefore, we divide *MSb* by *MSe*. This is called the value *F*, after the famous statistician Ronald Fisher (1925) who devised this test:

$$F(2, 57) = \frac{MSb}{MSe} = \frac{17.87}{4.67} = 3.83$$

If this value is greater than one, as here, it shows that the means differ more than would be expected by chance, assuming the population means are the same. If $F < 1$, the means differ less than expected. The question is how large a difference is necessary in order to reject the null hypothesis. As with the t tests, the F value can be looked up in an F table. One such table appears in Appendix D. It is necessary to know the degrees of freedom for the numerator (the number on the top) and the denominator (the number on the bottom). This table gives the critical values for a critical p of 5% and 1%. If we go to the second column and then go down to the row for df=50, the two critical values are 3.18 and 5.06. Therefore, we can say that the means are different at the 5%, but not at the1% level.

With growing technology, most statistical procedures are now run with the aid of a computer. Most programs produce what is called an ANOVA table:

	Sum of squares	df	Mean square	F	p	eta-sq.
Between groups	35.733	2	17.867	3.822	0.028	0.12
Within groups	266.450	57	4.675			
Total	302.183	59				

As with the t test, because the computer gives you a precise p value it is best to report that. So here you would say $F(2, 57) = 3.82$, $p = 0.03$, $\eta^2 = 0.12$.

This means that approximately 12% of the total variation of the sample scores can be attributed to variation between the groups. This does not mean that we would expect 12% of the variation in the population to be attributable to these group differences. A statistic called ω^2 (omega squared) is used for this. It is less common, so we will not focus on it, but some sources do (e.g., Kirk, 2007). It is:

$$\omega^2 = \frac{SS_b - (k - 1)MSe}{SS_{total} + MSe}$$

where k is the number of groups, here 3. The value for these data is:

$$\omega^2 = \frac{35.733 - 2 \cdot 4.675}{302.183 + 4.675} = 0.086 \ or \ 9\%$$

ω^2 can be thought of as an adjusted η^2 value. At the time of writing it is not printed by some of the main statistical packages (like SPSS) and because of this it is usually not reported. We discuss other adjusted effect size measures in Chapters 8 and 9.

At this point you can conclude that there is a difference among the means, but strictly speaking you should not say which means differ from which. To do this you have to do what is called *multiple comparisons*. There are entire books devoted to this subject (e.g., Toothaker, 1993). Most of these tests involve comparing each of the groups with each other using t tests, but requiring a lower p value to say that the difference is significant. The number of groups determines how much lower the p value needs to be. The more groups, the lower the p value should be. Here there are three groups. There are three possible pairwise comparisons.[4] Rather than get bogged down in details, we will simply say that you should lower your critical p value somewhat, depending on how many comparisons there are. One approach is to lower it by

---

4 These are control v. $1, control v. $20 and $1 v. $20. When there are four conditions, there are six comparisons. When there are five conditions, there are 10 comparisons. When there are 10 conditions, there are 45 comparisons. Thus, the number of comparisons rapidly increases. In general, dividing 5% by the number of comparisons is a conservative approach, meaning that you are likely to miss detecting many differences.

dividing by the number of comparisons, $0.05/3 = 0.017$. Using this approach, the p value from your t test would need to be less than 0.017 to be significant at the 5% level.

If t tests (which is what Festinger and Carlsmith, 1959, did) are done, the difference between the control and the $1 groups has $t(38) = 2.47$, $p = 0.02$, between the control and the $20 groups has $t(38) = 0.59$, $p = 0.56$, and between the $1 and $20 groups has $t(38) = 2.20$, $p = 0.03$. If we set a critical level of 0.017 then none of these would be statistically significant. As discussed in Chapter 6, most methodologists believe that p values are not the most important thing in deciding whether to accept or to reject a hypothesis. Here, the direction and size of the effect, and the compelling predictions by Festinger and Carlsmith, mean that most people would accept that the $1 group is higher. Looking at a graph with confidence intervals is much more important than relying on p values (see Figure 7.1).

THATCHER'S RESIGNATION

A common exercise for ANOVA questions is being given part of an ANOVA table and having to fill in the blanks. The following comes from data about people's memories and feelings when Margaret Thatcher resigned as Prime Minister of the United Kingdom (Wright et al., 1998). People were asked how important they thought the event was on a 0 to 4 scale, where 0 was 'not important at all' and 4 was 'extremely important'. Here we will look at whether these ratings differed by marital status. Figure 7.2 shows the 95% confidence intervals for four different groups: married (or cohabiting), single, widowed and divorced (or separated).

As can be seen, the mean for married is the highest, and the mean for widowed is the lowest. Below is the ANOVA table for these data. We have removed most of the numbers, and replaced them with letters. Try solving these for yourself, before reading further.

	Sum of squares	df	Mean square	F	Sig.	eta-sq.
Between groups	C	A	D	F	0.001	G
Within groups	2565.771	2106	E			
Total	2586.162	B				

Seriously, stop reading and try to do this yourself first.

Let's start with the degrees of freedom (the 'df' column). If you had the value for A, then you could calculate B by adding 2106 to A. Similarly, if you had B, you could calculate A by subtracting 2106 from it. You do not have these, however. You need to remember that the df_b for the between-groups sum of squares is equal to the number of conditions minus one, so 4–1=3. So, A=3, and therefore the value for B is 3+2106=2109.

C, the between-groups variation (or sums of squares), can be calculated by subtracting the variation within the groups (2565.771) from the total variation (2586.162), to produce 20.391. The values for D and E are the respective sums of squares divided by their degrees of freedom, so 20.391/3 = 6.797 and 2565.771/2106 = 1.218. The F value

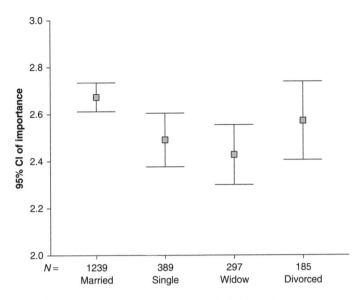

Figure 7.2   The means and 95% confidence intervals for how important an event
Thatcher's resignation was, broken down by marital status

(which is labelled F in the table) is the mean square for the between-groups divided by
the mean square for the within-groups, $6.797/1.218 = 5.580$. This is statistically significant. It is important to note that the sum of squares values, the degrees of freedom, the
mean square values, the F value and the significance level all have to be positive. If you
get a negative number you have made a mistake. It is important to estimate the size of
the effect, to say what proportion of the overall variation is accounted for by the difference between the groups. If we divide 20.39 by 2586.16 we get $\eta^2 = 0.8\%$. This is the
final value (labelled G) to put in the table. Less than 1% of the variation can be attributed to differences in marital status. It is important to stress that finding something that
is statistically significant does *not* mean that it is either a big or an interesting effect.
This will be expanded upon in Chapter 8.

Because the F value is significant, the next step is usually to see which groups differ.
Figure 7.2 shows that the mean for the married (and cohabiting) group is the highest. t tests
were run on each of the six possible pairs. Table 7.2 gives the t tests and their associated
p values. Because six tests are done, this increases the chance that a Type I error
(falsely rejecting a hypothesis) occurs. Therefore we would probably only be convinced
that the difference exists if p is less than about 0.01.[5] However, this increases the chance

5 We use 0.01 because 0.05/6 is 0.008, which is about 0.01. An obvious question is: why not use 0.008? We could
have. The reason that we did not was because we wanted to stress that there is no single correct value. Using
0.008 is not better than 0.01 or even 0.02. Using 0.02 would increase the chances of Type I errors, but decrease
the chances of Type II errors.

Table 7.2 *Pairwise t tests and their associated p values comparing self-rated importance of Margaret Thatcher's resignation as Prime Minister of the United Kingdom. Because there is more than one test, a more stringent critical level should be used. Here, we suggest p < 0.01 would be good*

	Marital status		
	Single	Widowed	Divorced (separated)
Married (cohabiting)	2.90 (0.004)	3.48 (0.001)	1.16 (0.245)
Single		0.70 (0.484)	0.83 (0.405)
Widowed			1.37 (0.171)

of missing a real effect, a Type II error. There are two comparisons which are statistically significant: the difference between married and single, and the difference between married and widowed.

Now at this point the researcher would be tempted to say that these effects are large – after all, the *p* values are 0.004 and 0.001. However, the *p* values do not tell you how large the effects are. They just say whether an effect has been detected. If you want to say how big an effect is you have to look at the actual difference. The *y* axis in Figure 7.2 only shows a very small area of the total. Figure 7.3 shows the 95% confidence intervals showing the

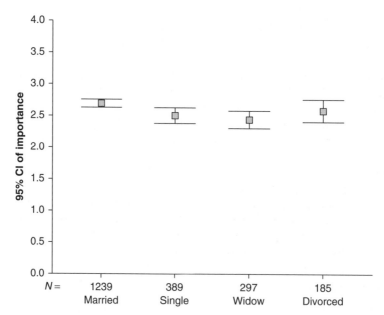

Figure 7.3 The means and 95% confidence intervals for how important Thatcher's resignation was for people of different marital status. The *y* axis now shows the entire range of responses

entire range of possible scores, from 0 to 4. This still shows that the married responses are the highest, but the differences look smaller. After all, the highest mean (2.67 for married) is less than a quarter of a unit on the 0 to 4 scale above the lowest mean (2.43 for widowed).

The confidence intervals tell you how precise your estimate of the mean is. When you increase the sample size confidence intervals tend to get smaller.

KRUSKAL–WALLIS TEST

The ANOVA procedure assumes that the data are normally distributed within groups. Single outliers can have a large influence on the resulting statistics. While a handful of outliers are unlikely to affect analysis with a data set the size of the Thatcher example, they often do with smaller samples. Consider the study of Shamay-Tsoory et al. (2005). They used the Kruskal–Wallis test to compare people with frontal lesions, posterior lesions and controls for how well they were able to understand sarcasm. They presented participants with several examples of sarcasm and counted the number of errors participants made in understanding the scenarios. Most of the posterior and control participants made no errors. To make this more interesting as a statistics example we will assume they gave a harder test, with scores ranging from 1 to 10. To make the example easier to present, we will also use smaller sample sizes than they used. Our data are:

Frontal ($n_1 = 6$)   5,   7,   3,   9,   4,   4
Posterior ($n_2 = 6$) 2,   1,   1,   6,   1,   3
Control ($n_3 = 10$) 1,   2,   8,   1,   3,   8,   2,   1,   1,   1

If you run a standard ANOVA you get $F(2, 19) = 2.68$, $p = 0.09$, $\eta^2 = 0.22$. It looks like a fairly large effect, but with the small sample it is non-significant. The non-significance is due in large part to the fact that a couple of the control participants made a lot of errors. If one of those 8s is removed, the F value becomes significant. The Kruskal–Wallis test is less affected by outliers. First, you rank all the values of the variable, ignoring which group they are in. The ranks (taking mid-ranks where appropriate) are:

Frontal ($n_1 = 6$)   17.0, 19.0, 13.0, 22.0, 15.5, 15.5
Posterior ($n_2 = 6$)   10.0, 4.5, 4.5, 18.0, 4.5, 13.0
Control ($n_3 = 10$)   4.5, 10.0, 20.5, 4.5, 13.0, 20.5, 10.0, 4.5, 4.5, 4.5

The ranks can be denoted R_{ij} where i stands for the different participants and j for which of the three groups the participants are in. Sum all the ranks within each group. This can be written ΣR_{ij} or we can use the shorthand: R_{+j}. This + means add up all the values in i. The sums are: $R_{+1} = 102.0$, $R_{+2} = 54.5$ and $R_{+3} = 96.5$. Let n be the total sample size ($n = 22$), although with this notation we could write it as n_+. We then calculate a statistic called H:

$$H = \frac{12}{n(n+1)} \sum \frac{R_j^2}{n_j} - 3(n+1)$$

For this example this is:

$$H = \frac{12}{22(22+1)} \left(\frac{102^2}{6} + \frac{54.5^2}{6} + \frac{96.5^2}{10} \right) - 3(22+1) = 5.95$$

This value can be looked up using the χ^2 table which is in Appendix E. The degrees of freedom is the number of groups minus 1. Thus, here $df = 2$ because there are three groups. The critical value for the 5% level is 5.99. The observed value is smaller than this so it is non-significant. Using the verbal labels of Efron and Tibshirani (1993: 204) introduced in Chapter 6, this is 'borderline evidence against H0'.

However, as with the ranked-based tests of Chapter 6, when there are a lot of ties in the data there is an adjustment which should be made. If there are no ties then the adjustment makes no difference, but if there are ties then the adjustment will increase the size of H. Therefore, if H is significant without the adjustment, then you know it will be significant with the adjustment. The adjustment factor is:

$$adj = 1 - \frac{\sum t_i^3 - t_i}{n^3 - n}$$

where t_i is the number of tied values for the variable at each possible value. Below are the ranked values in order and with the number with each ranking.

Value	Freq(t_i)	Ranks	$t_i^3 - t_i$
1	8	= 4.5, 4.5, 4.5, 4.5, 4.5, 4.5, 4.5, 4.5	$8^3 - 8 = 504$
2	3	= 10.0, 10.0, 10.0	$3^3 - 3 = 24$
3	3	= 13.0, 13.0, 13.0	$3^3 - 3 = 24$
4	2	= 15.5, 15.5	$2^3 - 2 = 4$
5	1	= 17.0	$1^3 - 1 = 0$ $\Sigma = 560$
6	1	= 18.0	$1^3 - 1 = 0$
7	1	= 19.0	$1^3 - 1 = 0$
8	2	= 20.5, 20.5	$2^3 - 2 = 4$
9	1	= 22.0	$1^3 - 1 = 0$

Table 7.3   *Company efficiency and seasons*

Company	Autumn	Winter	Spring	Summer	$\bar{x}_{j\cdot}$(*Mean$_j$.*)
1	30	24	35	28	29.25
2	34	31	52	47	41.00
3	30	45	41	42	39.50
4	51	58	66	52	56.75
5	67	55	77	69	67.00
6	35	56	58	61	52.50
$\bar{x}_{\cdot j}$(*Mean.$_j$*)	41.17	44.83	54.83	49.83	
		Grand mean (GM) or 'a mean for all seasons' – sorry!			47.67

We can ignore those with unique values since $1^3 - 1 = 0$. Thus, the adjustment value is: $1 - ((8^3-8) + (3^3-3) + (3^3-3) + (2^3-2) + (2^3-2))/(22^3-22) = 1-(504+24+24+6+6)/10626 = 0.947$. The adjusted *H* is: $H_{adj} = 5.95/0.947 = 6.28$. This value surpasses the critical value. Therefore we would write: $H(2) = 6.28$, $p < 0.05$, or if we were using a computer we would write $p = 0.04$. Usually the adjustment does not make this much difference because there usually are not this many ties. Siegel and Castellan (1988) say if 25% or fewer of the values within groups are tied then the adjustment is negligible.

REPEATED MEASURES ANOVA

In many cases researchers want to compare the means of different variables for the same group of people. This often occurs in time series (i.e., longitudinal) studies where the researcher is investigating if people change over time or when the researcher measures a series of variables and wants to see if these differ. The techniques for these repeated measures designs are more complex than the between-subjects designs. Here we describe a relatively simple example. Table 7.3 provides data for the efficiency of six companies during the four seasons. The scale ranges from 0 to 100, with 100 being spectacularly efficient. As can be seen, some companies are more efficient than others.

In general we recommend first graphing your data and then conducting statistical analyses. We recommend doing this for repeated measures ANOVAs, also, but for teaching purposes we will introduce the statistics for creating an ANOVA table and then use information calculated from this to create a table and graph.

When running repeated measures ANOVAs, you should always create a correlation matrix of the variables. This technique is covered in Chapter 8.

The first step in the calculations is adding together the sums of squares within each of the companies. We will refer to this as SS_{WITHIN}. It is sometimes called. $SS_{SUBJECTxTREATMENT}$. The equation is:

$$SS_{WITHIN} = \sum_{i=1}^{6} \sum_{j=1}^{6} \left(x_{ij} - \bar{x}_{i\bullet}\right)^2 = (30 - 29.25)^2 + (24 + 29.25)^2 + \ldots + (61 - 52.5)^2 = 1309.50$$

This looks complicated but you just square the difference between each value and its row mean, and add them together. This within-company variation will be part due to differences in the seasons (the 'treatment' effect) and part error (or residual). The amount attributable to the treatment is labelled $SS_{TREATMENT}$ (or SS_{MODEL}).

$$SS_{TREATMENT} = n\Sigma(x_{\bullet j} - GM)^2 = 6([41.17{-}47.67]^2 + \ldots + [49.83{-}47.67]^2) = 638.00$$

In words, find the difference between the column mean and the grand mean, square this, add them up, and multiply by the sample size. The final necessary sum of squares is for the error (SS_e) which is just the difference between these.[6]

$$SS_e = SS_{WITHIN} - SS_{TREATMENT} = 1309.50 - 638.00 = 671.50$$

The degrees of freedom are:

$k - 1$ for treatments, where k is the number of treatments (here $4 - 1 = 3$)
$(n - 1)(k - 1)$ for error, where n is the sample size (here $(6 - 1)(4 - 1) = 5{\cdot}3 = 15$)
$n(k - 1)$ for within (here $(6)(4 - 1) = 6{\cdot}3 = 18$)

These can be used to calculated the *MS* values in the same way as the between-subject ANOVAs. These are:

$$MS_{TREATMENT} = SS_{TREATMENT}/df_{TREATMENT} = 638.00/3 = 212.67$$

$$MS_e = SS_e/df_e = 671.50/15 = 44.77$$

Finally, $F = MS_{TREATMENT}/MS_e = 212.67/44.77 = 4.75$. The p value can be looked up in Appendix C or found with a computer ($p = 0.02$). The effect size is $\eta_p^2 = SS_{TREATMENT}/SS_{WITHIN}$, which here is $638.00/1309.50 = 0.49$ This is partial eta-squared because you have divided the sums of

---

6 You will often also see:

$SS_{TOTAL} = \Sigma\,(x_{ij} - GM)^2 = (30 - 47.67)^2 + \cdots + (61 - 47.67)^2 = 5029.33$

$SS_{SUBJECT} = SS_{TOTAL} - SS_{TREATMENT} - SS_{WITHIN} = 5029.33 - 638.00 - 1309.50 = 3719.83$

These are used for more complex ANOVAs.

Table 7.4   *The ANOVA table for the repeated measures data in Table 7.3*

	Sum of squares	df	Mean square	F	sig.	Partial eta-sq.
Treatment	638.00	3	212.67	4.75	0.016	0.487
Error	671.50	15	44.77			
Within	1309.50	18				

squares attributable to the condition by SS_{WITHIN} rather than the total sum of squares. You would write: $F(3, 15) = 4.75$, $p = 0.02$, $\eta_p^2 = 0.49$.[7] An ANOVA table is often produced as in Table 7.4.

You should always graph your data. Here this would include looking at histograms of the individual variables and something called scatterplots (which are discussed in Chapter 8) between pairs of variables. You should also graph the means for the four conditions. You could include the 95% confidence intervals calculated for each condition using the methods described in Chapter 5. This would be appropriate if the data were from a between-subjects ANOVA and informs you about the precision of each mean. Masson and Loftus (2003) describe how it would often be better to remove the variation among individuals when calculating these intervals. This would allow you to compare across groups. There are a few different ways to do this. The simplest uses the following equation:

$$95\% \ CI = mean \pm t_{0.05}\sqrt{\frac{MS_e}{n}}$$

Figure 7.4 shows a bar chart for the means of each condition. The larger confidence intervals are those found for each variable on its own. This is the standard produced by most statistical packages and they are sometimes called the between-subjects confidence intervals (BSCI). The smaller intervals are the so-called within-subject confidence intervals (WSCI). More details can be found in Masson and Loftus (2003) and Wright (2007).

Friedman's Test

The Kruskal–Wallis test is an alternative to the between-subjects ANOVA when you do not want outliers to have a large effect. Friedman's test does the same for the repeated measures ANOVA. Like many of the alternative procedures presented in this book, it is based on ranking the data. The first step in doing Friedman's test is ranking the values

---

7 An adjusted statistic, ω_p^2, can also be calculated for this situation:

$$\omega_p^2 = \frac{SS_{TREATMENT} - (k-1)MSe}{SS_{WITHIN} + MSe} = \frac{638 - 3(44.77)}{1309.50 + 44.77} = 0.37$$

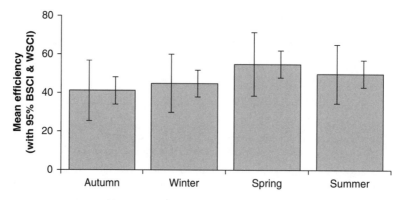

Figure 7.4   A bar chart of the means for the data in Table 7.3. Two sets of 95% confidence intervals are shown. The larger are the between-subjects confidence intervals (BSCI) and the smaller are the within-subject confidence intervals (WSCI)

within each case for all the different treatments. This is done in Table 7.5 for the company data from Table 7.3. There are a lot of 1s in the Autumn and Winter columns, which means these look like inefficient seasons, and a lot of 4s in Spring, which means most companies are more efficient then compared with the other seasons. If there are ties use the mid-ranks as done previously (see calculation for median in Chapter 1). The sum of the ranks for each company will be the same ($4 + 3 + 2 + 1 = 10$). Sum the ranks for each season. These are shown in the final row labelled R_{+j}.

Next, you calculate the statistic Q (sometimes this is denoted F_r, but given how prominent the F statistic is, using Q will be less confusing). You then use the following equation:

$$Q = \frac{12}{nk(k+1)} \sum R^2_{+j} - 3n(k+1)$$
$$= \frac{12}{6(4)(5)} (100 + 144 + 441 + 289) - 3(6)(5)$$
$$= 0.10(974) - 90 = 7.40$$

This can be looked up using the χ^2 table as was done with the Kruskal–Wallis test. The degrees of freedom (*df*) is $k - 1$, which here is 3. The critical value is 7.81 for the 5% level so this is not statistically significant. The *p* value found using a computer would be 0.06, so this is near the 5% critical value. This is the region Efron and Tibshirani (1993: 204) call 'borderline evidence against H0'. Thus, we would write $Q(3) = 7.40$, $p = 0.06$, or $Q(3) = 7.40$, *ns*.

As with the other ranked-based tests there is a correction for ties. As with the other procedures it is an ugly equation:

Table 7.5 *Company efficiency and seasons*

Company	Autumn	Winter	Spring	Summer
1	3	1	4	2
2	2	1	4	3
3	1	4	2	3
4	1	3	4	2
5	2	1	4	3
6	1	2	3	4
R_{+j}	10	12	21	17

$$Q = \frac{12 \sum R^2_{+j} - 3n^2 k(k+1)^2}{nk(k+1) + \dfrac{nk - \sum t^3_{ij}}{k-1}}$$

The t_{ij} is slightly different than with the Kruskal–Wallis $t_{i.}$. Here it is the values within each case. So, if the first company had the values 40, 50, 40, 60, and therefore the ranks 1.5, 3, 1.5, 4, the sum of the t_{ij}^3 for this company ($j = 1$) would be $2^3 + 1^3 + 1^3 = 10$. Fortunately here there were no ties so the correction would not be used. If you had, the $\sum t_{ij}^3$ would be 24 since there are 24 non-tied ranks and the results would be:

$$Q = \frac{12(974) - 3(36)(4)(25)}{6(4)(5) + \dfrac{6(4) - 24}{4-1}} = \frac{11688 - 10800}{120 - \dfrac{24 - 24}{3}} = \frac{888}{120} = 7.40$$

As with the correction for the Kruskal–Wallis test, this can only increase the value of Q. Thus, if your Q value is already statistically significant, this will not change by using the more complex formula.

SUMMARY

It is confusing that 'Analysis of Variance' is most commonly used to look for differences among means. The name is based on how the procedure looks for differences. The difference among means is measured by their variation. In a between-subjects t test, you look at the difference between two means. If the two means differ by a lot, then that set of two means has a large variation.[8] If you

---

8 A t test is just a special case of an ANOVA. If you run both a t test and an ANOVA on the same set of data you will get the same p value and t^2 will be equal to F.

have three or more means, then the more different they are from each other, the larger the variance among them. In both the *t* test and ANOVA you then divide this by a measure of how precise the estimate is. In both cases it is based on the amount of within-group variation and the sample size. As the within-group variation increases, the estimate becomes less precise (and *t* and *F* get smaller, and the confidence intervals get larger). As the sample size increases, the estimate becomes more precise (and *t* and *F* get larger, and the confidence intervals get smaller). The main point of this is that ANOVAs are about variance, but variance measures the differences among the means. Do not worry too much if any particular statistical procedure does not seem self-evident at first.

Four statistical tests were described in this chapter. First, the one-way ANOVA, where different people are in different conditions and you are interested in whether the means of these conditions differ, was described. This is one of the most common tests. Because it assumes that the data within each condition are normally distributed and because outliers have a very large impact, many people opt for the Kruskal–Wallis test as an alternative. This was the second test described. The third test described was the repeated measures (or within-subject) ANOVA. It is appropriate when you have one group of people and each person takes part in several treatment conditions. The final test was Friedman's ANOVA, which is an alternative to the repeated measures ANOVA when you do not want outliers to have a large impact.

EXERCISES

7.1 Barnier and McConkey (1998) gave participants 100 pre-paid postcards and said that they should post one of these every day. Seventeen participants were hypnotized when told this, 17 were told to act as if they have been hypnotized (simulators) and 17 were just told to do this. Their means and standard deviations for how many cards they posted are given below:

	Hypnotized	Simulator	Control
Mean (in % cards returned)	53.35	46.74	15.64
Standard deviation	37.36	41.03	27.73

(a) Construct, and graph, the 95% confidence intervals for these data.
(b) Below is the ANOVA table, with some numbers missing. Rewrite the table, filling in the missing values.

	Sum of squares	df	Mean square	F	eta-sq.
Between groups	XXXXX	2	XXXX	XX	XX
Within groups	65419	XX	XXXX		
Total	79205	58			

(c) Based on the graph and the ANOVA table, what, in a couple of lines, are your conclusions?

7.2 Suppose a researcher was interested in which animals, of cats, dogs and fish, made good pets. The researcher went to people's houses, and asked if they had cat(s), dog(s) or fish (no one with more than one type of pet could take part in the study). If they had one type of pet, they were asked how good a pet it made, on a 1 to 11 scale, with 11 being very good and 1 being very bad. The data are given in Table 7.6.

(a) Is there evidence that the ratings differ for cat, dog and fish owners?

(b) From what you found in part (a), does this mean that some pets are better than others?

7.3 There is much concern about witnesses being susceptible to misleading questions. Santtila et al. (1999) conducted a study to see how alcohol affected suggestibility. They had four conditions. A control group ($n = 13$) had a placebo, a glass of liquid containing no alcohol (the outside of the glass had been rubbed

Table 7.6   *How good a pet are cats, dogs and fish?*

Cat	Dog	Fish
6	2	4
11	4	2
10	10	6
2	6	3
10	8	2
4	5	5
6	6	4
8	4	6
8	9	4
7	11	5

(Cont'd)

Table 7.7 *Data on alcohol and suggestibility*

Condition	n	Mean (out of 35)	Standard deviation	Standard error
Control	13	8.2	4.1	1.14
Low	12	7.9	5.4	1.56
Medium	13	3.7	3.1	0.86
High	13	4.3	4.2	1.16

with alcohol so it smelled like the drinks for the other conditions). The three experimental conditions had alcoholic drinks: a low-dosage group ($n = 12$) with 0.13ml of 95% alcohol per kg of body weight, a medium group ($n = 13$) with 0.66ml, and a high group ($n = 13$) with 1.32ml. They administered a Finnish version of Gudjonsson's (1997) suggestibility scale. High scores mean more suggestible. The data are given in Table 7.7, along with some preliminary calculations.

Note: The condition means and standard deviations are taken directly from Table 2 of Santtila et al. (1999). All other numbers here, and in the ANOVA table, are calculated from these and therefore are slightly different from those in the paper owing to rounding error.

(a) Draw a graph showing intervals for *both* the standard deviation and the 95% confidence intervals.
(b) Rewrite the ANOVA table below, filling in the missing numbers.

	Sum of squares	df	Mean square	F	Sig.	eta-sq.
Between groups	212.57	X	X	3.92	0.014	0.014
Within groups	849.48	X	X			
Total	1062.05		X			

7.4 In a couple of sentences, when should you do an ANOVA as opposed to a *t* test?
7.5 When doing multiple comparisons, discuss, in about six lines, the issues involved in choosing a critical *p* value for the individual comparisons.
7.6 Imagine that you are the Statue of Liberty and you are unhappy. What is it that worries you about being the Statue of Liberty? Startup and Davey (2001) asked university undergraduates this. A response might be 'people will be walking around in my head'. Participants were then asked why this worried

them, and then why this new worry worried them, and so on. This 'catastro-phizing interview' continued until the student could come up with no more worries. Startup and Davey recorded the number of worry steps and com-pared three conditions. Before the interview participants listened to Gyorgy Ligeti's *Lux Aeterna*, Chopin's *Waltzes nos. 11 and 12*, or Vivaldi's *The Four Seasons, Spring*, which put them into a negative, a neutral, or a positive mood, respectively. The authors predicted that the negative group would cat-astrophize the most. Their data are:

Negative (*Lux Aeterna*)	3, 10, 12, 10, 10, 5, 11, 6, 15, 9, 6, 5, 7, 6, 12
Neutral (*Waltzes nos. 11 and 12*)	4, 2, 4, 6, 9, 4, 8, 5, 5, 9, 4, 3, 2, 5, 4
Positive (*The Four Seasons, Spring*)	4, 11, 4, 2, 4, 6, 1, 2, 16, 3, 7, 3, 2, 3, 2

Is there evidence that the different mood inductions create different amounts of catastrophizing?

7.7 Brighton & Hove Albion, the football team, are moving to a location right by the University of Sussex, in the town of Falmer. Falmer is a small town and the pro-posed location is an area of natural beauty. Not surprisingly, there is some con-cern. Luckin (2001) conducted a survey of people living in Falmer, of people living about a mile away, and of people living in two sections of Brighton. He hypoth-esized that people living in Falmer would be the most concerned. He developed a scale to measure concern which could range from 1.00 to 5.00. His data are:

In Falmer	5.00, 3.27, 4.18, 3.91, 3.40, 4.64, 1.00, 5.00, 4.36, 4.09, 3.82, 4.91, 4.91, 2.64, 5.00, 3.00, 4.36, 3.55, 5.00
Nearby	3.64, 1.27, 1.82, 4.45, 3.45, 1.09, 1.73, 1.55, 4.00, 1.36, 1.00, 3.45, 1.00, 1.70, 2.55, 1.00, 4.18, 3.27, 3.73, 1.00
In Brighton, location A	1.00, 4.55, 1.00, 1.00, 2.82, 2.27, 1.45, 1.73, 4.55, 1.45, 1.00, 1.27, 2.18, 2.36, 1.09, 1.82, 2.64, 2.64, 1.00, 1.00
In Brighton, location B	1.00, 1.00, 1.00, 1.00, 1.00, 1.00, 1.45, 1.00, 3.27, 1.91, 2.00, 1.00, 1.00, 1.00, 1.00, 2.64, 1.00, 1.55, 1.00, 1.55

(a) Conduct a Kruskal–Wallis ANOVA on these data to determine if the scores differ significantly. Interpret the results.

7.8 A representative sample of 100 voters was asked to rate four issues (taxation levels, environmental issues, foreign policy and political sleaze levels) for how likely it was

(Cont'd)

that policies about these would affect their voting preference. The scale ranged from 1 to 9, with 1 being 'no impact' and 9 being 'much impact'. The researchers assumed that the data were normally distributed. An ANOVA was done.

(a) What is the name of the ANOVA type that was done?
(b) An ANOVA was done and an ANOVA table produced. This is shown below with some XXXs that need to be filled in. Remake the table, filling in the XXXs.

	SS	df	MS	F	Sig.	Partial eta-sq.
Policy	228.77	XXX	XXX	XXX	0.08	XXX
Error	3133.48	XXX	XXX			

7.9 There is much interest in people's ability to perform complex tasks at different points in the day. Ten students volunteered to take part in a study exploring time-of-day effects. The volunteers answered 15 arithmetic problems at 6am, 11am, 3pm, 9pm and 1am. All the problems were ones that all the students should be able to do. The response variable was how many minutes it took. The data are shown below. Use Friedman's test to investigate if there are any differences.

6am	11am	3pm	9pm	1am
2	3	3	4	4
4	4	5	4	5
6	7	6	5	8
7	6	5	3	5
2	2	3	2	5
8	6	7	9	10
7	4	6	4	9
3	4	2	3	2
9	6	7	4	5
4	6	7	4	3

7.10 Shariff and Norenzayan (2007: Exp. 2) gave 75 participants a task where they could give another participant 0 to 10 one-dollar coins, and they would keep what they did not give. Before they decided how much to give they had to unscramble some sentences. They had three conditions. In the neutral condition the sentences did not contain words that were likely to evoke any specific concepts. In the secular condition the words included *civic, jury, court, police* and *contract*. In the God condition the target words were: *spirit, divine, God, sacred* and *prophet*. The following shows how much money people in each condition awarded:

Neutral	0	0	0	0	0	0	0	0	0	1	1	2	3	4	4	4	5	5	5	5	5	5	10
Secular	0	0	0	1	2	3	3	3	4	5	5	5	5	5	5	5	5	5	5	10	10	10	10
God	0	0	0	1	1	2	2	3	4	5	5	5	5	5	5	5	5	5	5	7	9	10	10	10

It is clear that the data are not normally distributed. Run an appropriate ANOVA on these data to compare the three groups.

📖 FURTHER READING

Field, A.P. (2009). *Discovering Statistics using SPSS for Windows* (3rd ed.). London: Sage. While this book focuses on conducting statistics using SPSS, it has several excellent chapters on ANOVA and extensions to the basic ANOVA models.

Kirk, R.E. (2007). *Statistics: An Introduction* (5th ed.). Belmont, CA: Wadsworth Publishing.
If we were going to recommend a long introductory textbook, this would be a good candidate. It has good coverage of ANOVA.

8

Regression and Correlation

A common situation in all of the sciences is when there are two variables and each of these varies along some kind of scale. A common question is whether these two variables are related. The procedures described in this chapter help you to answer this question. The most useful of the procedures is graphing the two variables using a scatterplot. The scatterplot is the basis for the remaining procedures: drawing a line, using a couple of equations to choose a line, and the correlation. We first show the standard approach, and then show alternatives that are less affected by outliers. The aims of this chapter are for you to learn how to interpret data with a scatterplot and to decide whether a certain model – that the relationship can be accounted for by a single straight line – is an acceptable description of the data.

Table 8.1 *Data and some preliminary calculations for estimating the velocity of cars. The final row is the sum of all the values in that column. Estimate$_i$ = E$_i$; Actual$_i$ = A$_i$; m(x) = mean(x); predicted value = pred$_i$; error (or residual) = e$_i$*

E_i	A_i	$E_i - m(E_i)$	$A_i - m(A)$	$(E_i - m(E_i))(A_i - m(A))$	$(E_i - m(E_i))^2$	$(A_i - (A_i))^2$	pred$_i$	e$_i$	e_i^2
8	12	−6.4	−6.8	43.5	41.0	46.2	10.5	−2.5	6.3
8	29	−6.4	10.2	−65.3	41.0	104.0	20.3	−12.3	150.1
35	24	20.6	5.2	107.1	424.4	27.0	17.4	17.6	310.4
13	16	−1.4	−2.8	3.9	2.0	7.8	12.8	0.2	0.0
5	7	−9.4	−11.8	110.9	88.4	139.2	7.6	−2.6	6.9
7	5	−7.4	−13.8	102.1	54.8	190.4	6.5	0.5	0.3
14	24	−0.4	5.2	−2.1	0.2	21.0	17.4	−3.4	11.4
22	21	7.6	2.2	16.7	57.8	4.8	15.7	6.3	40.2
27	26	12.6	7.2	90.7	158.8	51.8	18.5	8.5	71.8
5	24	−9.4	5.2	−48.9	88.4	27.0	17.4	−12.4	153.3
Sum =144 188		0	0	358.8	956.4	625.6	144	0	750.6

Note: Values printed have been rounded to the tenth place, but for calculations more decimals places are used.

MAKING A SCATTERPLOT

There is much interest in how accurately people are able to estimate the speed a car is travelling because witnesses and drivers are often asked how fast cars are going when an accident occurs (Hole, 2006). Suppose an eyewitness was asked to estimate the velocity of 10 cars to see how good the witness was at estimating car velocities because the eyewitness was going to testify about the velocity of a particular car involved in an accident. Table 8.1 gives the velocity of cars and the estimates given by the witness, plus some calculations that will be used in the next section.

The first step in analysing a problem of this type is to create a graph that shows the data. The appropriate graph for showing the relationship between two variables that are each measured on a scale is called a *scatterplot*. This is one of the most common graphs in scientific publications (Tufte, 2006; Wainer, 2005) and also frequently occurs in newspapers. A simple four-step scatterplot is shown below with the four steps labelled in Figure 8.1.

1   Decide which variable should be on the horizontal, or *x*, axis and find the minimum and maximum values. Sometimes it is arbitrary which variable you choose for which axis, but if it makes sense to think of one variable as predicting the other, or influencing values on the other, put that variable on the *x* axis. Here, it probably makes more sense thinking of the actual velocity predicting the estimated velocity so we chose to have the actual velocity on the *x* axis. The minimum value

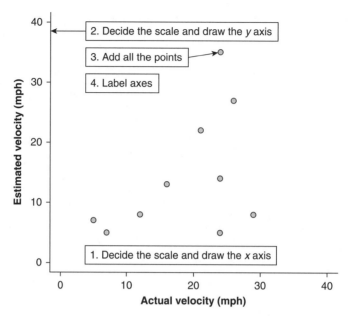

Figure 8.1 A scatterplot showing the relationship of estimated velocity with actual velocity. The four steps for making a scatterplot are labelled and discussed in the text

is 5mph and the maximum is 35mph, so we need to choose the length of the axis appropriately (like we did with histograms). Going from 0 to 40 makes sense (and we will actually leave a little space below 0 in case there is a velocity right at zero so that we will still be able to see it). We draw the axis and we label the points at 10mph increments because 10 is a nice round number.

2   We do the same thing for the vertical, or y, axis. Because these two variables are measuring velocity on the same scale, it will make sense to use the same axis range, so we also use a scale from 0 to 40mph. As with histograms, there are functions that computers use to decide how to create these axes, and most often the defaults are okay, but the programs usually allow you to choose your own values too.

3   Then, for each entry in Table 8.1 we add a dot into the appropriate location on the scatterplot. So, for the actual velocity of 35mph, the person estimated the velocity as 24mph, so we move along to 35mph on the x axis and then move up to 24mph on the y axis, and draw a dot. The computer does this automatically (and allows you to choose different symbols, and you can also add a name for each data point as with the name histogram from Chapter 1). If you have multiple data points on the same location, so two people estimating a 35mph car is travelling at 24mph, the norm is not to draw the second point. An alternative is to draw an additional point really close to it so that readers see that there were two points there. When making these with a computer there are several other alternatives (sunflowers and jitters are covered below).

4   The final step is labelling the axes and the labels. It is important to do this and to include the appropriate units (here mph). We can pretty much guarantee that if you do not label your axes you will lose points on your assignments!

Figure 8.1 is a very simple scatterplot and much additional information can be added to it. Computer programs make this relatively easy to do. It is important, however, that you only add information that is useful and that you do discuss. Because computers make it easy to add 'bells-and-whistles' to graphs, some people are tempted to do this, but it is important to make clear why you are presenting any additional information. (We should also add when you make your scatterplots you should not add the little boxes we have included for the four steps!)

CALCULATING THE REGRESSION LINE

After making a scatterplot it is often useful to draw a curved line or a straight line through the data points to show if there is a relationship between the variables. Methods for drawing curved lines can be fairly complex and are covered in Wright and London (2009). Here we describe how to choose a good straight line to draw. First, it is worth drawing one by hand on a scatterplot. Get a ruler out and decide upon a straight line that you think fits the data. This is subjective and everybody will come up with slightly different lines, but it is a good method to begin with. Because everybody will come up with different lines, and that humans can bias their choice of lines to fit with what they want to find, scientists use agreed upon conventional procedures to produce lines. There are several different procedures that could be used, and in fact the most popular procedure is one that most methodologists now think is not the best in many situations. Still, it is by far the most used and is based on many of the procedures already considered in this book (e.g., the mean, the t tests, ANOVA). It requires fitting a line that minimizes the sum of squares of all the distances from the line to the points. This is called the ordinary least squares (OLS) regression line or, because it is so common, often just the regression line. In mathematical terminology, the line found is the one which minimizes $\sum e_i^2$, where e_i are called residuals or the distance between the line and the observed value for the y variable. The e stands for *error* (also called residual) since if the straight line is a model for how we think people will estimate the velocity, the difference between the model and the observed value is error. In the remainder of this section we describe how to calculate this line.

The mean for estimated velocity is 14.4mph. Without knowing the actual velocity of a car, if somebody asked you to guess the estimated velocity of any car in the study a good guess would be the mean. There will be some error associated with your guess. The difference between the observed value, in Table 8.1 labelled E_i, and the mean is shown in third column of Table 8.1. Sometimes the value is close to the mean, sometimes it is not. As can be seen in the final row, the sum of all these is 0. If we square each of these values (in the sixth column) we get what is called the total sum of squares, or SS_{total}. If we divide this by n-1 or 9, we get the variance (so, 956.4/9 = 106.3). Both SS_{total} and the variance are measures of the error of our guesses. The basis of regression is whether using information about the other variable, here the actual velocity, and assuming that there is a straight line relationship between the two, we can lessen the amount of error by a worthwhile amount.

A line for the relationship between two variables (here estimated and actual velocity) is described by two values, the intercept and the slope. We describe this as a *model*. The norm is to denote the variable on the y axis as y_i, the variable on the x axis with x_i, the intercept with $\beta 0$, and the slope with $\beta 1$.[1] The regression equation can be written as: $y_i = \beta 0 + \beta 1 x_i + e_i$. In previous mathematics courses you may have learned the equation for a line as: $y = \beta 0 + \beta 1 x$, without the subscripts or the error term (sometimes as: $y = ax + b$). This is one of the main differences between mathematics and statistics. In statistics we assume our model does not perfectly capture each data point, there is uncertainty.

The equations for finding the regression line, shown below, look complicated and their derivation requires knowing a little calculus so will not be covered here. The mean for both variables should be found first (you should always perform univariate descriptive statistics before these complicated ones). The means are 18.8mph for actual velocity and 14.4mph for estimated velocity. The following are the equations for the slope ($\beta 1$) and the intercept ($\beta 0$) of the regression line:

$$\beta 1 = \frac{\sum (x_i - \bar{x})(y_i - \bar{y})}{\sum (x_i - \bar{x})^2}$$

and

$$\beta 0 = \bar{y} - \beta 1 \bar{x}$$

Most of the calculations have already been done in Table 8.1. The numerator (top part) of the $\beta 1$ equation is 358.8 and the denominator (bottom part) is 625.6, which means $\beta 1 = 358.8/625.6 = 0.5735$. The $\beta 0$ estimate is: $14.4 - 0.5735(18.8) = 3.62$.

Figure 8.2 shows a scatterplot with all the estimated and actual velocities, and we have included the regression line. We have also included vertical lines from each point to the regression line. These are the e_i for each point. The regression line is the one which minimizes the sum of the squares of these vertical lines. The larger the sum of these squared

---

1 Some statistics books spend much time differentiating the population parameters we are trying to estimate, say β, from the estimate for this which is denoted $\hat{\beta}$. Providing that you realize that the values you find based on data are just empirical estimates of the true population values (i.e., the plug-in principle), this extra layer of notation can usually being avoided. The only statistics that psychology texts usually differentiate are the sample mean ($\bar{x}$) as an estimate for the population mean (μ) and the respective values for the standard deviation (sd and σ).

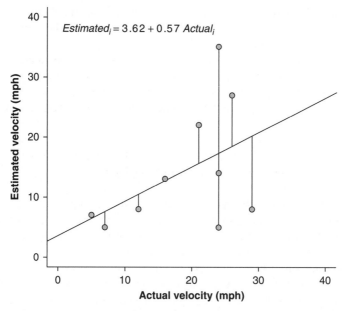

$Estimated_i = 3.62 + 0.57\ Actual_i$

Figure 8.2 A scatterplot showing estimated with actual velocity, with the regression line. The vertical lines, from each data point to the regression line, are the residuals, the e_i

values, the more error there is in the model. Here, the sum is 750.6. This is called the error or residual sum of squares, SS_{error}. The total sum of squares is equal to the amount accounted for by the model, SS_{model}, plus SS_{error}. Thus: $956.4 = 750.6 + SS_{model}$. We can rearrange these values to get: $SS_{model} = 956.4 - 750.6 = 205.8$. This tells us that 205.8 of the total 956.4, or $205.8/956.4 = 0.22$ or 22% can be accounted for by the model. This is called R^2 and is the same as the η^2 covered in Chapter 7.

In the same way as was done with the sums of squares in Chapter 7, it is possible to test whether this reduction is greater than expected by chance. This is the same as testing whether the population value for $\beta 1$ is 0. In words, this tests whether the line in Figure 8.2 is flat. We calculate the mean sum of squares by dividing each sum of squares by their associated degrees of freedom. For the model the number of degrees of freedom is the number of variables that we are using in the equation, which we will label k. In this chapter this is 1 (for the actual velocities). Thus, the MSS_{model} is SS_{model} or 205.8. The number of degrees of freedom associated with the error term is: $n - k - 1$. Here this is: $10 - 1 - 1 = 8$. Therefore, MSS_{error} is $750.6/8 = 93.8$. We can calculate the F value by dividing these: $205.8/93.8 = 2.19$. We write $F(1, 8) = 2.19$. Many statistical packages produce a t value for this, which is simply the square root: $t(8) = \sqrt{2.19} = 1.48$. The probability values of these can be looked up in Appendices C and D or calculated with most statistical packages. The p value is approximately 0.18. This shows that we should not, on the basis of these data, reject the hypothesis that there is no relationship between the actual and estimated velocities. Of course, because the sample is small we would want to be cautious with any conclusions.

Let's consider another example. Many questionnaires attempt to measure people's attitudes on a variety of topics. Suppose someone was interested in the relationship between attitudes towards gun control and views on tougher prison sentencing. The researcher might ask a sample of 100 people to rate their agreement on the following two statements:

'Gun control laws should be relaxed'
'The laws on prison sentencing are far too weak'

using a scale from 1 ('totally disagree') to 11 ('totally agree'). Figure 8.3 shows two scatterplots between the responses to these two variables. In the left-hand panel we have used what are called *sunflowers*. Because there are a large number of people in the sample, there are many coordinates, or points, on the scatterplot that have more than one person at them. If there is just a single person at a point then there is just the circle for the bud of the sunflower. If there are two people, like the pair giving the response 2 to each question, then the sunflower has two petals. The point above that (2 to the 'guns' question and 3 to the 'sentencing' question) has four people, and therefore four petals are drawn. Drawing sunflowers is a common option in many statistical computing programs. The right-hand panel denotes multiple cases with the same response by making the numbers slightly different. A small random number, called a *jitter*, has been added to all the responses. These are called sunflower and jitter scatterplots, respectively. The regression line is also printed on both these graphs. It shows an increase in agreeing with 'sentencing' is associated with an increase in the 'guns' question. It is left as an exercise to find the exact form of this equation.

Regression is often used for prediction. Complex types of regression are used for predicting the weather (and the climate), the stock market and the spread of diseases. Here we consider a simpler problem. At the end of most courses, students are asked to fill out a form to provide feedback to help the instructor improve the course for the following year. Sometimes these forms are also used when making decisions about tenure, therefore the instructor wants as many high marks as possible. Neath (1996) describes 20 ways to improve these marks,[2] including carefully looking at the feedback forms to make sure the numbers are correct. We are going to put you into one of those moral dilemma situations, in the shoes of your instructor.

---

2 Including: be male (and teach only males), grade leniently, be present when the forms are being filled out, have them filled out before the exam, but after the review session, teach small classes, teach upper division classes, do not allow non-majors, teach options, show (even unrelated) films in class, and pretend you have the same likes and dislikes of your students.

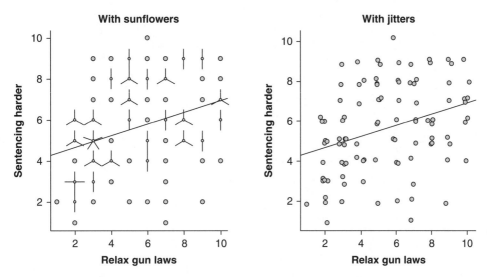

Figure 8.3   Scatterplots comparing the views on sentencing and gun control

You have finished your first term of teaching, worked your socks off, and just received 15 feedback forms. The head of department will hire you if your mean on the 'How satisfied with the course' question is above 4 on the 1–7 scale (7 being good). Students were also asked 'How organized was the instructor', also with a 1–7 scale. Here are the responses:

Satisfied	2	6	4	3	6	2	⅂	1	2	5	5	1	3	7	7
Organized	1	2	3	4	5	6	7	2	3	4	5	2	3	4	5

One of the responses looks either like a 1 or a 7. If it is a 1 the mean is 3.67 and you are fired. If it is a 7 the mean is 4.07, and you keep your job. If you exclude that person's data, the mean is 3.86 so you are fired. It is anonymous so you cannot find the person. What do you do? Because students also filled out a question about 'organization', it is worth seeing if that provides any information about whether it is more likely to be a 1 or a 7. The 14 readable questionnaires can be used for the following regression:

$$Satisfied_i = 1.57 + 0.65 \, Organized_i + e_i$$

If you knew nothing about what the person had written for 'Satisfied', but knew they had written 7 for 'Organized', you can put the number 7 into the equation to get a predicted value for 'satisfied':

$$Satisfied_i = 1.57 + 0.65{\cdot}7 + e_i = 6.12 + e_i$$

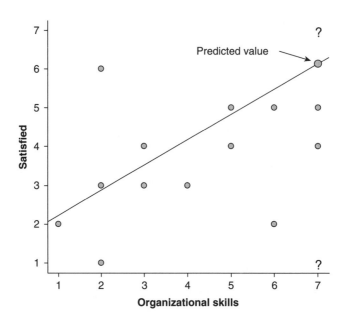

Figure 8.4   A scatterplot of satisfaction with organization for the 14 students with perfectly legible responses. The line is the regression line for these. ?s are placed at the two options for interpreting the illegible student's ratings. A large dot is placed where the regression predicts how satisfied someone who gives a 7 to an organization should be

This means that our best guess is that this person would have said '6.12'. Of course, students could only provide whole number responses, so 6 looks the most likely response. We can see this on Figure 8.4. The predicted values, for any value of *Organized*$_i$, will be along the regression line. The one for *Organized*$_i$ = 7 is where the large circle is. As the regression line is much closer to the 7, you would probably be okay arguing that the scribbled character should be interpreted as a 7. But, it is worth noting that someone has given a 6 on organized and a 2 on satisfied. We recommend while arguing this with your head of department that you describe how your ratings will improve next term so that you are not this close to being fired.

PEARSON'S CORRELATION

Sometimes the data points in a scatterplot are close to the regression line, sometimes they are not. It would be useful to have some statistic that measures how close the points are to the regression line, what is sometimes called the 'fit' of the regression line. Not surprisingly, given this section's title, *Pearson's correlation* is just such a statistic. Pearson's correlation, described by Karl Pearson in 1896,[3] is so common that often people just call it 'correlation', but as we will see later this chapter, other correlations exist. Pearson's correlation gives a value, ranging from −1 to +1, which measures the fit of a straight line to the data. Negative scores mean that as the values of one variable go up, the values of the other variable tend to go down. Positive scores mean that as the values of one go up, so do the values of the other. Values near either −1 or +1 mean that the regression line has a nearly perfect fit. Values around 0 mean that the regression line does not fit the data well.

The correlation value is denoted with the letter r. The equation for it is:

$$r = \frac{\sum (x_i - \bar{x})(y_i - \bar{y})}{\sqrt{\sum (x_i - \bar{x})^2 \sum (y_i - \bar{y})^2}}$$

If we consider the data in Table 8.1, all the information needed for the above equation has already been calculated. These values can be entered into the correlation equation:

$$r = \frac{358.8}{\sqrt{(625.6)(956.4)}} = \frac{358.8}{773.5} = 0.46$$

As this is positive, we know that as the actual velocity goes up, the estimated velocity also tends to increase (as also evident by the regression line going up and that the estimate for $\beta 1$ is positive). It is often useful to square the correlation: $0.46 = 0.46 = 0.21$. This value is the amount of variation that the two variables share. In other words, it is the R^2 calculated earlier.

The statistic r is a standardized effect size, which means that it is often reasonable to compare r values across studies. Some people tell you to square r to interpret the size, because then you can talk about the proportion of shared variance, but given most people do not have a working concept of shared variance at their disposal this is often not useful. Others (e.g., Rosenthal, et al., 2000) prefer the unsquared r because it conveys information about the success rate if both measures were binary (though, as we will see in Chapter 10, there are other measures of effect size in this situation) and because r^2 sometimes looks so small that people think it is not important. As a very rough rule of thumb,[4] Cohen (1992) describes $r = 0.1, 0.3$ and 0.5, as 'small', 'medium' and 'large', respectively. These verbal labels should not be applied without consideration of what the correlation is of, and should not be interpreted as a measure of importance. With this caveat in mind, the observed $r = 0.46$ is a fairly 'large' correlation.

---

3 Pearson acknowledges that Bravais had created this formula previously, and he gives much credit to Galton. Stigler (1986) notes that Edgeworth had also created this formula prior to Pearson, had informed Pearson of this, but that Pearson seemed to give little credit to Edgeworth. 'Stigler's Law of Eponymy' states that all scientific findings are not named after their creator, but usually after the person who popularized them (see also Vicente & Brewer, 1993).

4 'Rule of thumb' is an old phrase (from at least the seventeenth-century) referring to using one's thumb to help with the measurement of various things (http://www.phrases.org.uk/meanings/307000.html; accessed 15 April 2007). An eighteenth-century cartoon and a twentieth-century cult movie (The Boondock Saints) suggest the phrase was used to refer to the maximum width of stick you were allowed to hit your wife with according to English law, but these seem to be sources of an urban myth rather than this being actual English Law!

The next step is usually to see if the observed r differs significantly from 0. This can be done by testing the t or F values above, or by changing the r value into one of these using the following formulae:

$$t = \frac{r\sqrt{n-2}}{\sqrt{1-r^2}}, \quad F = \frac{r^2(n-2)}{1-r^2}$$

From these, using $r = 0.46$, you get $t(8) = 1.47$ and $F(1, 8) = 2.15$, which are within the rounding error of the values printed above (using $r = 0.464$, which is the more precise value of r, produces $t(8) = 1.48$ and $F(1, 8) = 2.19$, as found above).

We have produced a table in Appendix A that allows you to look up whether the observed value of r exceeds the critical value for $\alpha = 0.01$, $\alpha = 0.05$ and $\alpha = 0.10$ (these are all two-tailed tests), without having to translate r into a t or an F value. You need to know the sample size to use this table. Here the sample size is 10. You go to the row corresponding to $n = 10$. The critical values are 0.765, 0.639 and 0.549 for $\alpha = 0.01$, $\alpha = 0.05$ and $\alpha = 0.10$, respectively. All of these are larger than the observed value of 0.46. Therefore, this correlation is not significantly different from 0. As the sample size increases, the critical values for the correlation become smaller and smaller. If there had been an n of 20, 0.46 would have been significant at $\alpha = 0.05$. As with the other tests discussed in this book, when done on a computer, the computer usually writes a precise p value. You should usually write this value when it is available (the exception being if $p < 0.001$, then just write $p < 0.001$).

As mentioned in previous chapters, it is more informative to report the confidence interval of a measure than just to do a test of whether it is *significantly* different from 0. Calculating this for r requires a couple of steps. First you have to use what is called the Fisher (1921) transform called r' :[5]

$$r' = 0.5 \ln\left(\frac{1+r}{1-r}\right)$$

This is necessary because the values for r are constrained between -1 and 1, and therefore r is not normally distributed (particularly as it approaches -1 or 1). It is worth repeating what the *ln* transformation is: *ln* is the natural logarithm. If $\ln(x) = y$, then $e^y = x$. e is a number, approximately 2.72, which has some useful mathematical properties. e^y means e multiplied by itself y times. So, 2^3 is $2 \times 2 \times 2 = 3$, and e^3 is $e \times e \times e \approx 20.1$. Thus, $\ln(20.1)$ 3.00. In more practical terms, to do a natural logarithm on your calculator, there is probably a button with ln or log on it. To do the opposite, or to exponentiate, there is probably an e^x or an exp button.

The 95% confidence interval around r' is:

---

5 Sometimes Fisher's transformation is written with absolute values signs around the $(1 + r)/(1 - r)$ part. This is unnecessary when transforming correlations because that value will always be positive, but Fisher's transform is used in other situations, not covered in this book, where this is necessary.

$$95\% CI_{r'} = r' \pm 1.96\sqrt{\frac{1}{n-3}}$$

This produces the limits for r', not r, so the limits have to be transformed back into r values using the following formula:

$$r = \frac{e^{2r'} - 1}{e^{2r'} + 1}$$

The button on most calculators to get e^x is either e^x or EXP.

Consider the gun control example, with $r = 0.46$ and $n = 100$. The t value is:

$$t = \frac{0.46\sqrt{100 - 2}}{\sqrt{1 - 0.46^2}} = 5.13$$

which surpasses the critical values for $\alpha = 0.01$ and $\alpha = 0.05$ with 98 degrees of freedom (which from the appendix for $df = 100$, are 2.63 and 1.98, respectively). The r' value is:

$$r' = 0.5 \ln\left(\frac{1 + 0.46}{1 - 0.46}\right) = .50$$

r' is usually close to r, the exceptions being when r gets near -1 or 1. The 95% confidence interval (and for the 99% confidence interval just replace the 1.96 with 2.56) for r' is:

$$5\% CI_{r'} = 0.50 \pm 1.96\sqrt{\frac{1}{100 - 3}} = 0.50 \pm 0.20$$

This means the confidence interval boundaries are 0.30 and 0.70, but in r' values. Back-transforming these yields:

$$r = \frac{e^{2(0.30)} - 1}{e^{2(0.30)} + 1} = \frac{1.82 - 1}{1.82 + 1} = 0.29$$

and

$$r = \frac{e^{2(0.70)} - 1}{e^{2(0.70)} + 1} = \frac{4.06 - 1}{4.06 + 1} = 0.60$$

So, the 95% confidence interval for $r = 0.46$ with $n = 100$ is (0.29, 0.60). Notice that the observed value is closer to the upper boundary than the lower one. Confidence intervals for r are not symmetric around r, so the style of writing confidence intervals 0.46 ± 'some value' will not work. Sometimes you will see people still doing this, which means they are relying on old-fashioned tables, have not used the $r \rightarrow r'$ transformation, or are just printing an approximate value.

Karl Pearson was born Carl Pearson. A popular belief is that he changed his name in honour of Karl Marx. Pearson was greatly enamoured with Marx. In 1881 Pearson wrote to Marx offering to translate *Das Kapital*. Apparently Marx was less enamoured with Pearson's translation skills, so that project never materialized. Pearson had in fact been using *Karl* for several years prior to reading Marx, and Porter (2004) described how the change was likely Pearson's homage to German culture, rather than to Marx.

AN ALTERNATIVE PROCEDURE: SPEARMAN'S r_S

In previous chapters there have been two broad approaches suggested when you want out-lying points to be less influential: statistics based on ranking the data and the median. There are many so-called robust methods for correlation and regression (Wilcox, 2005). Here we examine two approaches: Spearman's r_S (also called ρ or rho) correlation and transforming the data.

We will start with Spearman's r_S. The crime statistics in Sussex, England, for 2005–6 were published in the local Brighton paper and broken down by neighbourhood and type of offence. The left-hand panel of Figure 8.5 shows for the different neighbourhoods the number of thefts and drug offences. Clearly there is a positive relationship between the two types of offences, but one point stands out: 'Regency', which corresponds to the centre of Brighton, where people drink, get high and thieve. Regency is an outlier for both types of crime because it has far more of both. It is the region where Fat Boy Slim DJs to happy clubbers, not where he lives.

Spearman's r_S addresses problems with cases like Regency which are univariate outliers. By univariate outlier, we mean that it is an outlier just looking at the drug variable, and it is an outlier just looking at the thefts variable. Spearman's r_S involves taking the ranks of each of the variables on their own (as done in previous chapters), and then conducting Pearson's r on the ranks. Ranking the variables lessens the impact of any univariate outlier. Thus, Pearson's r on raw data is $r = 0.94$, but it is very influenced by this one data point and also by a couple of the other HTDs (the sociologists' abbreviation of *havens for thieving druggies*). Ranking the data on both of these variables means that all the wholesome areas squished into the lower left-hand corner are spread out and Regency and other HTDs are pulled in. When the cor-relation is run on the ranks, what is Spearman's r_S, you get 0.78. We recommend that if you are doing a Spearman's by hand, you rank the data, conduct the Pearson cor-relation, and calculate the significance and confidence interval as if it was a Pearson correlation. In fact, many computer programs use slightly different methods, but the deviation is small.

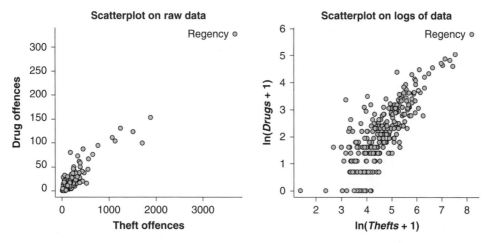

Figure 8.5   Scatterplots of different Sussex neighbourhoods by the number of drug offences and thefts in 2005–6. The left panel shows the raw data. The right panel shows the data after using the *ln* transformation on both variables. We took the *ln* of the variable plus 1

A common question is whether you should try both Pearson's and Spearman's methods and use whichever you like better. If you do use both approaches, heed Helena Kraemer's advice:

if both r_p [Pearson's] and r_s are applied to the same data and substantially differ from each other, it is a strong indication that the assumptions underlying r_p are not satisfied and that r_s should be preferred. (Kraemer, 2006: 531)

However, careful examination of the scatterplot should be done prior to conducting either of these procedures, so that you should know, prior to calculations, if there are any large outliers.

Ranking is a particular transformation, and when it is done all meaning about the distances between adjacent points is lost. You would know that there were more drug offences in Regency than elsewhere, but you would not know how much more and there is nothing you could do with these ranks to get back to the original data. The inference becomes about the ranks of data, and this can make it difficult to describe the results. Here, a better alternative might be to take the natural logarithms (ln) of the variables plus 1 (the +1 prevents negative infinities for the places with 0 of a particular type of offence). For these

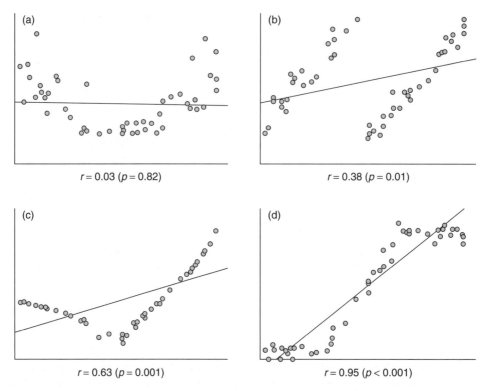

Figure 8.6   Four different scatterplots with their corresponding Pearson's correlation values

transformed values, $r = 0.76$ and $r_s = 0.74$, and Regency no longer stands out as much (see the right-hand panel of Figure 8.5). The ln transformation is a useful transformation for many positively skewed variables (so is the square root transformation ... though neither of these works with negative values).

TWO CONSIDERATIONS OF REGRESSIONS AND CORRELATIONS

There are two additional issues which we wish to stress. First, the regressions/correlations described here are just for straight lines. In many cases there is a clear relationship, but it is not linear. Figure 8.6 shows some examples where there are clear relationships, but they are not linear. The correlations may be high, as with panel (d), but clearly a straight line does not describe these data. There are more complex regressions that can be used to model these relationships (Wright & London, 2009). The most important technique, however, remains using scatterplots to allow you to understand the nature of any relationships.

Finally, there is an oft-cited adage, 'correlation does not imply causation', which is stated in every introductory statistics book. What often happens after people run a correlation is that they state their conclusions in 'causal' language. So, a researcher might find a positive correlation between ice-cream sales and crimes in Central Park (more people are there in summer), and wrongly conclude that there is a causal connection between the two (and might suggest banning ice-cream to reduce crime). This adage applies equally to other statistical tests, like the t test (see the pet ownership exercise, 7.2, in Chapter 7). While a large correlation does suggest that there is probably some causal relationship that may connect these two variables in some complex way (perhaps: hot weather $\rightarrow$ more people wanting ice-cream; hot weather $\rightarrow$ more people in Central Park; more people $\rightarrow$ more crimes), it does not say what this relationship is (Wright, 2006). It is often tricky to make sure that you avoid accidentally using causal language inappropriately. Randomly allocating people to conditions makes reaching causal conclusions much easier.

SUMMARY

With respect to technical details, this chapter introduced you to the equations for regression and the 'fit' statistic for it, the correlation. Regression is used to plot a straight line that describes the points in a scatterplot. This can be used to describe the relationship between two variables and for predicting the scores of one variable from another. The correlation is simply a measure of how good the fit of the regression line is. Any time a correlation is reported you should have produced a regression line and a scatterplot. As a correlation is only meaningful with respect to a regression line, and the fit of a regression line is best understood by looking at it with a scatterplot of the data, it is best to start with a scatterplot, run a regression, and then look at the correlation.

In assessing the fit of a regression line sometimes people simply see if the correlation is significant, and then say that the regression has a good fit. Figure 8.7 shows that this on its own is not good; it gets the sad face. The next step is to look at the size of the correlation. A correlation can be significant although extremely small in size, simply because the sample is large. It is worth looking at the size of the correlation and its 95% confidence interval. Looking just at the correlation and its significance is not enough. Your conclusions should not change too much if a couple of people's data are removed and, as shown with the Sussex crime data, a few points can have a large impact on the correlation. If they do change, then your regression is not *robust* and you should be cautious in your interpretation. These first three ways to assess the fit of a regression line are all mechanical applications of statistics and are not enough, on their own, to assess the fit of a model.

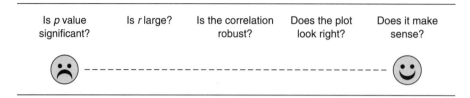

| Is p value significant? | Is r large? | Is the correlation robust? | Does the plot look right? | Does it make sense? |

Figure 8.7   Five ways for assessing the fit of a regression model. All should be used. Using just the ones on the left is discouraged

It is critical to see from the scatterplot if it looks as if the regression line fits the data well. This is subjective, but important. If you were assessing the fit of Figure 8.6(d), it has a large, significant and robust correlation. However, the straight line clearly does not capture the full essence of the data. The final criterion is: does the regression make sense? If, for example, your regression contradicts the law of gravity, the odds are your model is wrong and you should be very cautious with any conclusions. All five of these assessments should be used in evaluating the fit of a model, and for all the statistics you use.

Finally, there were a few places where we mentioned that there are more advanced regression techniques. This is an understatement. Regression procedures, of one form or another, underlie almost all statistics. Statisticians are busy working on many new types of regressions, but the basic ordinary least squares (OLS) regression and Pearson's correlation are the most common. A couple of alternatives to these were presented here and we describe one extension in Chapter 9, but these are just the tip of the iceberg (see Wright & London, 2009, for a little more of the iceberg). Understanding the basics of regression, therefore, is a necessary building block for further advancement in statistics.

EXERCISES

8.1   At the beginning of the chapter we described an example of having people estimate the speeds of cars. Peter Wright (a former honours student of one of us) actually found that most of his participants were fairly accurate. Figure 8.8 shows the data from one of his participants along with the regression line. The following may be useful information:

Mean of actual velocity	25.17mph
Mean of estimated velocity	23.05mph

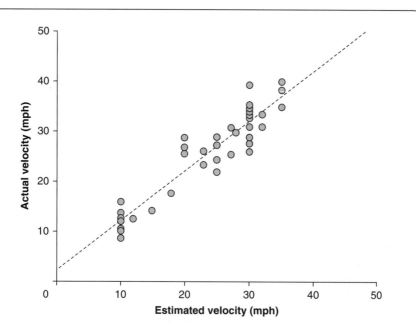

Figure 8.8   Data from one participant showing actual and estimated vehicle velocities

$$\sum(actual_i - \overline{actual})^2 = 3225.37$$

$$\sum(estimate_i - \overline{estimate})^2 = 2813.90$$

$$\sum(actual_i - \overline{actual})/(estimate_i - \overline{estimate}) = 2833.37$$

where the 'over-lined' variable names are their means. Suppose you were a police officer and this participant had been a witness to a car crash. The driver said he was only driving at 10mph, but this witness said the car appeared to be going 25mph. What would you predict is the actual speed from the regression? Do you think the driver's estimate is accurate? (Do not do any formal test for the final part of this question, just write what you think.) Why does it make sense to put estimated velocity on the x axis here?

8.2   Zelinsky and Murphy (2000) were interested in the relationship between how long it takes to say the name of an object and the amount of time that a person looks at the object when encoding the object for a recognition test.

(Cont'd)

Table 8.2   *Data based on Zelinsky and Murphy (2000)*

Name	Gaze
0.34	0.52
0.37	0.38
0.45	0.50
0.54	0.37
0.59	0.62
0.63	0.53
0.54	0.78
0.83	0.64
0.70	0.93
0.76	0.78

Suppose participants were shown 10 different pictures of common objects that varied in the amount of time that it takes to name the object, and the researchers recorded the mean time that the participants gazed at the objects. The times, in seconds, that might be found if such a study was run were as given in Table 8.2.

Find whether there is a relationship between these two variables:

(a)   Draw a scatterplot for these data and add the regression line.
(b)   Find Pearson's correlation.
(c)   Find Spearman's r_S correlation.

8.3   Find the regression equation shown in Figure 8.3. Let the variable *guns$_i$* be denoted x_i and the variable *sentencing$_i$* be denoted y_i. The following may be useful information:

$$\text{mean for } x_i = 5.42$$
$$\text{mean for } y_i = 5.65$$
$$\Sigma(x_i - \bar{x})(y_i - \bar{y}) = 187.70$$
$$\Sigma(x_i - \bar{x})^2 = 660.36$$
$$\Sigma(y_i - \bar{y})^2 = 484.75$$
$$n = 100$$

Write out the regression equation and remember to include subscripts where appropriate and a term for the residuals.

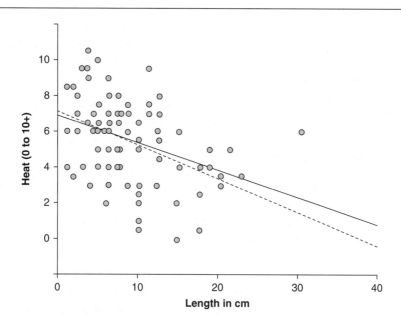

Figure 8.9   A scatterplot showing the relationship between the length of a chile and the heat. The solid line going through it is the regression line for all the data. The dashed line is the regression line without Nu Mex Big Jim

8.4   Find the correlation for the 'sentencing' and 'guns' in Exercise 8.3. Is this statistically significant? Is the correlation larger than the correlation for the data in Table 8.1? Are your answers to these questions contradictory?

8.5   If cooking with chiles, it is important to recognize that some are much hotter than others. A good chile database is on http://easyweb.easynet.co.uk/~gcaselton/chile/chile.html. On it, we found 85 chiles where both the length (in centimetres) and heat (on a 0 to 10 scale, but one of the Habaneros got a 10+ which we recorded as 10.5) were listed.[6] The resulting scatterplot is shown in Figure 8.9. The solid line going through the data is the regression line, and has the following equation:

$$Heat_i = 6.86 + 0.15Length_i + e_i$$

(Cont'd)

6 The Habaneros chiles are very hot. These should be avoided as they can cause great discomfort and illness. However, if you do get past the heat, they have an apple-like scent and come in a variety of pretty colours.

(a) Which tend to be hotter, small or large chiles?

(b) If you found a chile that was 12cm long, how hot on average, on the 0 to 10+ scale, would you expect it to be? From the scatterplot, describe (in words) how confident you would be that the chile's heat was approximately what you found from the equation.

(c) There is an outlier in the upper right area of the graph. Many of you will immediately recognize this as Nu Mex Big Jim, the world's largest chile. It was engineered to be big (and in fact some specimens are much larger than the 30.5cm average in the graph). As it was engineered to be big, it might be worth re-running the regression without this chile. Will the correlation be larger or smaller after this outlier has been removed?

(d) The regression line without Nu Mex Big Jim is shown by the dashed line on Figure 8.9. Its equation is

$$Heat_i = 7.1 + 0.19Length_i + e_i$$

If you came across a 30cm chile, growing naturally, what heat level would you predict? How confident would you be in the accuracy of this estimate and why?

8.6 Do you ever see signs saying that a garage or driveway is 'In *constant* use'? If you are like us, when you see one of these signs *and* see that it is not currently in use, you park there. When the owner arrives he (always it's a *he*) rants and raves that he can't park his car and 'Didn't you see the sign?' We each reply: 'Yes, I saw your sign, which is why I park there'. Why are we in the right, and why is the garage/driveway owner in the wrong (and annoying)?

8.7 One of the great baseball teams was the early 1970s Oakland A's. They won three consecutive World Series from 1972–4. Back in those days home runs were less common. Here are the A's 1974 batting statistics for at bats, home runs (HR) and stolen bases (SB).

	At bats	HR	SB
Gene Tenace	484	26	2
Pat Bourque	96	1	0
Dick Green	287	2	2
Sal Bando	498	22	2
Bert Campaneris	527	2	34
Joe Rudi	593	22	2
Billy North	543	4	54

Reggie Jackson	506	29	25
Jesus Alou	220	2	0
Angel Mangual	365	9	3
Claudell Washington	221	0	6
Ted Kubiak	220	0	1
Ray Fosse	204	4	1
Deron Johnson	174	7	1
Larry Haney	121	2	1
Dal Maxvill	52	0	0
Jim Holt	42	0	0
Gaylen Pitts	41	0	0
Manny Trillo	33	0	0
Phil Garner	28	0	1
Champ Summers	24	0	0
Vic Davalillo	23	0	0
John Donaldson	15	0	0
Tim Hosley	7	0	0
Rich McKinney	7	0	0
Herb Washington	0	0	29

(a) Decide what type of correlation (Pearson's r or Spearman's r_s) is appropriate to see if there is an association between the number of home runs and the number of stolen bases.

(b) Decide if there are any outliers and whether they should be removed. Say why (it might help learning from the web who one of the players was).

(c) Run whichever correlation that you think is appropriate. What is its value and its confidence interval? Is it significant?

📖 FURTHER READING

Abelson, R.P. (1995). *Statistics as Principled Argument*. Mahwah, NJ: Lawrence Erlbaum.
This book, like Figure 8.7, describes how it is important to look at more than just p values to convince people that your data have something to say.

Miles, J., & Shevlin, M. (2001). *Applying Regression & Correlation: A Guide for Students and Researchers*. London: Sage.

This is a really nice book covering the two variable regressions discussed here and more complicated ones.

Wright, D.B. & London, K. (2009). *Modern Regression Techniques Using R: A Practical Guide for Students and Researchers.* London: Sage.
This book covers the next stage of regressions that we feel is appropriate for psychologists and other social scientists.

9

Factorial ANOVAs and Multiple Regression

In Chapters 7 and 8 you were introduced to ANOVAs with one variable and simple linear regression. In those chapters you had to consider just two variables. In the ANOVA chapter (7) you had a single categorical variable and you were interested in whether there were differences in the means of some response variable either among multiple groups or for the means of multiple variables. In the regression chapter (8) you examined the association between two quantitative variables. In much psychology, the situations are more complex. Often you want to see the relationships among several variables simultaneously. More advanced textbooks focus on these situations and the mathematics can get complex. Here we describe two extensions: two-way ANOVAs and multiple regressions. We restrict ourselves to situations with just three variables.

TWO-WAY ANOVA

Recall from Chapter 7 that ANOVAs can be used to compare means for several different groups. In Chapter 7 these groups were described by a single categorical variable. The grouping variables in ANOVAs are often called *factors*. The different values that these factors can have are called the variable's *levels*. Suppose, however, you had two categorical variables and you wanted to see how the means of a third variable related to these two variables. A concrete example will make things clearer. The simplest type of two-way ANOVA is when both variables have only two levels. This is called a 2×2 design. Suppose the researcher is testing the effect of two different forms of psychotherapy and medication dosage (low or medium) on the amount of improvement in depression measured on a scale of 1–20 where higher scores are better. Table 9.1 shows data from 20 people (five per group) constructed for illustrative purposes. We will call the variables *IMPROVE*, *PSYCH*, and *DOSE*.

Some terms to learn:

- *Factor:* What the categorical variables used in ANOVAs are often called.
- *Levels:* The different values for a categorical variable.
- *Main effect:* The effect of one of the variables, averaged across the levels of all other variables.
- *Interaction effect:* How the effect of one variable depends on the levels of one or more of the other variables.

The first step should be graphing the data for the different groups. It is best to look first at the distribution of the variable *IMPROVE* for each group. With only five people per group you can just look at Table 9.1, but in general a good way to do this is with boxplots (see Chapter 1). These are shown in the left-hand panel of Figure 9.1. In the right-hand panel the means are shown with their 95% confidence intervals with a bar chart. Sometimes line charts are used, but these should only be used if the variable placed on the *x* axis could have intermediate values. Because there could be doses between low and medium it is acceptable to use a line graph if *DOSE* is on the *x* axis. It would not be appropriate to use a line graph if *PSYCH* was on the *x* axis as it is unclear what Psychotherapy 1.5 might entail. The most obvious thing from both these graphs is that the people in Psychotherapy 2 with a low dose show the least improvement. This is an interaction because the effect of one variable depends on the level of the other. So, the dose level only matters for Psychotherapy 2.

As with the one-way ANOVA, you calculate the sums of the squared deviations within each group (SS_{within}) and sum these (see Chapter 7). For the first group, SS_{within} is:

$$(11-15)^2 + (13-15)^2 + (15-15)^2 + (17-15)^2 + (19-15)^2 = 16 + 4 + 0 + 4 + 16 = 40$$

Table 9.1   *Data for a 2×2 two-way ANOVA showing the amount of improvement in depression depending on the type of psychotherapy and drug dose*

Drug dose:	Psychotherapy 1		Psychotherapy 2	
	Low	Medium	Low	Medium
Improvement	11	11	1	11
	13	13	3	13
	15	15	5	15
	17	17	7	17
	19	19	9	19
Mean (*M*)	15	15	5	15
Variance	10	10	10	10
SS_{within}	40	40	40	40

The total for all four groups is 40+40+40+40 = 160. You then calculate the SS attributable to each variable on its own for the main effects. This is done in a similar way to Chapter 7. To find the effect for which Psychotherapy is used, find the mean of all the data (i.e., the grand mean or GM) which is 12.5, and square the difference between this and the mean for each psychotherapy. The mean for Psychotherapy 1 is 15 and for Psychotherapy 2 is 10, so you subtract the grand mean from these (resulting in 2.5 and −2.5, respectively), square these values (6.25 for both), multiply these by the number of cases which is 10 since there are 10 people in each psychotherapy (resulting in 62.5 for each group), and then sum these together. In short,

$$SS_{PSYCH} = 10(15-12.5)^2 + 10(10-12.5)^2 = 125$$

You do the same for *DOSE* (and you also get 125). These are the sums of squares for the main effects of *PSYCH* and *DOSE*.

The interaction is calculated by finding the total sum of squares, which is the total variance multiplied by $n-1$,[1] and subtracting the sums of squares for the main effects. Here you get 19(28.16) −125 −125 −160 = 535 − 410 = 125, which is labelled $SS_{interaction}$ or $SS_{PSYCH \times DOSE}$. This gives us the sums of squares for each part of the ANOVA. As with one-way ANOVAs, you divide these by the degrees of freedom associated with each effect to get mean square (MS) values. For main effects this is k-1 where k is the number of levels of that variable (here $k = 2$ for both variables), and the interaction has ($k1$-1)($k2$-1) degrees of freedom, where $k1$ and $k2$ are the number of levels for variable 1 and variable 2, respectively. Here,

---

1 Or take each value, subtract the grand mean, square this, and sum them up (i.e., $\Sigma(x_i-GM)^2$). This is what you are doing when calculating the variance.

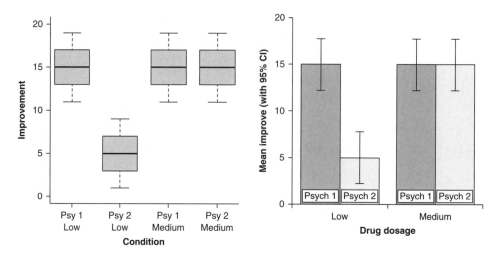

Figure 9.1   The left hand panel shows boxplots for the data in Table 9.1. The right hand panel shows a bar chart with 95% confidence intervals for the same data

$k1 = k2 = 2$, so $(k1-1)(k2-1) = 1$. The degrees of freedom for the error term is $n - k1k2$ or here $20-2(2) = 16$.

The F value for each is the MS associated with that effect divided by the MS associated with the within-condition variation (MS_{within} also called the MS_{error} and $MS_{residual}$). These are all shown in Table 9.2. The F value can be looked up in the same manner as Chapter 7, in Appendix D or found with a statistical package. The values here all have $p = 0.003$. We have also included η_p^2 (pronounced partial eta squared). This is the sum of squares for that effect divided by SS_{within} plus the sums of squares for the effect. So, $\eta_p^2 = SS_{effect}/(SS_{effect} + SS_{within})$, which here is $125/(160/125) = 0.44$. This is the most common effect size for ANOVAs and it is printed by some of the main statistical packages. η_p^2 is the proportion of variation accounted for by that variable after the other variables' effects have all been considered.[2]

Within the text of a paper you should write something like:

There were main effects of the type of psychotherapy, $F(1, 160) = 12.50$, $p = 0.003$, $\eta_p^2 = 0.44$, and of the level of dose, $F(1, 160) = 12.50$, $p = 0.003$, $\eta_p^2 = 0.44$, but these must be viewed within the context of a significant interaction, $F(1, 160) = 12.50$, $p = 0.003$, $\eta_p^2 = 0.44$.

---

2 Sometimes people refer to this errantly as just η^2, the measure introduced in Chapter 7. Plain η^2 is the SS of the effect over the SS_{total}. Levin and Hullett (2002) and Pierce et al. (2004) discuss the differences between these and that many people (including some statistics packages) errantly describe one when they mean the other. With the one-way designs in Chapter 7, η^2 is the same as η_p^2, but with more complex designs this is not true.

Table 9.2 *An ANOVA table for the data in Table 9.1. The main effects and interaction are all statistically significant*

Effect	SS	df	MS	F	p	η_p^2
Psychotherapy	125	1	125	12.50	0.003	0.44
Dose level	125	1	125	12.50	0.003	0.44
Interaction	125	1	125	12.50	0.003	0.44
Within (error)	160	16	10			
Total	535	20 (including 1 for the constant)				

Finally, it is often worth reporting an *F* value for the entire ANOVA. To find this, first find MS_{model} which is the sum of the $SS_{effects}$ divided by the sum of their degrees of freedom; here this is 375/3 = 125. Divide this by MS_{within}, which is 10, and you get 12.5. You would write this $F(3, 16) = 12.50, p = 0.001, \eta^2 = 0.70$. This is the same value that you would get if you ran a one-way ANOVA with the four groups. Note that we wrote η^2 here. This is the same as η_p^2 when the entire model is included.

Since the effect of the individual variables differs according to the levels of the other variable, it is common practice to stress that any main effects must be interpreted in light of the interaction, rather than on their own. In this example, while drug dosage showed a main effect with the medium dose leading, on average, to better outcomes than low dosage, this effect only held for patients receiving Psychotherapy 2. Hence, the researcher might conclude that if side-effects are a concern with higher dosages, Psychotherapy 1 combined with low-dose medication leads to equal symptom improvement as when the patients receive the medium dosage.

What does $\eta_p^2 = 0.44$ mean? It means 44% of the variation that the variable could account for, it does.[3] This is a very large effect. We created these data ourselves. Most effects in real examples are smaller. It is important, where practical, to report the confidence intervals for any effects. Smithson (2003: Example 5.2) goes through how to do this for η_p^2. It is a complicated process which requires a computer. Thus, here it is not practical to introduce, but if your computer software reports the interval you should also.

---

3 As in Chapters 7 and 8 there is an adjustment that is sometimes made to this effect size. η_p^2 is $SS_{effect}/(SS_{effect} + SS_{within})$. This value will always be above zero because SS_{effect} will always be positive. η_p^2 is a measure of the proportion of variation accounted for in the sample. As we did with η^2 and R^2 in previous chapters, this can be adjusted so that it is an estimate of the proportion in the population. The adjusted value is calle ω_p^2 (partial omega squared) and is:

$$\omega_p^2 = \frac{SS_{effect} - df_{effect}MS_{within}}{SS_{effect} + (n - df_{effect})MS_{within}} \quad \text{which for DOSE is } \omega_p^2 = \frac{120 - 1.10}{120 + (20 - 1)10} = \frac{110}{310} = 0.35$$

As with the other adjusted effect sizes the value shrinks. It shrinks more when the vairable associated with the effect has lots of levels and when there are few cases.

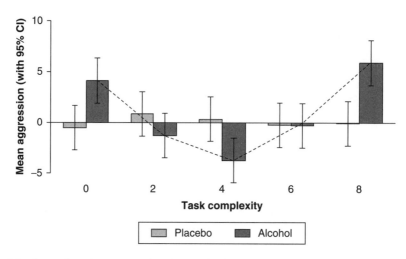

Figure 9.2   Data showing aggression depending on whether alcohol has been consumed and the task difficulty. These data are based on Giancola and Corman (2007). The dotted line connects the means for the alcohol group

$k \times c$ EXAMPLE

A 2×2 ANOVA is the simplest type of factorial ANOVA. Here we go through an example with a slightly more involved design, a 2×5 design. Giancola and Corman (2007: Exp. 2) were interested in how ingesting alcohol affects aggression so they split 120 people into two groups. People in the first group were given the equivalent of three to four alcoholic drinks and people in the second group were given non-alcoholic drinks (i.e., placebo), but the rims of the drinks were sprayed with alcohol so that they thought they were drinking. This is the first factor, *DRINK*, and it has two levels (alcohol and placebo). Participants performed a task in which they had to administer electric shocks to a confederate (Gabriel, 1986). The second factor was task complexity, *TASK*, and it had five levels (0, 2, 4, 6 and 8, where 0 is an easy task and 8 is difficult). The response variable was the number and duration of the electric shocks administered. This is a proxy for aggression, so we will label this variable *AGGRESS*. We constructed these data to be similar to their findings. Figure 9.2 shows the means with their 95% confidence intervals.

   Figure 9.2 shows that aggression levels remain relatively constant for the placebo participants. However, there is a V-shaped relationship for those who have had alcohol. At low levels of complexity, they give lots of shocks, but as complexity increases they give fewer shocks than controls (presumably they are concentrating on the task rather than shocking the confederate), and then at high levels of complexity they zap the confederates a lot, the authors argue, because of the stress caused by the difficult task.

Table 9.3   *The variances for each of the 10 conditions, as well as the means for the two alcohol groups, the five task groups, and the whole sample*

	Task complexity					
	0	2	4	6	8	Row means
Placebo	27.38	21.38	19.50	20.21	19.74	0.068
Alcohol	13.25	40.35	20.54	19.77	28.17	0.943
Column means	1.79	−0.22	−1.69	−0.27	2.92	$var_{++} = 27.94$ $mean_{++} = 0.506$

Table 9.3 shows the variances for the different groups. These are used to calculate the SS for the different effects. Below are the calculations. Let var_{ij} be the variance for the i_{th} row and the j_{th} column, and n_{ij} be the corresponding cell size. Let $mean_j$ be the mean for those in column j, and n_{+j} be the column size. Let $mean_{i+}$ and n_{i+} be the values for the rows, and var, $mean$ and n be the values for the entire sample. We have used more digits in these calculations than are printed in Table 9.3 to avoid rounding errors, so if you re-calculate these SS your values will be slightly different from ours (the data are on the book's website).

$$SS_{total} = var(n_{++} - 1) = 27.94 \cdot 119 = 3325.34$$

$$SS_{within} = \sum_{ij} var_{ij}(n_{ij} - 1) = 27.38 \cdot 11 + \ldots + 28.17 \cdot 11 = 2532.89$$

$$SS_{DRINK} = \sum_{i+} (mean_{i+} - mean_{++})^2 n_{i+}$$

$$= (0.068 - 0.506)^2 \cdot 60 + (0.943 - 0.506)^2 \cdot 60 = 23.03$$

$$SS_{TASK} = \sum_{+j} (mean_{+j} - mean_{++})^2 n_{+j}$$

$$= (1.79 - 0.506)^2 \cdot 24 + \cdots + (2.92 - 0.506)^2 \cdot 24 = 322.20$$

$$SS_{DRINK \times TASK} = SS_{total} - SS_{within} - SS_{DRINK} - SS_{TASK}$$

$$= 3325.34 - 2532.89 - 23.03 - 322.20 = 447.42$$

Table 9.4 shows an ANOVA table for these data, though many of the cells are missing. We have included the SS calculations above, and will go through how to calculate the rest.

- *df:* For the main effects, the degrees of freedom are k-1 where k is the number of levels for that variable. So, df_{DRINK} is 2–1=1 and df_{TASK} is 5–1=4. The interaction is the product of these two: $df_{DRINK \times TASK} = 1.4 = 4$. The df_{total} is n–1=120–1 = 119. The df_{within} can be found by subtracting the dfs for all the others from df_{total}: 119–1–4–4=110, or by summing the values of each cell minus 1: $\sum (n_{ij} - 1) = 10.11 = 110$.

Table 9.4 *An ANOVA table for the data depicted in Figure 9.3. Calculations for the missing values are given in the text*

Effect	SS	df	MS	F	p	η_p^2
DRINK	23.03					
TASK	322.20					
Interaction	447.22					
Within (error)	2532.89					
Total	3325.34					

- *MS*: The mean square (MS) for each row is the SS/df. So, $MS_{TASK} = SS_{TASK}/df_{TASK} = 322.20/4 = 80.55$.

- *F*: The *F* statistic is the MS of the effect divided by MS_{within}. So, $F_{TASK} = MS_{TASK}/MS_{within} = 80.55/23.03 = 3.50$. We write this with the degrees of freedom for both of these effects, $F(4, 110) = 3.50$.

- *p*: These need to be looked up in a table or found with a computer package. All the main statistical packages allow you to calculate *p* values from the *F* value and the degrees of freedom. Here the values are: $= 0.32$, $= 0.01$, and $= 0.001$, the effects of drink, task and their interaction. The appendix would allow you to say: *ns*, < 0.01, and < 0.01.

- η_p^2: The effect size is $SS_{effect}/(SS_{effect} + SS_{within})$. For the task, this is $322.20/(322.30 + 2532.89) = 0.11$.

If conducting an ANOVA when one or more factors have several levels, the ANOVA table tells us that there is an interaction, but it does not describe the nature of this interaction. There are more complex models that can be used to examine these effects. These are covered in more advanced textbooks. For our purposes you should examine the graph, and the pattern in Figure 9.2 looks fairly clear.

Factorial designs can take on more complex forms than the examples above and include more factors. Thus, a 2×2×3 design has three factors, where two of them have two levels and one has three levels. This design requires 12 different groups of participants. With designs that have more than two factors, several different interaction effects are possible. With a three-factor design we can have three different two-way interactions (Factor 1 with Factor 2, Factor 1 with Factor 3, and Factor 2 with Factor 3) and a three-way interaction. With these more involved factorial design studies, the nature of interactions can be determined by comparing group means in order to determine if a unique condition stands out or from different patterns of means. As the number of factors increases it can become difficult to provide a theory to account for these higher-order interactions. Often they can arise through measurement bias (like a floor or ceiling effect), so caution is urged. As the number of factors and levels increases, the number of groups also increases. A 4×3×4×5 design would require 240 groups! Factorial designs can also include within-subject factors, where participants take part in all levels of the factor. Further, the examples we looked at all had equal numbers of people in each condition. This makes the computations easier. Fortunately, most of the time you are dealing with more complex examples a computer calculates the values for you.

Table 9.5   *An ANOVA table with the values filled in*

Effect	SS	df	MS	F	p	η_p^2
DRINK	23.03	1	23.03	1.00	0.32	0.01
TASK	322.20	4	80.55	3.50	0.01	0.11
Interaction	447.22	4	111.80	4.86	0.001	0.15
Within (error)	2532.89	110	23.03			
Total	3325.34	119				

MULTIPLE REGRESSION

In Chapter 8 you were introduced to scatterplots, correlations and regressions as statistical tools when examining the relationship between two continuous variables. In many situations you have more than two variables. In some cases you are interested in how several variables predict a single response variable. In these cases you often use multiple regression. We will focus on situations where there are only three variables: two predictor variables and one response variable. For illustrative purposes we will go through the mechanics with a small data set constructed to show the procedure.

Table 9.6 shows data for three variables for 50 individuals. The variables are a measure of kindness on a 1–11 scale, a person's annual income in $1000s, and the amount the person gave to charities in $1000s. We will go through how to make scatterplots, appropriate correlations and, finally, a regression for this example.

Table 9.6   *Data for the multiple regression example. These are available on the book's web page*

No.	Kindness	Income	Charity	No.	Kindness	Income	Charity	No.	Kindness	Income	Charity
1	4	37	3.852	18	3	24	3.709	35	5	28	2.953
2	11	16	3.270	19	8	28	3.958	36	8	23	3.730
3	10	19	2.772	20	6	16	2.644	37	6	31	4.234
4	3	31	3.973	21	5	27	3.209	38	9	24	4.156
5	9	17	2.623	22	1	34	4.599	39	6	32	3.950
6	7	26	3.987	23	8	22	2.934	40	1	32	3.958
7	7	29	3.068	24	8	24	3.786	41	2	21	2.793
8	11	31	5.132	25	7	20	1.800	42	1	26	2.559
9	9	17	3.265	26	1	33	3.363	43	7	28	3.595
10	7	14	2.941	27	9	12	2.993	44	1	38	3.992
11	9	24	4.095	28	5	24	4.488	45	5	29	4.399
12	8	16	3.117	29	0	19	3.052	46	2	23	2.710
13	7	24	3.867	30	1	37	3.852	47	6	19	2.950
14	10	24	3.775	31	1	25	2.524	48	3	33	4.154
15	5	17	3.089	32	7	20	2.453	49	5	32	4.242
16	6	21	2.391	33	3	17	1.434	50	7	26	4.402
17	9	25	3.846	34	2	24	1.583				

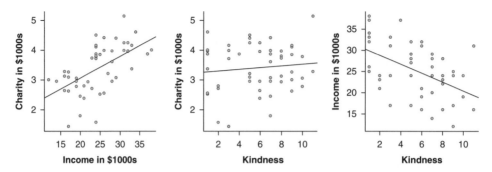

Figure 9.3 Scatterplots between each pair of variables for the data in Table 9.6

Scatterplots for Three Variables

There are several ways to plot three variables in a scatterplot. We consider four of them here. First, you can make scatterplots between each pair of variables and this is shown in Figure 9.3. The left panel shows that there is a positive relationship between somebody's income and their contributions to charity. The middle panel shows that there appears no relationship (or only a slight positive relationship) between kindness and the amount you give to charity (which should seem a little counter-intuitive). The right panel shows a negative relationship between kindness and income. This method has the advantages that each scatterplot is easily read and interpreted, and that it can be expanded to more variables. Most statistics packages make *scatterplot matrices*, which show the scatterplots between large numbers of variables. The difficulty with this approach is, if you are interested in how all three variables are associated, this does not allow this to be looked at very easily.

Figure 9.4 shows a scatterplot using the 3D option available in many statistics packages. The scatterplot is now in three dimensions. Most of these packages allow you to spin this scatterplot around, but because the paper that the graph is printed on is still only two dimensions these are always difficult to visualize. Sometimes spinning the scatterplot around reveals interesting aspects of the data, but most of the time we find this approach does not aid our understanding of the data.

The third approach, shown in Figure 9.5, displays the third dimension by using the symbol plotted for each point to refer to the third variable. In the left panel the amount that people give to charity is shown by the width of the circle. The bigger the circle is, the more that is given to charity. In the right panel the amount contributed to charity, in $1000s, is shown. For both of these we added a slight jitter[4] to the kindness scores so that they do not overlap as much. These scatterplots show that the highest values are for people with high incomes who are also kind. The advantage of this approach is that you get all the information about three variables simultaneously in a single graph. The difficulties are that when you have a large number of data points it becomes difficult to see each symbol and while there are methods (e.g., Chernoff, 1973) to extend this to more variables, they are problematic.

---

4 Meaning we add or subtract a small number, so instead of a kindness score of 4, it may become 4.10. This is often done with scatterplots when the variables can only take on a small number of discrete values (see Chapter 8).

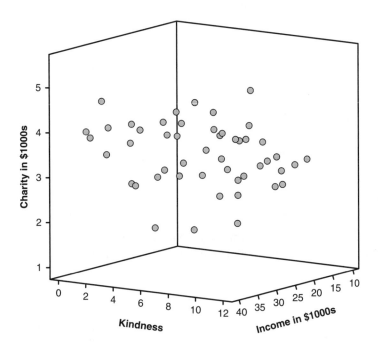

Figure 9.4   A three-dimensional scatterplot for the data in Table 9.6

The fourth method is to split the figure into separate graphs for different levels of one of the predictor variables. In Figure 9.6 this is done by splitting income into three bins: low, middle and high incomes. It shows a positive relationship between kindness and charity contributions for each of the three income groups. This approach has the difficulty that you lose information within each bin about one of the variables. This approach works best with larger data sets ($n > 50$). It is often called a *trellis graph*. It is important when making these that you use the same scales on the axes.

Each of these different methods for creating scatterplots shows different aspects of the data. It is usually necessary to try a couple of different methods, and then decide which method best conveys the information embedded within the data. None of them is the best approach for every data set.

Partial Correlations

Using the procedures in Chapter 8 you should find the Pearson correlations between each pair of variables before looking at multiple variables together. For notational ease let kindness = x, charity = y, and income = z. The correlation between x and y can be denoted r_{xy} and the equation for it is:

$$r_{xy} = \frac{\sum (x_i - \bar{x})(y_i - \bar{y})}{\sqrt{\sum (x_i - \bar{x})^2 \sum (y_i - \bar{y})^2}}$$

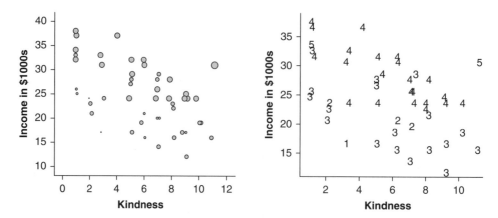

Figure 9.5 Two scatterplots of income with kindness. In the left panel the amount given to charity is proportional to the width of the circles. In the right panel the amount given is shown with its numeral

With multiple variables, correlations are often shown in a correlation matrix (see Table 9.7). These show, like the scatterplots in Figure 9.3, that there is a negative relationship between kindness and income, and a positive relationship between income and charity.

There is a lot of empty space in this table. Some packages will write 1.00 along the diagonal to tell the person that the correlation between a variable and itself is 1, and then print on the upper triangle the same information as the lower triangle. Since you know that the correlation between a variable and itself is 1, and that the correlation between x and y is the same as between y and x, you should not do this. It is a waste of ink. Useful information about the variable can be placed on the diagonal (often the standard deviation is used, though below we put histograms). It is worth putting something useful in the upper triangle of the table.

One useful statistic is called the *partial correlation* (other information, like the 95% confidence interval of r or Spearman's correlation, could also be used). It is the correlation between two variables after partialling out the effects of a third variable (or several variables). It is usually denoted $r_{xy.z}$ (or occasionally $r_{xy|z}$). This would be read as 'the correlation between x and y partialling out z'. When you have three variables the partial correlation can easily be calculated from the r values printed in Table 9.7.

$$r_{xy.z} = \frac{r_{xy} - r_{xz}r_{yz}}{\sqrt{1 - r_{xz}^2}\sqrt{1 - r_{yz}^2}}$$

For the partial correlation of kindness (x) with charity (y), partially out income (z), we get:

$$r_{xy \cdot z} = \frac{0.11 - (-0.50 \cdot 0.59)}{\sqrt{1 - (-0.50)^2}\sqrt{1 - (0.59)^2}} = \frac{0.405}{0.87 \cdot 0.81} = 0.57$$

This is a much larger value than the bivariate correlation. It shows removing the effects of income, kindness does increase with charity contributions. This is shown best in Figure 9.6. The calculations for the other partial correlations can be done in the same way. These are listed in the upper triangle in Table 9.8.

Table 9.7   *The correlations for between kindness, charity and income*

	Kindness	Charity	Income
Kindness			
Charity	+0.11		
Income	−0.50	+0.59	

When doing a correlation matrix with several variables you would print the partial correlation between pairs of variables partialling out all the other variables. Thus, you would provide a measure of the shared variance (the correlation) and the unique shared variance (the partial correlation).

Table 9.8   *The correlations are shown in the lower left-hand triangle, the partial correlations are shown in the upper right-hand triangle, and histograms showing the distributions are plotted along the diagonal*

	Kindness	Charity	Income
Kindness		0.57	−0.69
Charity	+0.11		0.74
Income	−0.50	+0.59	

Multiple Regression

These data show two seemingly different messages. The correlation between kindness and charity is only 0.11. However, the partial correlation is 0.57 when income is partialled out. While these two statistics are examining related issues, the issues are

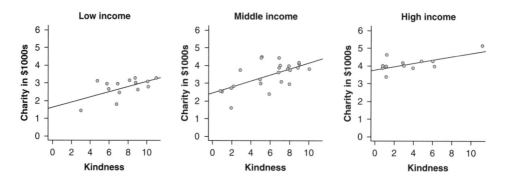

Figure 9.6 Scatterplots between charity contributions with kindness plotted separately for low, middle, and high income individuals

different. If somebody asked you to predict the amount of charitable contribution and told you that the person was kind this would not help you to predict their contribution. However, if somebody told you they were kind and rich, then you would be able to make a prediction.

Multiple regression is appropriate when you want to look at the combined effects of more than one variable in predicting a response variable. The computations underlying multiple regression mean that it is almost invariably taught with computers to help with the number-crunching. As such, we will assume that you are using a statistics package for this. Almost all the main packages work in a very similar way. You tell them what the response (sometimes called dependent) variable is and what the predictor (sometimes called independent variables or covariates) variables are. If we told it that *CHARITY* was the response variable and *INCOME* and *KIND* were the predictor variables, it would construct the following equation:

$$CHARITY_i = B0 + B1\ INCOME_i + B2\ KIND_i + e_i$$

The logic is the same as in Chapter 8. The *B* values (here *B0*, *B1* and *B2*) are what the computer tries to estimate optimally. The computer defines 'optimally' as the set of *B* values which result in the smallest sum of the squared residuals.[5] The output for statistical packages comes in different formats. When presenting the information in laboratory reports and papers you will probably want to alter how this is done. Here we present the output in two ways. In Table 9.9 the output is organized in such a way to emphasize the regression equation. The problem with this approach

---

5 In many texts these are written as $\beta0$, $\beta1$ and $\beta2$ (beta, the Greek letter). However, SPSS calls them *B* and, given SPSS is very popular among social scientists, we will use their notation.

Table 9.9   *Regression output emphasizing the regression equation*

CHARITY$_i$	= −0.024 +	0.139 KIND$_i$	+ 0.106 INC$_i$ + e$_i$
se	0.463	0.030	0.014
t(47)	−0.051	4.702	7.559
p	.96	<0.001	<0.001
$R^2 = 0.554$, Adjusted $R^2 = 0.535$, $F(2, 47) = 29.18$, $p < 0.001$			

Table 9.10   *Regression output that allows for large numbers of predictor variables*

Variable	B	seB	t (47)	p
Intercept	−0.024	0.463	−0.051	0.96
KIND	0.139	0.030	4.702	<0.001
INC	0.106	0.014	7.559	<0.001
$R^2 = 0.554$, Adjusted $R^2 = 0.535$, $F(2, 47) = 29.18$, $p < 0.001$				

is that often people have several predictor variables, and the page would not be wide enough to write the equation. Therefore, the values are presented vertically as in Table 9.10.[6]

The output in Tables 9.9 and 9.10 tells the reader that, controlling for income, there is a positive relationship between kindness and charitable contributions. They also say that, controlling for kindness, there is a positive relationship between income and charitable contributions. Thus, if you had two people who had the same income, you would expect the kinder person to give more to charity. In fact, for every unit increase in kindness, you would expect them to give, on average, $139 more to charity. Similarly, if you had two equally kind people, the one with the higher income would be expected to give more. For each $1000 extra income, you would expect them to give, on average, an extra $106.

It is worth stressing two important caveats. The regression above is making some assumptions. Many of these are similar to those assumptions made in Chapter 8, but there is an additional one, and that is that there is not an interaction between the two variables. Interactions can be included in multiple regressions by multiplying the two

---

6 In these tables we have included adjusted R^2. This lowers the R^2 value. The amount of shrinkage depends on the number of participants. Shrinkage also increases with the number of predictor variables. Therefore a new equation is used:

$$adj. R^2 = 1 - \frac{(1 - R^2)(n - 1)}{n - k - 1}$$

where n is the sample size and k is the number of predictor variables. There are different types of adjusted R^2, but this is the most common.

predictor variables together and including that product in the model (for these data there is not an interaction). The second caveat is to stress that people were not randomly allocated into a kindness condition or a high income condition. Without the random allocation it is difficult to make causal statements. Wright (2006) goes into some detail on this at an introductory level.

Common Mistake

Sometimes people have one response variable and want to see how each of several predictor variables relates to it. Because they have one response variable and several predictor variables they think this means that they should run a multiple regression. They shouldn't, at least the way the researcher's aim is phrased. They should run a series of correlations. If you were presented with the data in Table 9.3 and asked to find whether kindness and charitable contributions were correlated, and you ran a multiple regression and came to the conclusion that they were, you have answered the wrong question (sometimes this is called a Type III error, running the wrong statistical procedure). You should have done the simpler procedure, the ordinary bivariate correlation. On the whole, simpler procedures are better than more complicated ones.

SUMMARY

ANOVAs and regression are the two most used procedures in statistics. ANOVAs are actually a type of regression, but within psychology they have different developmental tracks. Chapters 7 and 8 covered the simplest forms of these procedures. The purpose of this chapter was to take one further step. We showed how to conduct factorial ANOVAs. These are appropriate when you have multiple categorical predictor variables. We showed how this is done when there are separate people in each condition, so called between-subject designs. There are ANOVA procedures available for within-subject designs, designs with both within- and between-subject factors, continuous predictor variables, etc. There are also special procedures when there are not equal numbers of people in conditions, when the variances differ, etc. In other words, there are lots more things you can do with ANOVAs.

Similarly, the multiple regression technique we introduced is one step above the regressions of Chapter 8, but there is more that can be done. Statisticians have produced methods to allow different types of variables as both response and predictor variables, to allow different relationships among all the variables, to search for parsimonious sets of predictor variables, etc.

This chapter is new to this edition. While the other chapters we think legitimately comprise the 'First Steps' in statistics, this chapter's contents are a sneak preview of the 'Next Steps'.

EXERCISES

The procedures described in this chapter are usually analysed with the aid of a computer. With that in mind we do not require much by-hand computation in these exercises. The first few require interpreting data, and the final three computation with a computer.

9.1   Taylor et al. (2007) were interested in cultural differences in dealing with stress. They had 41 Asians and Asian Americans and 40 European Americans take part in a series of stressful behaviours, like counting backwards by 3 aloud and giving speeches. They measured stress before these tasks and afterwards, and their response variable was the difference between these two. The way they calculated this makes it so the mean pre-experiment stress and mean post-experiment stress were both 0, so the change in stress as measured this way was also 0. They randomly assigned participants to three groups. In the *implicit-support* group participants wrote about a group of people they were close to. In the *explicit-support* group participants wrote about how this group could offer advice for the stressful tasks. And there was a *no support* control group. Figure 9.7 shows their results. Their numeric results were: $F(2, 74) = 3.84$, $p = 0.03$, $\eta_p^2 = 0.10$. In a few sentences describe their findings.

9.2.   Brown et al. (2007) were interested in what predicts social anhedonia, which is where people do not want social contact. The authors used experience-sampling methodology where a beeper went off telling their participants ($n = 245$) to respond to several questions at different time points in their study. We will simplify their data/output for illustrative purpose. Suppose they compared social anhedonia (0 low to 10 high) with whether the participant reported being alone (0, with others; 1, alone) when the beeper beeped, and their rating of positive affect (0–10 scale, where 10 stands for lots of positive emotions). Suppose the regression equation they found was:

$$Anhedonia_i = 7.00 + 1.50\,Alone_i - 0.5\,PosAffect_i + e_i$$

where the standard errors were, for the intercept 1.00, for $Alone_i$ 0.50, and for $PosAffect_i$ 0.20.

(Cont'd)

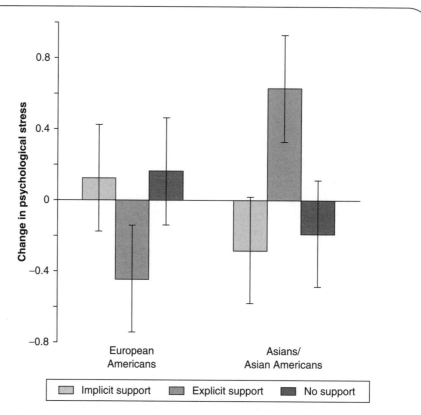

Figure 9.7 Change in psychological stress from pre test to post test as a function of culture and support condition (Taylor et al., 2007, Figure 1, reprinted with permission of the author and publisher)

(a) In a few sentences write what you would conclude from this study.
(b) How was your answer to part (a) different than it would have been if the analyses had been done separately using $Alone_i$ to predict $Anhedonia_i$ and using $PosAffect_i$ to predict $Anhedonia_i$?
(c) In a single plot, try graphing the regression equation. (*Hint:* try inputting different values of $PosAffect_i$ for those alone and those with other people.)

9.3 Wright et al. (under review) presented participants with a brief crime scenario where a woman was raped and then tried to identify her assailant from an identification parade (i.e., a line-up). The study had a 2×3 design. The identification was either conducted by a person who knew which person in the parade was the suspect or they did not know which person was the suspect (Factor 1 called *BLIND*, where 0 is blind administration, where the administrator does not know the suspect's identity, and where 1 is non-blind). The second factor is whether the victim made no identification ($ID = 0$), identified the suspect ($ID = 1$), identified one of the other people (known innocents) in the parade ($ID = 2$). Participants were asked to provide a belief in guilt on a 0–100% scale. It was negatively skewed, so the variable was squared; this is called *SQBELIEF* and scaled to run from 0 to 1. A random sample of 100 of their participants' data are below, and also on this book's website in a couple of formats.

(a)   Produce descriptive statistics for these data.
(b)   Create an appropriate graph for these data.
(c)   Conduct the appropriate ANOVA for these data.

9.4   Tramo and colleagues (1998) compared the IQs of 10 monozygotic twin pairs with the size of their brains. We will just look at the second-born twin's measured IQ (call this *IQ2*). We will use their twins' IQ (called *IQ1*) and the total volume of their brain in cubic centimetres (called *VOLUME*). The data are from http://lib.stat.cmu.edu/datasets/IQ_Brain_Size. Here they are for the 10 second-born twins on the three variables considered here:

IQ2	VOLUME	IQ1
89	963	96
87	1027	87
103	1272	101
96	1079	103
126	1070	127
101	1173	96
93	1067	88
94	1347	85
114	1100	97
113	1204	124

Use $VOLUME_i$ and $IQ1_i$ to predict $IQ2_i$. First graph the data in whichever way you feel is most appropriate and then, using a statistical analysis package, conduct the regression.

(Cont'd)

BLIND	ID	SQBELIEF	BLIND	ID	SQBELIEF	BLIND	ID	SQBELIEF
1	0	0.26	1	0	0.72	0	0	0.81
0	1	0.90	1	1	0.64	1	1	0.16
1	0	0.42	0	0	0.25	0	1	0.56
0	1	0.69	1	2	0.06	1	0	0.42
1	2	0.49	0	1	0.25	1	2	0.25
0	2	0.72	0	1	0.72	1	2	0.36
1	2	0.36	0	2	0.56	0	0	0.12
1	1	0.90	0	1	0.96	0	2	0.25
0	2	0.25	1	2	0.49	0	2	0.00
0	1	0.90	0	0	1.00	1	0	0.01
1	1	0.72	0	2	0.56	0	2	0.25
0	1	0.56	0	0	0.96	0	1	0.76
1	0	0.25	1	0	0.09	1	2	0.42
0	2	0.49	1	1	0.09	1	1	0.81
1	0	0.04	1	2	0.64	1	1	0.25
0	0	0.72	1	0	0.06	1	1	0.49
1	1	0.04	0	0	0.25	1	0	0.16
0	0	0.77	1	0	0.16	1	2	0.36
0	1	0.85	0	2	0.16			
0	2	0.25	1	0	0.09			
0	1	0.25	1	0	0.12			
0	0	0.06	1	0	0.81			
1	2	0.36	1	1	0.90			
1	0	0.06	1	1	1.00			
1	1	1.00	1	0	0.12			
0	0	0.25	0	2	0.64			
1	0	0.36	0	2	0.42			
1	1	0.81	1	0	0.56			
0	0	0.02	1	2	0.01			
0	2	0.64	0	1	0.76			
0	2	0.49	1	2	0.64			
0	2	0.09	0	0	0.04			
1	1	0.49	1	2	0.25			
1	1	0.25	0	0	0.81			
1	0	0.64	0	0	0.00			
1	2	0.30	0	0	0.36			
0	0	0.36	0	0	0.00			
0	0	0.01	1	0	0.79			
0	0	0.72	1	0	0.36			
0	2	0.36	1	1	0.12			
1	1	0.99	1	0	0.81			

Data from 100 participants sampled at random from Wright et al. (under review).

📖 FURTHER READING

Maxwell, S.E., & Delaney, H.D. (2004). *Designing Experiments and Analyzing Data: A Model Comparison Perspective* (2nd ed.). Mahwah, NJ: Lawrence Erlbaum.
Chapter 7 is particularly useful.

Wright, D.B. & London, K. (2009). *Modern Regression Techniques Using R: A Practical Guide for Students and Researchers*. London: Sage.
This book was designed as a follow-up to the current text, so it is the next step in regression. It uses the statistical software R (which is free).

10

Categorical Data Analysis

You have now learned much about the concepts and procedures of statistics. This will have provided you with both the ability to analyse many kinds of data and the foundations to learn more statistics. There is one more set of statistical tests to learn from this book. They are appropriate when you are looking for a relationship between two categorical variables. We discussed what categorical (also called qualitative and nominal) data are in Chapter 3. They place the cases in categories and it is not appropriate to conclude anything about the distances between these categories. We will begin with the situation when both variables can take only two possible values. At the end of the chapter a more complex example will be examined.

CROSS-RACE IDENTIFICATION

About 10 years ago the UK football (soccer) commentator, John Motson, said 'There are teams where you have got players who, from a distance, look almost identical. And, of

Table 10.1 *A contingency table, sometimes called cross-tabs or cross-tabulation, for the frequency of correct and incorrect choices for each of the four confederates broken down by race of the participant and whether the confederate was identified. The first number is the frequency. The numbers in parentheses are the percentages. Below these are the odds of a correct response. Data are from Wright et al. (2001: Table 1)*

Sample	Black confederate		White confederate	
	Blacks	Whites	Blacks	Whites
South Africa				
Number correct	17 (68%)	8 (68%)	15 (60%)	21 (84%)
Number incorrect	8 (32%)	17 (32%)	10 (40%)	4 (16%)
Odds of correct response	2.125	0.471	1.500	5.250
England				
Number correct	19 (95%)	24 (77%)	8 (35%)	14 (52%)
Number incorrect	1 (5%)	7 (23%)	15 (65%)	13 (48%)
Odds of correct response	19.000	3.419	5.333	1.077

course, with more black players coming into the game, they would not mind me saying that that can be very confusing' (BBC Radio 5's *Sportsweek*, 4 January 1998). This caused immediate uproar for being politically incorrect, but there is a substantial literature showing that people have relatively more difficulty making cross-race identifications than own-race identifications (John Motson is white). This is called the own-race bias. Almost all of the research on this topic has used laboratory settings and has shown participants dozens of faces. In most real-world cases people are only asked whether they recognize a single individual. Wright, Boyd & Tredoux (2001) wanted to test the own-race bias hypothesis in a more naturalistic setting.

In shopping centres in South Africa and England, either a black or a white confederate (someone working for Wright et al.) went up to either a black or white member of the public. The confederate asked a couple of questions, for example what time it was. A few minutes later the experimenter approached the person and identified herself as a memory researcher. She asked if the person could identify the confederate with whom the participant had just spoken from a set of 10 faces. Table 10.1 gives the number of people in each condition who accurately identified the person. This is called a *contingency table*.

Here these data are analysed separately for each confederate. For the black confederate in South Africa, 17 of the 25 black participants (68%) correctly identified the confederate. It is often useful to think of the *odds* of a correct response. The odds of a correct response are the number of correct responses (17) divided by the number of incorrect responses (8), which is 17/8 = 2.125. This means that it is about twice as likely that a black participant will make a correct response than an incorrect response. Of the white participants, eight correctly identified the confederate while 17 did not. The odds of a correct response for white participants are 8/17 = 0.471. These data show the own-race bias: black participants are more accurate than white participants at identifying the black confederate.

Effect Size Measures for 2 × 2 Tables

There are several ways to measure the strength of the association between two binary variables, and much debate about which is best. We will cover three. First, the *odds ratio* (OR), which is the most common in the medical sciences and is the building block for a technique called 'logistic regression', which extends the regression techniques covered in Chapters 8 and 9 to situations with categorical response variables. The second is called phi (sometimes denoted with the Greek letter φ), and it is easily interpreted within the hypothesis testing procedures used in these circumstances. Further, it can be generalized to comparisons between variables with more than two categories. Finally, a statistic called *Cohen's kappa* (κ) will be discussed because it has good statistical properties and is relatively easy to interpret.

The *odds ratio* (OR) is the most common measure of effect size in medicine and is one of the most popular elsewhere so you are likely to run across it often. It is the odds for one group divided by the odds for the other group. If the odds were the same in the two groups their ratio would be 1. Consider the data in Table 10.2 for the white confederate in South Africa. The own-race hypothesis is that the odds for a correct response should be higher for the white participants (because they are viewing a white confederate). Because of this it is better to divide the odds for the white participants (21/4 = 5.250) by the odds for the black participants (15/10 = 1.500), and get 5.250/1.500 = 3.50. Values above 1 are those in the predicted direction, so this result lends further support to the own-race bias. The odds ratio can be calculated more directly as: 21(10)/(15)4 = 210/60 = 3.50. This means that the odds of correctly choosing the confederate are three and a half times higher if you are a white participant than if you are a black participant. The odds ratio is a different class of effect size than the correlation, and Cohen's (1992) descriptions of small, medium and large effect sizes do not translate perfectly into the odds ratio, but roughly an odds ratio of 1.5 is small, 3.5 is medium and 9.0 is large.

If you had divided the odds for black participants by the odds for white participants, or had just arranged the columns (or rows) in Table 10.2 the other way around (as in Table 10.1), the odds ratio would be 1.00/3.50 = 0.286. When you get an odds ratio below 1 it is often useful to find the reciprocal of it; in English this means take one over the value.

One problem with the odds ratio is that while it cannot be smaller than 0, it can increase to infinity. There are two ways to address this problem. The first is to transform it so it has a range like Pearson's *r*, from −1 to 1. If you take $(OR − 1)/(OR + 1)$ you get such a measure. This is used enough so it has its own name: the gamma (γ) correlation (here it is 0.56). The second

Table 10.2   *Data for identifying the white confederate in the South African data from Wright et al. (2001). Also shown are the equations for three measures of effect size: the odds ratio, phi and Cohen's κ*

	Participants' race			
	White	Black		Three measures of effect size
Correct	A 21	B 15	odds ratio	AD/BC
Incorrect	C 4	D 10	phi	$\dfrac{(AD - BC)}{\sqrt{(A+B)(C+D)(A+C)(B+D)}}$
			Cohen's κ	$\dfrac{2(AD - BC)}{(A+B)(B+D)+(C+D)(A+C)}$

way is to take the natural logarithm of OR, ln (OR). It turns out that this is centred on 0 because ln $(1) = 0$. It is approximately normally distributed when there is no association. This allows us to calculate the 95% confidence interval for the odds ratio. This is done in four steps.

1   Take the ln of the observed OR. Here, ln $(3.50) = 1.253$.
2   Calculate the standard error on the log odds ratio:

$$se(\ln OR) = \sqrt{\frac{1}{A} + \frac{1}{B} + \frac{1}{C} + \frac{1}{D}} \quad \text{here} \quad \sqrt{\frac{1}{21} + \frac{1}{15} + \frac{1}{4} + \frac{1}{10}} = 0.681$$

3   Calculate the 95% confidence interval of ln OR:
   lower bound = ln OR – 1.96 se(ln OR)   here $1.253 – 1.96(0.681) = -0.082$
   upper bound = ln OR + 1.96 se(ln OR)   here $1.253 + 1.96(0.681) = 2.588$
4   Back-transform these into odds ratios by exponentiating them (with the EXP or e^x key on your calculator):

   $\exp(-0.082) = e^{-0.082} = 0.92$
   $\exp(2.588) = e^{2.588} = 13.30$

Thus, the 95% confidence interval goes from 0.92 (just below chance which is 1.00) to 13.30. Note that the observed value (3.50) is not halfway between these.

An alternative measure is called phi (it is usually written phi rather than the Greek letter φ) and is calculated thus:

$$phi = \frac{(AD - BC)}{\sqrt{(A+B)(C+D)(A+C)(B+D)}}$$

Here this is:

$$phi = \frac{(21 \times 10 - 15 \times 4)}{\sqrt{(21+15)(4+10)(21+4)(15+10)}} = \frac{150}{\sqrt{315000}} \frac{150}{561.25} = 0.267$$

This is like an r value in that a negative value simply means that the effect is in one direction. If the table is re-structured so that $A = 15$, $B = 21$, $C = 10$, $D = 4$, you will get phi $= -0.267$. In fact, phi is *very* much like Pearson's r. If you calculated Pearson's r on two binary variables, you get phi!

There are a few different ways to calculate the confidence interval of phi. Because it is calculated in the same way as Pearson's r it is reasonable to use the same procedures as used there. You begin using Fisher's r' transformation which here would mean $r' = 0.273$. The 95% confidence interval for r' then is: 0.273 ± 0.286, or from -0.012 to 0.560. Back-transforming these values (see Chapter 8) yields a lower bound of -0.01 and an upper bound of 0.51. There are more complex methods that can be used to calculate this,[1] and the bootstrap procedures described in previous chapters can also be used, but this method provides accurate enough intervals for most purposes.

Finally, we report Cohen's kappa (κ).[2] The history of this statistic is interesting because it was first put forward by Cohen (1960), not for its statistical properties, but because it seemed to communicate the association well to non-mathematicians. Since its creation, its mathematical properties have been studied and it has been found to have good properties (Kraemer, 2006). The equation for Cohen's kappa is shown in Table 10.2. When we calculate it for these data we get 0.24.

Cohen's kappa is often described as the percentage agreement, but correcting for chance. It is worth seeing what is meant by this. For over 100 years people have used weather forecasting to illustrate the problems using percentage agreement without correcting for chance as a measure of association (Finley, 1884, and numerous papers in the 1880s about this, see Murphy, 1996), so we will keep with tradition. Suppose we wanted to see how good a weather forecaster was at forecasting tornados in Toledo, Ohio, over a 100-day period one summer. Suppose 10 tornados touched down in the Toledo area that summer. Table 10.3 shows the contingency table for this with the predictions of two forecasters.

---

1 Smithson (2003: Example 4.4) goes through another method which is more complicated and computationally demanding than treating phi like r. He provides computer code for it, but the web page he lists in his book has moved to https://www.anu.edu.au/psychology/people/smithson/details/CIstuff/CI.html.

2 There is a statistic called weighted kappa. Cohen's (1960) version is a particular instance of it. The equation for weighted kappa is: $(AD - BC)/(w(A + B)(B + D) + (1 - w)(C + D)(A + C))$. When $w = 0.5$ this is Cohen's kappa. Cohen's is sometimes called unweighted kappa.

Table 10.3   *Forecasting tornados*

	Forecaster A says			Forecaster B says		
	No tornado	Tornado	Totals	No tornado	Tornado	Totals
No tornado	90	0	90	70	20	90
Tornado	10	0	10	0	10	10
Totals	100	0	100	70	30	100

Forecaster A is right 90% of the time; Forecaster B is right 80% of the time. Which fore-caster would you trust more? You should say 'Forecaster B'. This is because Forecaster A's predictions do not relate to whether there is a tornado or not. If you just knew that there were going to be 90 tornado-less days then you would know that saying 'no tornado' was probably going to be right. Because of this, Cohen's kappa is 0 for Forecaster A. The value for Forecaster B is 0.41. The equation shown in Table 10.2 is the easiest way to calculate kappa, but to conceptually understand it, consider the following. Suppose that you knew the total number of tornados (10, or 10%) and the total number of tornados that Forecaster B predicted (30, or 30%). If there was no association between the weather and the prediction then only 10% of the forecaster's tornado predictions should be for tornado days. This would be 3. This means 27 would be for non-tornado days. Similarly, if 3 of the 10 tornado days were pre-dicted, 7 would not be predicted. This would leave 63 non-tornado days correctly predicted. In total there would be 63 + 3 = 66 correct predictions, even if there were no association between the forecasts and the weather. This would leave 100 − 66 = 34 errors. Forecaster B made 80 correct predictions, or 14 more than predicted by chance.[3] Cohen's kappa is this dif-ference (14) divided by the number of errors if using the chance proportions (34), so 14/34 is 0.41. Landis and Koch (1977) have applied verbal labels to different numerical values of kappa: 0–0.20 is poor, 0.21–0.40 is fair, 0.41–0.60 is moderate, 0.61–0.80 is substantial, and above that is almost perfect.

The standard equation to calculate the confidence interval of kappa requires, according to Everitt (1996: 291), a 'strong stomach' so we do not recommend calculating by hand. For reference, see Fleiss et al. (1969). For these data the resulting 95% confidence interval is from 0.23 to 0.60.

Three different measures of association were discussed in this section, and in fact there are dozens more. There is much disagreement about these, but one thing that is agreed is that no single measure is always the best.

---

3 If the number of correct predictions made is less than the number predicted by chance, this number (and the resulting kappa) should be negative.

The χ^2 (Chi-Square) Test for the 2 × 2 Test

As in previous chapters, a common approach to data analysis is to test a specific hypothesis, here that there is no association between two variables. In the previous examples this would be between the race of the participant and whether their memory was accurate, and between whether the forecaster said that there would be a tornado, and if there was a tornado. To test this you need to calculate the χ^2 (chi-square) statistic. We will describe three ways to compute this. The first is the easiest if you have already calculated phi. The second is a method to directly calculate χ^2 if you have not already calculated phi. The third is a general method for calculating χ^2 values that extends to more complex problems. It is also the method that best illustrates what χ^2 is (and is related to Cohen's kappa).

> The null hypothesis is that there is no association between the two variables. If there is no association, the χ^2 value should be small. If there is an association, this value should be larger. As such, χ^2 is a measure of how bad the model (no association) fits the data.
>
> - Small χ^2 value: No association. Do not reject H0.
> - Large χ^2 value: An association detected. Reject H0.

If you have already calculated phi, calculating κ^2 is simply: n phi^2, where n is the total sample size. For the own-race bias example it is: $50 (0.267)^2 = 3.56$. Sometimes people calculate χ^2 first and then calculate phi from this. In this case phi is the square root of χ^2/n.

For the 2 × 2 case χ^2 can also be calculated directly from the values A, B, C and D from Table 10.2. Given the close relationship between phi and χ^2 it is not surprising the equations look similar: This can be calculated direct.

$$\chi^2 = \frac{n(AD - BC)^2}{(A+B)(C+D)(A+C)(B+D)}$$

which yields: $50(-150)^2/315000 = 3.57$. This is within rounding of the value found previously (this value is correct; the 3.56 had a small amount of rounding error).

The third method of calculating the χ^2 value looks the longest (well, it is the longest), but it has two big advantages. First, it shows conceptually what the test is doing. Second, it is a very general procedure which extends to more complex problems. As with all hypothesis testing, you begin assuming that the null hypothesis is correct. Then you find out how far away the observed values are from those predicted by the null hypothesis. If they are a long way away then you reject the null hypothesis.

We will use this method to calculate the χ^2 value for the White confederate in South Africa. Before showing how this is done it is worth introducing a convenient notation to use

Table 10.4   *Observed data (O_{ij}) for the white confederate in South Africa (Wright et al., 2001), showing the calculations for expected values (E_{ij}) and the standardized residuals (SR_{ij}) for each cell. These can be used to calculate the χ^2 statistic for the entire contingency table*

	Black	White (RT_i)	Row total	
Correct	$O_{11} = 15$ $E_{11} = 18$ $SR_{11} = -0.71$	$O_{12} = 21$ $E_{12} = 18$ $SR_{12} = 0.71$	$RT_1 = 36$	$E_{ij} = \dfrac{RT_i CT_j}{n}$
Incorrect	$O_{21} = 10$ $E_{21} = 7$ $SR_{21} = 1.13$	$O_{22} = 4$ $E_{22} = 7$ $SR_{22} = -1.13$	$RT_2 = 14$	$SR_{ij} = \dfrac{O_{ij} - E_{ij}}{\sqrt{E_{ij}}}$
Column total (CT_j)	$CT_1 = 25$	$CT_2 = 25$	$n = 50$	

with contingency tables. This is similar to those we used with the ANOVAs in Chapters 7 and 9. Each cell can be denoted with two numbers placed as subscripts. The first number corresponds to the row number, the second to the column number. For example, the first cell in Table 10.4 shows $O_{11} = 15$. This means that the observed value for the cell in the first row in the first column is 15. The second cell in the first row has the subscript 12 because it is in the first row and the second column. As we have done with other variables, the observed values can be denoted with a general term, O_{ij}, where the subscript i denotes the row and the subscript j the column.

The first step is to calculate the expected values, denoted E_{ij}, if there was no relationship between the two variables. Overall, 36 of the 50 people, or 72%, correctly chose the confederate. If there were no association between being correct and the participant's race, then you would expect about 72% of black participants and about 72% of white participants to choose the confederate correctly. There are 25 people in each group and 72% of 25 is 18. Therefore, the expected value for both of these groups, for the correct number, is 18. For each, if 18 of 25 are expected to be correct, then seven are expected to be incorrect. An alternative and computationally easier method for calculating the expected value for each cell is to multiply the total number of people in the row (RT_i) by the total number of people in the column (CT_j) and divide by the sample size (n).[4] This is done in Table 10.4.

The difference between the observed value and the expected value is the residual. As with the regression procedure, the residual shows how far away the observed value is from

---

4 To be consistent with Chapter 9, we could label the row totals as RT_{i+}, the column totals as CT_{+j}, and the total sample size as n_{++}, but this is not necessary for the problems in this book. This notation is used for more complex analyses of contingency tables.

the value predicted by the model (here the model is that there is no association between the two variables). It is often useful to show the *standardized residuals*, abbreviated SR. This gives a measure for how far off the expected value is from the observed value, taking into account the row and column totals. It is the residual divided by the square root of the expected value. These equations are shown in the right-hand portion of Table 10.4. The larger the standardized residual for a given cell, the more that cell contributes to the overall χ^2 value.

Now you are ready to calculate the χ^2 value. It is the sum of the squared standardized residuals:

$$\chi^2 = \sum \text{SR}_{ij}^2 = \sum \left(\frac{(O_{ij} - E_{ij})}{\sqrt{E_{ij}}} \right)^2 = \sum \frac{(O_{ij} - E_{ij})^2}{E_{ij}}$$

If you sum the squares of all the standardized residuals in Table 10.4, remembering that the square of a negative number is a positive number, you get

$$(-0.71)^2 + (0.71)^2 + (1.13)^2 + (-1.13)^2 = 0.50 + 0.50 + 1.28 + 1.28 = 3.56$$

The far right-hand side of the above equation shows a more direct way to calculate the χ^2 value. Take each residual, square it, divide by the expected value and then sum these up. For the first cell this is $(15 - 18)^2/18$, 9/18 or 0.50. Either method of calculating these produces the same number.

This value can be looked up in the χ^2 distribution in Appendix E at the back of this book. As with the t and F tests you need to know the degrees of freedom. A handy rule of thumb is to take the number of rows, minus one, and multiply this by the number of columns, minus one. Here, that is: $(2-1)(2-1) = (1)(1) = 1$. For all 2×2 χ^2 tests there is always just one degree of freedom. The critical values are 3.84 and 6.63 for the 5% and 1% levels, respectively.

The big question is: what conclusions should you make? The observed χ^2 value is 3.57 (or 3.56 depending on rounding), which is smaller than the critical value of 3.84 found in Appendix E. Therefore it is non-significant. You should write this as: $\chi^2(1) = 3.57$, *ns*, or if you have access to a computer $\chi^2(1) = 3.57$, $p = 0.06$. However, from Figure 10.1 it is clear that in this sample the white participants were more accurate at identifying the white confederate than were black participants. The effect is just not large enough, given the sample size, to be statistically significant. However, as it is in the predicted direction and is of a similar magnitude as for the black confederate, it does support the hypothesis (see Berkowitz, 1992, for further arguments about how even non-significant replications lend support to a theory). The analyses of the English data are left as exercises.

NOT PROPAGATING THE SPECIES: THE DARWIN AWARDS

A fundamental tenet of the theory of evolution is that the fittest people are more likely to reproduce, passing their genes on to future generations. Wendy Northcutt (2000) has

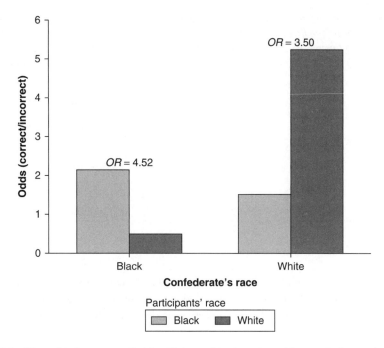

Figure 10.1   The odds for correctly identifying a black and a white confederate for black and white participants in South Africa (from Table 1 of Wright et al., 2001)

explored the converse, that there are people who should, and do, stop their genes being passed on to future generations. People who die (or at least end their chances of reproducing) doing particularly stupid things can be given Darwin Awards. There is even a Darwin Awards movie starring Winona Ryder. For example, a 1994 winner tipped a Coke machine over trying to get a free soda and when it fell on him he died. This meant he could not pass his genes on. Some people do stupid things that do not kill them, like Larry Walters who connected 45 helium-filled weather balloons to his lawn chair, grabbed some Miller Lite beer (presumably he is health-conscious so drinks lite beer), and planned to float just above his backyard looking down at his neighbours. Instead, his aircraft shot up. Two pilots from nearby Los Angeles International Airport (surprised to hear this happened in LA?) radioed to report a man drinking lite beer in their air space. Eventually he came down, was arrested, but still alive and able to reproduce (and some women find this kind of behaviour attractive). Therefore, he only received an Honourable Mention. Northcutt, who began the Darwin website (www.darwinawards.com) while researching neuroscience at Stanford University, also describes Urban Legends, which did not really happen, and Personal Accounts, where people write in about themselves or other people doing stupid things.

Table 10.5   The breakdown, by gender, of the different classifications in Northcutt's (2000) book, The Darwin Awards. The first number is the observed frequency. The second number is the expected value if the null hypothesis were true. The gender of the recipient was unclear in some of the descriptions. Some of these we did not use, while for others we tried to infer the gender

	Category				
	Darwin Award	Honourable Mention	Urban Legend	Personal Account	Row total (*RT*)
Males	131	23	16	35	205
	130.76	23.62	20.25	30.37	
Females	24	5	8	1	38
	24.24	4.38	3.75	5.63	
Column total (*CT*)	155	28	24	36	243

Table 10.5 shows the number of males and females in each of these four categories, and the expected values if there was no association between gender and the breakdown of awards. For example, the expected value for the males with Darwin Awards is:

$$E_{11} = \frac{(RT_1)(CT_1)}{n} = \frac{(205)(155)}{243} = 130.76$$

The odds for a Darwin Award winner being male are $131/24 = 5.46$, meaning that a Darwin Award winner is 5.46 times more likely to be male rather than female. It is left as an exercise to calculate the odds of a recipient being male for the other categories.

The standardized residuals can be calculated in the same way as for the 2×2 problem: subtract the expected value from the observed value, then divide this difference by the square root of the expected value. For example, for males being in the Urban Legend category, it is $(16 - 20.25)/ \sqrt{20.25} = -0.94$. Figure 10.2 shows the standardized residuals for each cell.

The next step is squaring the standardized residuals and adding them together to find the observed χ^2 of 10.32. The degrees of freedom are the number of rows minus one ($2-1 = 1$), multiplied by the number of columns minus one ($4 - 1 = 3$), which makes $df = 3$. The critical values at the 5% and 1% levels are 7.81 and 11.34, respectively. The value is significant at the 5% level, though not the 1% level. Using the 5% level, the hypothesis that there is no association between which category someone is in and their gender can be rejected. It is important to realize that this is not saying that males are more likely to be represented in the table. It is clear that they are (see Box 10.1 for the method to show this). These statistics already take into account that males are far over-represented in the Darwin book. What these data show is that there are more urban myths about women and more

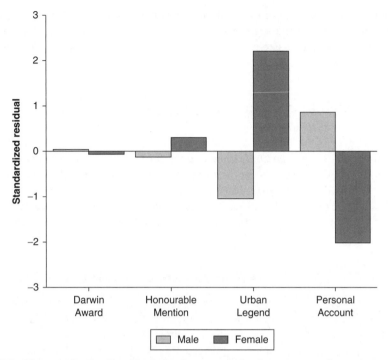

Figure 10.2   The standardized residuals for the association between gender and classification from *The Darwin Awards*. The figure shows that there are more females in Urban Legends than predicted, and fewer females in the Personal Accounts

personal accounts about men than predicted by the null hypothesis. You can think up your own explanations for this.

It is worth noting that the method of squaring the residuals and dividing by the expected value for the cell, and then adding up all of these values, will also produce the correct value. The equation for this is.

$$\chi^2 = \sum \frac{(O_{ij} - E_{ij})^2}{E_{ij}}$$

When discussing phi in the last section it was pointed out that sometimes people calculate χ^2 and use that to calculate phi. When there are more than two rows or columns this is the method used, with a slight change. Instead of calculating 'phi', there is a statistic called Cramer's V, which is like phi when there are more than two rows or more than two columns. Because of its similarity to phi it is sometimes called Cramer's phi. To find it, first count the number of rows ($\#r$) and the number of columns ($\#c$) in the contingency table. Take the smaller of these. Here $\#r = 2$ and $\#c = 4$, so $\#r$ is smaller. Then subtract 1 from this. Then, take the square root of χ^2 divided by n times this number. This is usually written as:

$$Cramer's\ V = \sqrt{\frac{\chi^2}{\min(\#r - 1, \#c - 1)n}} \quad \text{here} \quad \sqrt{\frac{10.32}{1 \cdot 243}} = .21$$

As with phi and kappa, the confidence interval for Cramer's V is difficult to calculate (Smithson, 2003). Calculating it requires repeatedly using what is called the non-central chi-square distribution. Computers can handle this without difficulty, but they are needed for the task. Therefore, we do not recommend doing it by hand and suggest consulting Smithson (2003). Using his procedures the confidence interval goes from 0.12 to 0.33.

Box 10.1   The χ^2 Test for a Single Binary Variable

Most of the people discussed in Northcutt's book (2000: 254) are male rather than female (if you can't figure out why, think about Homer and Marge Simpson). It is a common situation where a researcher has one binary variable, like gender, and the researcher wants to know if the two values are equally likely. The logic is the same as with the other tests described in this chapter. The first step is to calculate the number of people that the model predicts will be in each cell. If the model was that the two values are equally likely, then the prediction is that half the people should be male and half should be female. As there are 243 people in the sample the prediction is that 121.5 should be male and 121.5 should be female. There will not be exactly 121.5 of either gender, but the prediction if the model is right is that the observed frequencies should be close.

   Clearly in this case the model does not fit well. The residuals, standardized residuals and standardized residuals squared are as given in Table 10.6. The alternative method of squaring the residuals, dividing by the predicted value, and then summing these, also works:

$$\chi^2 = \frac{(205 - 121.5)^2}{1215} + \frac{(38 - 121.)^2}{1215} = \frac{6972.25}{1215} + \frac{6972.25}{1215} = 114.77$$

The difference between these numbers is just due to rounding (the 114.77 is right). There is one degree of freedom for this problem. For contingency tables with only one variable the number of degrees of freedom is the number of categories minus one, here $2 - 1 = 1$. This value greatly exceeds the critical value so that the hypothesis that

Table 10.6   *Males and females in Northcutt (2000)*

	Observed	Expected	Residuals	*SR*	*SR²*
Males	205	121.5	83.5	7.585	57.38
Females	38	121.5	−83.5	−7.585	57.38
Total	243	243	0	0	$114.76 = \chi^2$

males and females are equally likely to show up in Northcutt's (2000) book can be rejected. Write this as $\chi^2(1) = 114.77$, $p < 0.001$. You should also include either the proportion of males (205/243 = 84% male) or the odds (205/38 = 5.39 odds of being male).

In general, if you have a contingency table, even complex ones with several variables, the basic procedure of calculating expected values and using these to calculate a χ^2 value can be used. Suppose that you were checking someone for extra-sensory perception (ESP). From a normal deck of playing cards you look at a card, and ask the person the suit of the card. You then thoroughly shuffle the deck, and repeat this test. You do this 100 times and the person is right 35 times and wrong 65 times. The question is if this is higher than chance. At first glance some people might think this is lower than chance because it is lower than 50%. However, with four suits, chance guessing predicts only 25 of the 100 being correct. Thus the residual for correct responses is 35 − 25 = 10, and is 65 − 75 = −10 for incorrect responses. Dividing by the square roots of their respective expected values yields $10/\sqrt{25} = 2.00$ and $−10/\sqrt{75} = −1.15$. These are the standardized residuals. If they are squared (yielding 4.00 and 1.32, respectively) and summed, this makes $\chi^2(1) = 5.32$, which is significant with one degree of freedom at the 5% level. Therefore the null hypothesis of no ESP can be rejected.

SUMMARY

This chapter introduced you to statistical procedures for exploring the association between two categorical variables. The main test that psychologists use is the χ^2 test. This tests if the observed values are different enough from the expected values to reject the hypothesis that there is no association. If the χ^2 value is large enough, it means that the observed data are further away from the predicted values than you would expect, assuming that there was no association between the variables. In these cases, you reject the null hypothesis and say that there is an association between the two variables.

We stressed two other concepts in this chapter that are often not covered in textbooks. The first is reporting effect sizes and that there is a choice of which effect size to use. The most used of these for categorical data is the odds ratio. It is a measure of the size of the effect for 2×2 contingency tables. As psychologists increasingly recognize the importance of reporting effect sizes (Wilkinson et al., 1999), it is becoming the norm to report them. There are several measures of effect size that could have been introduced. We also discussed phi, kappa and Cramer's V. These are all useful in different circumstances.

The second extra concept we stressed was the standardized residual. As with other statistics it is important to look at the residuals to ascertain where any effect may be present. The standardized residual adjusts the value to take into account the row and column totals. For most purposes this is worth doing. As with the odds ratio, there are alternatives we could have introduced. We used the standardized residual because it is closely related to the impact that each cell has on the overall χ^2 value. If you square the standardized residuals, and sum these, you get χ^2.

FINAL SUMMARY

We hope that you found this book useful. Statistics textbooks differ in their aims and audiences. The main aim of this textbook was to introduce the most common statistical tests used in psychology in a relatively non-threatening manner. The expected audience is people wanting to learn about statistics but not in the detail presented in the 600 + -page introductory textbooks. This book is meant for people who want to think about their statistics, not those who simply want to follow a 'how-to' chart without understanding.

As is true with any book, there will be certain biases that the authors will have. We have not tried to hide these. We think that the biggest problem for statistics students is not understanding the conceptual aspects. We have tried to stress the commonalities among the procedures so that you can generalize your conceptual knowledge of one statistical procedure to others. All the statistical procedures in this book have the form

$$\text{Data} = \text{Model} + \text{Residuals}$$

Further, for every statistical test, the fit of the model is based, among other things, on the size of the residuals. If you start thinking with this simple equation in mind, then generalizing among the tests that you have learned, and to other tests, will become easier.

We also stressed that graphing, in particular good graphing, is extremely important. We have included a paper (Wright & Williams, 2003) as an appendix (F) showing bad graphs. But a good graph can communicate data extremely efficiently. Equally important, it can convey the information simply to people without statistical expertise. You should always try presenting your data to non-scientists. Sometimes we read manuscripts where the authors try to use the longest words possible, and present their ideas in the most compli-cated manner. These are signs of poor writing and generally lower how bright the reader thinks the author is (Oppenheimer, 2006).

Finally, these are just the first (and second) steps. The ANOVA, regression and contin-gency tables presented all are the basis for more complex procedures. The steps that you have taken throughout this book should allow you to take further steps in statistics.

EXERCISES

10.1   Calculate the odds for white English participants and black English partici-pants identifying the black and white confederates (from Table 10.1). For each confederate, calculate the odds ratio. Do these data support the own-race bias?

10.2   Find the odds of being male for those given an Honourable Mention in the Darwin Awards from Table 10.5.

10.3   The two cities we live in (at the time of writing this question) are Toledo (USA) and Brighton (UK). Suppose that you wanted to compare two people for their ability to predict whether it was going to rain or not, and that one person was in Toledo and one was in Brighton. Table 10.7 shows the days that each pre-dicted rain by whether it rained or not. First, what is the percentage of time each is accurate in their prediction? Second, what is the odds ratio for each of the amateur meteorologists? Calculate the 95% confidence interval for the odds ratio of one of the two meteorologists. Calculate phi and kappa, too. Discuss why your answers may seem contradictory.

10.4   The Sixth Conference of the European Society for Cognitive Psychology was held at Elsinore, Denmark, in 1993. Martin and Jones (1995) asked delegates which way the queen was facing on the 20-Kroner coin. The correct answer is to the right. Seventy-two participants were asked this and only 21 cor-rectly said that the queen faced to the right. What are the odds of a correct answer? Assuming chance guessing is 50%, is this significantly different from chance?

10.5   In Martin and Jones's (1995) study (Exercise 10.4), half of the participants were Danish and half were not. Of the Danish participants, 10 of 36 correctly said that the queen was facing to the right. Of the non-Danish participants, 11 of 36 said she was facing to the right. What is the odds ratio for the relationship between nationality and the direction that people thought the queen was fac-ing on the 20-Kroner coin? Is this significantly different from 1? What is the 95% confidence interval for this.

(Cont'd)

Table 10.7 *For amateur meteorologists in Toledo and Brighton, whether they say it is going to rain by whether it does rain*

	Toledo			Brighton		
	Says rain	Says dry	Total	Says rain	Says dry	Total
It rains	9	48	57	120	61	181
It is dry	52	256	308	118	66	184
Total	61	304	365	238	127	365

Table 10.8 *Data based on Kuhn and colleagues' (2000) study of youth homicide in Milwaukee, Wisconsin*

	Race of suspect			
Victim	White	Black	Other	Total
White	35	9	8	52
Black	9	250	1	260
Total	44	259	9	312

10.6 Kuhn and colleagues (2000) explored whether there was an association between the race of the victim and the suspect in youth homicides in Milwaukee County during the 1990s. Table 10.8 provides data based on their Figure 1 showing the race of the suspect for the 52 homicides of white youths and the 260 homicides of black youths.

What are the odds of a white victim having a white suspect? What are the odds of a black victim having a white suspect? Is there an association between the race of the victim and the race of the suspect? Looking at just the black and white victims and suspects (i.e., ignore the 'Other' column), what is the odds ratio and what is the 95% confidence interval for this?

10.7 According to Darwin Awards data, males appear much more likely to win Darwin Awards than females. From the biological fact that females can only

Table 10.9   *A sample of data from Schuman and Rieger (1992) where respondents were asked whether they thought the Hitler or Vietnam analogy was better for the elder George Bush's Gulf War*

	Oct. 1990	Nov. 1990	Dec. 1990	Jan. 1991	Feb. 1991	Totals
Hitler analogy	16	14	12	17	22	81
Vietnam analogy	12	11	12	9	5	49
Totals	28	25	24	26	27	130

reproduce a relatively few number of times, but that males can spread their genes much more, why might the overall gender difference in Darwin Awards be good for the species?

10.8   In the run up to, and during, George Bush Senior's Gulf War, those trying to persuade public opinion tended to be suggesting one of two analogies for the West's role: either the Hitler analogy or the Vietnam analogy. Acceptance of each of these implies a different attitude towards the war. Schuman and Rieger (1992) conducted six surveys in which US respondents were asked which analogy they thought was better. The war began in January 1991. Did the proportion of people preferring each analogy change over time? A small sample of their data are in Table 10.9.

   Sometimes it is best to re-organize the data, for example combining all the data before the war with those data collected during the war. If you do this, do your conclusions change?

10.9   Table 10.10, based on Nightingale (1993), shows the number of guilty and not guilty verdicts from 179 university students who read a trial summary about a case in which a young girl was hit by a truck. The victim was 6, 9 or 12 years old. Is there any evidence that the victim's age influenced the verdict about whether the truck driver was negligent?

Table 10.10   *Data based on Nightingale (1993) on the relationship between a verdict of negligent or not, and the victim's age*

	6 years old	9 years old	12 years old	Total
Negligent	42	39	34	115
Not negligent	20	22	22	64
Totals	62	61	56	179

📖 FURTHER READING

Agresti, A. (2002). *Categorical Data Analysis* (2nd ed.). Hoboken, NJ: John Wiley & Sons. This is a more advanced book, but it covers almost everything you are likely to want to know about categorical data analysis.

Northcutt, W. (2000). *The Darwin Awards: Evolution in Action*. New York: Dutton. The UK title is *The Darwin Awards: 150 Bizarre True Stories of How Dumb Humans Met their Maker*. Not sure why there is a difference, but this is a very entertaining book. The webpage, www.darwinawards.com, is also recommended.

Appendix A The *r* Table

n	Significance level			n	Significance level		
	1%	5%	10%		1%	5%	10%
3	1.00	1.00	0.99	23	0.53	0.41	0.35
4	0.99	0.95	0.90	24	0.52	0.40	0.34
5	0.96	0.88	0.81	25	0.51	0.40	0.34
6	0.92	0.81	0.73	30	0.46	0.36	0.31
7	0.87	0.75	0.67	35	0.43	0.33	0.28
8	0.83	0.71	0.62	40	0.40	0.31	0.26
9	0.80	0.67	0.58	45	0.38	0.29	0.25
10	0.76	0.63	0.55	50	0.36	0.28	0.24
11	0.73	0.60	0.52	60	0.33	0.25	0.21
12	0.71	0.58	0.50	70	0.31	0.24	0.20
13	0.68	0.55	0.48	80	0.29	0.22	0.19
14	0.66	0.53	0.46	90	0.27	0.21	0.17
15	0.64	0.51	0.44	100	0.26	0.20	0.17
16	0.62	0.50	0.43	150	0.21	0.16	0.13
17	0.61	0.48	0.41	200	0.18	0.14	0.12
18	0.59	0.47	0.40	300	0.15	0.11	0.10
19	0.58	0.46	0.39	400	0.13	0.10	0.08
20	0.56	0.44	0.38	500	0.12	0.09	0.07
21	0.55	0.43	0.37	1000	0.08	0.06	0.05
22	0.54	0.42	0.36				

Note: Table created in SPSS.

In order to find if your observed *r* value has reached statistical significance at $p = 1\%$, $p = 5\%$ or $p = 10\%$, you first need to know the number of people in your sample. Go to the first column, labelled *n*, and go down to the appropriate number. If your number is not listed, go to the one above it in the table. For example, if you had 47 participants in your study, you would go to the row with $n = 45$. In order to be significant at the 1% level you need $r = 0.38$ or higher. To be significant at the 5% level you need $r = 0.29$ or higher.

Appendix B   The Normal (z) Distribution

z	p	z	p	z	p
0.00	1.000	1.19	0.234	1.58	0.114
0.05	0.960	1.20	0.230	1.59	0.112
0.10	0.920	1.21	0.226	1.60	0.110
0.15	0.881	1.22	0.222	1.61	0.107
0.20	0.841	1.23	0.219	1.62	0.105
0.25	0.803	1.24	0.215	1.63	0.103
0.30	0.764	1.25	0.211	1.64	0.101
0.35	0.726	1.26	0.208	1.65	0.099
0.40	0.689	1.27	0.204	1.66	0.097
0.45	0.653	1.28	0.201	1.67	0.095
0.50	0.617	1.29	0.197	1.68	0.093
0.55	0.582	1.30	0.194	1.69	0.091
0.60	0.549	1.31	0.190	1.70	0.089
0.65	0.516	1.32	0.187	1.71	0.087
0.70	0.484	1.33	0.184	1.72	0.085
0.75	0.453	1.34	0.180	1.73	0.084
0.80	0.424	1.35	0.177	1.74	0.082
0.85	0.395	1.36	0.174	1.75	0.080
0.90	0.368	1.37	0.171	1.76	0.078
0.95	0.342	1.38	0.168	1.77	0.077
1.00	0.317	1.39	0.165	1.78	0.075
1.01	0.312	1.40	0.162	1.79	0.073
1.02	0.308	1.41	0.159	1.80	0.072
1.03	0.303	1.42	0.156	1.81	0.070
1.04	0.298	1.43	0.153	1.82	0.069
1.05	0.294	1.44	0.150	1.83	0.067
1.06	0.289	1.45	0.147	1.84	0.066
1.07	0.285	1.46	0.144	1.85	0.064
1.08	0.280	1.47	0.142	1.86	0.063
1.09	0.276	1.48	0.139	1.87	0.061

z	p	z	p	z	p
1.10	0.271	1.49	0.136	1.88	0.060
1.11	0.267	1.50	0.134	1.89	0.059
1.12	0.263	1.51	0.131	1.90	0.057
1.13	0.258	1.52	0.129	1.91	0.056
1.14	0.254	1.53	0.126	1.92	0.055
1.15	0.250	1.54	0.124	1.93	0.054
1.16	0.246	1.55	0.121	1.94	0.052
1.17	0.242	1.56	0.119	1.95	0.051
1.18	0.238	1.57	0.116	1.96	0.050
1.97	0.049	2.21	0.027	2.45	0.014
1.98	0.048	2.22	0.026	2.46	0.013
1.99	0.047	2.23	0.026	2.47	0.013
2.00	0.046	2.24	0.025	2.48	0.012
2.01	0.044	2.25	0.024	2.49	0.012
2.02	0.043	2.26	0.024	2.50	0.012
2.03	0.042	2.27	0.023	2.51	0.012
2.04	0.041	2.28	0.023	2.52	0.012
2.05	0.040	2.29	0.022	2.53	0.011
2.06	0.039	2.30	0.021	2.54	0.011
2.07	0.038	2.31	0.021	2.55	0.011
2.08	0.038	2.32	0.020	2.56	0.010
2.09	0.037	2.33	0.020	2.57	0.010
2.10	0.036	2.34	0.020	2.58	0.010
2.11	0.035	2.35	0.019	2.59	0.010
2.12	0.034	2.36	0.018	2.60	0.009
2.13	0.033	2.37	0.017	2.70	0.007
2.14	0.032	2.38	0.016	2.80	0.005
2.15	0.032	2.39	0.016	2.90	0.004
2.16	0.031	2.40	0.016	3.00	0.003
2.17	0.030	2.41	0.015	3.50	<0.001
2.18	0.029	2.42	0.015	4.00	<0.001
2.19	0.029	2.43	0.014	4.50	<0.001
2.20	0.028	2.44	0.014	5.00	<0.001

Note: This table was produced by the author using SYSTAT's Data Basic.

Suppose we were adopting a significance level of 0.05 or 5%. This is the conventional level adopted by many researchers, but there is nothing particularly special about it (except that it has become a convention). We would need to find a z either greater than 1.96 or less than -1.96 to reject the hypothesis. Only the positive values are shown in the table. The 5% is based on there being 2.5% of the area under the curve greater than $z = 1.96$ and 2.5% less than $z = -1.96$.

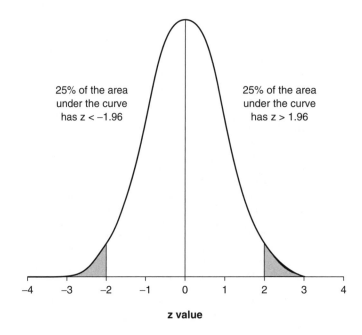

25% of the area
under the curve
has z < −1.96

25% of the area
under the curve
has z > 1.96

z value

Appendix C Student's t Distribution

df	Critical p value					
	0.001	0.010	0.050	0.100	0.200	0.500
2	31.60	9.92	4.30	2.92	1.89	0.82
3	12.92	5.84	3.18	2.35	1.64	0.76
4	8.61	4.60	2.78	2.13	1.53	0.74
5	6.87	4.03	2.57	2.02	1.48	0.73
6	5.96	3.71	2.45	1.94	1.44	0.72
7	5.41	3.50	2.36	1.89	1.41	0.71
8	5.04	3.36	2.31	1.86	1.40	0.71
9	4.78	3.25	2.26	1.83	1.38	0.70
10	4.59	3.17	2.23	1.81	1.37	0.70
11	4.44	3.11	2.20	1.80	1.36	0.70
12	4.32	3.05	2.18	1.78	1.36	0.70
13	4.22	3.01	2.16	1.77	1.35	0.69
14	4.14	2.98	2.14	1.76	1.35	0.69
15	4.07	2.95	2.13	1.75	1.34	0.69
16	4.01	2.92	2.12	1.75	1.34	0.69
17	3.97	2.90	2.11	1.74	1.33	0.69
18	3.92	2.88	2.10	1.73	1.33	0.69
19	3.88	2.86	2.09	1.73	1.33	0.69
20	3.85	2.85	2.09	1.72	1.33	0.69
21	3.82	2.83	2.08	1.72	1.32	0.69
22	3.79	2.82	2.07	1.72	1.32	0.69
23	3.77	2.81	2.07	1.71	1.32	0.69
24	3.75	2.80	2.06	1.71	1.32	0.68
25	3.73	2.79	2.06	1.71	1.32	0.68
30	3.65	2.75	2.04	1.70	1.31	0.68
35	3.59	2.72	2.03	1.69	1.31	0.68
40	3.55	2.70	2.02	1.68	1.30	0.68
45	3.52	2.69	2.01	1.68	1.30	0.68
50	3.50	2.68	2.01	1.68	1.30	0.68
60	3.46	2.66	2.00	1.67	1.30	0.68
70	3.44	2.65	1.99	1.67	1.29	0.68
80	3.42	2.64	1.99	1.66	1.29	0.68
90	3.40	2.63	1.99	1.66	1.29	0.68
100	3.39	2.63	1.98	1.66	1.29	0.68
$\infty(z)$	3.29	2.58	1.96	1.64	1.15	0.67

Note: This table was produced by the author using SYSTAT's Data Basic.

Suppose you were comparing the means of two groups of people and did not know the population standard deviations. The usual test in this circumstance is the group t test (Chapter 6). Suppose one group had 28 people in it and the other group had 24. The number of degrees of freedom is $20 + 24 - 2$, which is 42. If you were using $p = 0.05$ for rejecting hypotheses then you would need a t value greater than 2.02. When the exact number of degrees of freedom is not listed, as in this case, most researchers recommend using the higher critical t value. This lessens the chances of a Type I error (rejecting a true hypothesis), but it does increase the chances of a Type II error (failing to reject a false hypothesis).

Appendix D   The *F* Distribution

Numerator degrees of freedom

df	1	2	3	4	5	6	7	8	9	10	20	50	1000
1	161.45	199.50	215.71	224.58	230.16	233.99	236.77	238.88	240.54	241.88	248.01	251.77	254.19
	4052.18	4999.50	5403.35	5624.58	5763.65	5858.99	5928.36	5981.07	6022.47	6055.85	6208.73	6302.52	6362.68
2	18.51	19.00	19.16	19.25	19.30	19.33	19.35	19.37	19.38	19.40	19.45	19.48	19.49
	98.50	99.00	99.17	99.25	99.30	99.33	99.36	99.37	99.39	99.40	99.45	99.48	99.50
3	10.13	9.55	9.28	9.12	9.01	8.94	8.89	8.85	8.81	8.79	8.66	8.58	8.53
	34.12	30.82	29.46	28.71	28.24	27.91	27.67	27.49	27.35	27.23	26.69	26.35	26.14
4	7.71	6.94	6.59	6.39	6.26	6.16	6.09	6.04	6.00	5.96	5.80	5.70	5.63
	21.20	18.00	16.69	15.98	15.52	15.21	14.98	14.80	14.66	14.55	14.02	13.69	13.47
5	6.61	5.79	5.41	5.19	5.05	4.95	4.88	4.82	4.77	4.74	4.56	4.44	4.37
	16.26	13.27	12.06	11.39	10.97	10.67	10.46	10.29	10.16	10.05	9.55	9.24	9.03
6	5.99	5.14	4.76	4.53	4.39	4.28	4.21	4.15	4.10	4.06	3.87	3.75	3.67
	13.75	10.92	9.78	9.15	8.75	8.47	8.26	8.10	7.98	7.87	7.40	7.09	6.89
7	5.59	4.74	4.35	4.12	3.97	3.87	3.79	3.73	3.68	3.64	3.44	3.32	3.23
	12.25	9.55	8.45	7.85	7.46	7.19	6.99	6.84	6.72	6.62	6.16	5.86	5.66
8	5.32	4.46	4.07	3.84	3.69	3.58	3.50	3.44	3.39	3.35	3.15	3.02	2.93
	11.26	8.65	7.59	7.01	6.63	6.37	6.18	6.03	5.91	5.81	5.36	5.07	4.87
9	5.12	4.26	3.86	3.63	3.48	3.37	3.29	3.23	3.18	3.14	2.94	2.80	2.71
	10.56	8.02	6.99	6.42	6.06	5.80	5.61	5.47	5.35	5.26	4.81	4.52	4.32
10	4.96	4.10	3.71	3.48	3.33	3.22	3.14	3.07	3.02	2.98	2.77	2.64	2.54
	10.04	7.56	6.55	5.99	5.64	5.39	5.20	5.06	4.94	4.85	4.41	4.12	3.92
11	4.84	3.98	3.59	3.36	3.20	3.09	3.01	2.95	2.90	2.85	2.65	2.51	2.41
	9.65	7.21	6.22	5.67	5.32	5.07	4.89	4.74	4.63	4.54	4.10	3.81	3.61
12	4.75	3.89	3.49	3.26	3.11	3.00	2.91	2.85	2.80	2.75	2.54	2.40	2.30
	9.33	6.93	5.95	5.41	5.06	4.82	4.64	4.50	4.39	4.30	3.86	3.57	3.37

(Cont'd)

Numerator degrees of freedom

df	1	2	3	4	5	6	7	8	9	10	20	50	1000
13	4.67	3.81	3.41	3.18	3.03	2.92	2.83	2.77	2.71	2.67	2.46	2.31	2.21
	9.07	6.70	5.74	5.21	4.86	4.62	4.44	4.30	4.19	4.10	3.66	3.38	3.18
14	4.60	3.74	3.34	3.11	2.96	2.85	2.76	2.70	2.65	2.60	2.39	2.24	2.14
	8.86	6.51	5.56	5.04	4.69	4.46	4.28	4.14	4.03	3.94	3.51	3.22	3.02
15	4.54	3.68	3.29	3.06	2.90	2.79	2.71	2.64	2.59	2.54	2.33	2.18	2.07
	8.68	6.36	5.42	4.89	4.56	4.32	4.14	4.00	3.89	3.80	3.37	3.08	2.88
16	4.49	3.63	3.24	3.01	2.85	2.74	2.66	2.59	2.54	2.49	2.28	2.12	2.02
	8.53	6.23	5.29	4.77	4.44	4.20	4.03	3.89	3.78	3.69	3.26	2.97	2.76
17	4.45	3.59	3.20	2.96	2.81	2.70	2.61	2.55	2.49	2.45	2.23	2.08	1.97
	8.40	6.11	5.18	4.67	4.34	4.10	3.93	3.79	3.68	3.59	3.16	2.87	2.66
18	4.41	3.55	3.16	2.93	2.77	2.66	2.58	2.51	2.46	2.41	2.19	2.04	1.92
	8.29	6.01	5.09	4.58	4.25	4.01	3.84	3.71	3.60	3.51	3.08	2.78	2.58
19	4.38	3.52	3.13	2.90	2.74	2.63	2.54	2.48	2.42	2.38	2.16	2.00	1.88
	8.18	5.93	5.01	4.50	4.17	3.94	3.77	3.63	3.52	3.43	3.00	2.71	2.50
20	4.35	3.49	3.10	2.87	2.71	2.60	2.51	2.45	2.39	2.35	2.12	1.97	1.85
	8.10	5.85	4.94	4.43	4.10	3.87	3.70	3.56	3.46	3.37	2.94	2.64	2.43
25	4.24	3.39	2.99	2.76	2.60	2.49	2.40	2.34	2.28	2.24	2.01	1.84	1.72
	7.77	5.57	4.68	4.18	3.85	3.63	3.46	3.32	3.22	3.13	2.70	2.40	2.18
30	4.17	3.32	2.92	2.69	2.53	2.42	2.33	2.27	2.21	2.16	1.93	1.76	1.63
	7.56	5.39	4.51	4.02	3.70	3.47	3.30	3.17	3.07	2.98	2.55	2.25	2.02
40	4.08	3.23	2.84	2.61	2.45	2.34	2.25	2.18	2.12	2.08	1.84	1.66	1.52
	7.31	5.18	4.31	3.83	3.51	3.29	3.12	2.99	2.89	2.80	2.37	2.06	1.82
50	4.03	3.18	2.79	2.56	2.40	2.29	2.20	2.13	2.07	2.03	1.78	1.60	1.45
	7.17	5.06	4.20	3.72	3.41	3.19	3.02	2.89	2.78	2.70	2.27	1.95	1.70
75	3.97	3.12	2.73	2.49	2.34	2.22	2.13	2.06	2.01	1.96	1.71	1.52	1.35
	6.99	4.90	4.05	3.58	3.27	3.05	2.89	2.76	2.65	2.57	2.13	1.81	1.53
100	3.94	3.09	2.70	2.46	2.31	2.19	2.10	2.03	1.97	1.93	1.68	1.48	1.30
	6.90	4.82	3.98	3.51	3.21	2.99	2.82	2.69	2.59	2.50	2.07	1.74	1.45
1000	3.85	3.00	2.61	2.38	2.22	2.11	2.02	1.95	1.89	1.84	1.58	1.36	1.11
	6.66	4.63	3.80	3.34	3.04	2.82	2.66	2.53	2.43	2.34	1.90	1.54	1.16

Note: The top value in each row is the necessary F value to reject the hypothesis at $p = 0.05$. The second value is for $p = 0.01$.

To find whether an F value is significant you need to know both the degrees of freedom of the numerator and the degrees of freedom of the denominator. Usually these are the degrees of freedom of the model and of the residuals, respectively, but for certain hypotheses this need not be the case. Suppose for 45 subjects that we had divided them into five groups. Our model would therefore have four degrees of freedom (four dummy variables to represent the five values). The residuals would have 40 degrees of freedom. The critical values are 2.61 and 3.83 for $p = 0.05$ and $p = 0.01$, respectively.

Appendix E   The χ^2 Distribution

	Critical level				Critical level		
df	0.10	0.05	0.01	df	0.10	0.05	0.01
1	2.71	3.84	6.63	23	32.01	35.17	41.64
2	4.61	5.99	9.21	24	33.20	36.42	42.98
3	6.25	7.81	11.34	25	34.38	37.65	44.31
4	7.78	9.49	13.28	30	40.26	43.77	50.89
5	9.24	11.07	15.09	35	46.06	49.80	57.34
6	10.64	12.59	16.81	40	51.81	55.76	63.69
7	12.02	14.07	18.48	45	57.51	61.66	69.96
8	13.36	15.51	20.09	50	63.17	67.50	76.15
9	14.68	16.92	21.67	60	74.40	79.08	88.38
10	15.99	18.31	23.21	70	85.53	90.53	100.43
11	17.28	19.68	24.72	80	96.58	101.88	112.33
12	18.55	21.03	26.22	90	107.51	113.15	124.12
13	19.81	22.36	27.69	100	118.50	124.34	135.81
14	21.06	23.68	29.14	200	226.02	233.99	249.45
15	22.31	25.00	30.58	300	331.79	341.39	359.91
16	23.54	26.30	32.00	400	436.65	447.63	468.73
17	24.77	27.59	33.41	500	540.93	553.13	576.50
18	25.99	28.87	34.81	600	644.80	658.09	683.52
19	27.20	30.14	36.19	700	748.36	762.66	789.98
20	28.41	31.41	37.57	800	851.67	866.91	895.99
21	29.62	32.67	38.93	900	954.78	970.90	1001.63
22	30.81	33.92	40.29	1000	1057.72	1074.68	1106.97

Note: This table was produced by the author using SYSTAT's Data Basic.

All probabilities in this table refer to the extreme tail (see figure). Suppose you were analysing some categorical data and there were five degrees of freedom in the residuals. This might happen if you were looking to see if there was an association in a 2×6 contingency table (one variable has two possible values, the other six). If you were using the $p = 0.05$ level then you would need a χ^2 value of 11.07. The area beyond this point on the graph is 5% of the total area under the curve. Only 5% of the time would you expect a value this high (or higher) if there is no association in the population (providing proper sampling and procedures are used).

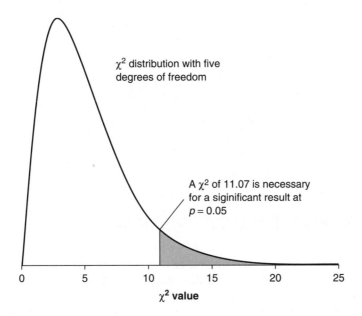

χ^2 distribution with five degrees of freedom

A χ^2 of 11.07 is necessary for a siginificant result at $p = 0.05$

χ^2 **value**

Appendix F   How to …
Produce a Bad Results Section[1]

DANIEL B. WRIGHT AND SIÂN WILLIAMS

Complicated equations, confusing figures, arcane technical expressions; all commonly found in psychology results sections. In this article we'll show you how to achieve these lofty heights of mind-numbingly boring techno-babble. Inappropriate use of statistical procedures, bad graphs, poor writing style … we'll cover the lot. Your findings will be so obscure that even you won't understand them.

Our approach follows Howard Wainer (1984), who described how to make graphs as uninformative as possible. His approach was to 'concentrate on methods of data display that leave the viewers as uninformed as they were before seeing the display or, worse, those that 'induce confusion' (p. 137). But perhaps Wainer didn't go far enough: we show how entire results sections can be made to 'induce confusion'. Many authors of results sections published in the most respected journals already recognize the value of obscurity. Indeed, the American Psychological Association created a task force to discover why so many follow our approach (Wilkinson *et al.*, 1999).

STATISTICAL TESTS: FAILING THE FOUR RS

There are three basic ways to miscommunicate findings: numerical, graphical and verbal. The first, numerical, relates to the statistical tests that people conduct.

To produce a results section that is completely misleading, the author could conduct statistical tests that are clearly wrong. Easily achieved when you consider that when questioned, many researchers do not even understand concepts fundamental to much of the statistics that they use, like what *p* means or what a confidence interval is (Oakes, 1986). But, unfortunately, reviewers have a tendency to notice when wrong tests are used. A subtler tactic that can often

---

1 This paper is taken from *The Psychologist*, December 2003, *16* (12): 646–648.

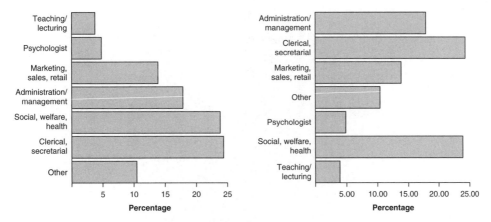

Figure 1   Destination of psychology graduates in the UK: same data, different presentation styles

get past reviewers is only conducting and reporting the final hypothesis-testing statistics, and not exploring the data. Failing to explore the data adequately can mean that interesting facets of the data will not be discovered by the researcher and thus will be hidden from the reader.

Hoaglin *et al.* (1983) discuss the four Rs of understanding data:

- *Resistance* Some statistics are not 'resistant' – they are heavily influenced by a small fraction of the data. (This concept is closely related to statistic being robust. Resistance is a characteristic of robust statistics.) The mean, ANOVAs, ordinary regressions, and so on, are not resistant, so you should use them (or you could always see Wilcox, 2001, for an introduction to some alternatives).
- *Residuals* This refers to how different points do not fit with the model. Much as Piaget showed how focusing on children's errors could shed light on cognitive development, it is necessary to examine the residuals to judge the worth of any model.
- *Re-expression* Should the raw data be rescaled to make the analyses and interpretation simpler? Often this is to make the scale of the data more appropriate for the theories being investigated or to make the data more resistant (usually more like the normal distribution). For example, reaction time data are often transformed so that the distribution is not as positively skewed.
- *Revelation* Your methods of analysis can often reveal interesting and unexpected aspects of the data and help inform theories. Following our advice should limit this possibility.

As our goal is to help people create misleading and uninformative results sections, we recommend ignoring the four Rs. Instead, find an introductory textbook that has a flowchart that presents simple questions like 'Are you interested in an association, or group differences?'

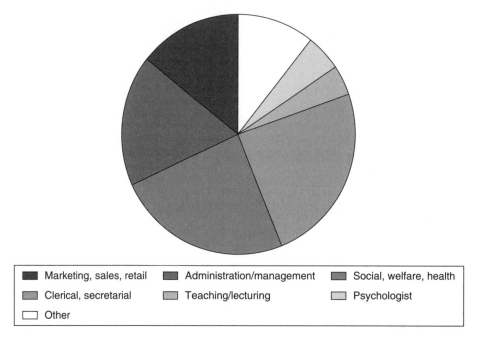

Figure 2 A pie chart of the data

and 'What is the level of measurement of the data?' and directs the reader to one particular test. This approach, used on its own and with little consideration of the questions, should leave you with just an r, F or χ^2 value as the only means to decide whether the statistical model being considered is appropriate. Don't bother with graphing and examining the descriptive statistics before performing any inferential statistics.

MAKING BAD GRAPHS

For decades the science of graphical display developed so that politicians could construct misleading graphs, with the assumption that the audience was not interested in the numbers unless they were made artistically appealing. Tufte (2001) and Wainer (1984) show some graphs, from highly respected sources, that hide the data from readers, display data inaccurately and present them in a cluttered and confused manner. Many of these methods have arisen because computers can add extra frills to graphs – what is called 'chartjunk'. While computers have made making graphs that clearly communicate the findings easier, they have also created a fertile environment for you to smother your data with technology: 'like weeds, many varieties of chartjunk flourish' (Tufte, 2001, p. 107).

Figure 3   Dilbert. © Copyright 1996 UFS, Inc. Reproduced by permission

As an example, Figure 1 shows two graphs giving the destinations of psychology graduates in the UK in 1999 (data from the BPS document *Studying Psychology,* 2001). In the first graph the reader can see the frequency increasing from 'teaching/lecturing' to 'clerical, secretarial', but the reader won't know that with most graphics software you can tick lots of fancy options. In the second graph we've alphabetised the items and altered the axis labels. Looks pretty and makes the information more opaque. Many of the patterns that can be used to fill bars create visual illusions about the size, the shape and even the apparent motion of the bars. Figure 2 is a pie chart, which generally makes it more difficult for the reader to extract information (Hollands & Spence, 2001). Then the boss from Dilbert shows (or he'd say 'demonstrates') the pinnacle of bad graphs (Figure 3). According to the SYSTAT manual, these false 3–D pie charts 'incorporate nearly every visual illusion discussed in this chapter' (Wilkinson, 2000, p. 13).

Being creative with colour can further demonstrate how technology can triumph over communication. Consider using red and green, to make the graph particularly bad for the approximately 10 per cent of males who have difficulty distinguishing these colours.

MISCOMMUNICATING WITH THE WRITTEN WORD

Even if you have written a brilliant literature review, have meticulously and clearly described your study, and have written a fluent and informative discussion, there are still several ways to make your paper 'induce confusion'.

Assume all rules of writing style are not applicable for results sections. Many readers expect results sections to be confusing. This is because the standards of good writing do not apply to results sections. In their book *The Elements of Style* Strunk and White (1979) argue the case for 'cleanliness, accuracy, and brevity' (p. xiii) in the use of language. Messiness, inaccuracy and extravagance will ensure that people avoid even reading the results section.

Sometimes it is worth doing more than just inducing confusion. Sometimes it is worth producing annoyance. Most scientists are driven by a sense of curiosity (Grigorenko,

2000). We question things. You can feed this curiosity by reporting only some of the information. For instance, omitting the degrees of freedom for an analysis may leave your audience curious about your sample size. It is also possible, and very easy, to neglect to describe any transformations you have made to the data, or how you dealt with any outliers. However, our favourite method is conducting a statistical test, sat a *t* test, and not reporting the means. Imagine telling someone in a pub about a study and instead of saying 'the group who were given the drug answered, on average, 10 per cent more questions correctly, and this much of a difference would be unlikely if the drug had no effect', you said '*t*(18) 2.30' and nothing else. The American Psychological Associations task force on statistical inference (Wilkinson *et al.*, 1999) stressed the importance of reporting descriptive statistics. If you wish to produce a bad results section, ignore everything in their report.

Try to make the statistical techniques sound as complicated as possible. Some statistical techniques are very complex. Assume that the reader has a PhD in statistics and knows every statistical technique. Use lots of a jargon, particularly if you are using some esoteric technique that you have just learnt. Explain every minute mathematical aspect of the technique. This is easily done by paraphrasing statistics books and manuals – you don't need to understand them yourself. Use a thesaurus to slightly change the meanings of words so that it is not copying word-for-word from the manual. Given that some words have precise technical meanings, this should also confuse readers who felt that they understood the techniques. For example, the words *components* and *factors* have different meanings, and result from different statistical procedures, but are sometimes interchanged.

Use the word *significant* as if it meant the effect was large and important. Some words have a different meanings in English and Statisticalese. Usually the words have the same basic meaning, but have a more precise definition in scientific jargon than in English. But sometimes the meanings are very different. *Significant* in Statisticalese means that assuming the null hypothesis is correct, data as extreme as observed should occur less than 5 per cent of the time. The word *significant* means something very different in English: important. One way to confuse readers is to assume being statistically significant means that the effect is significant in the English sense of the word.

Be careless about using causal language when describing correlational studies. Both causal and associative hypotheses are important in psychology, However, they are different with respect to the theories that are being investigated, and they require different research designs. We recommend casually using words like *cause* and *influence* when conducting studies where there has been no manipulation.

BUT IF YOU INSIST ON DOING IT PROPERLY…

Irony aside, many of the techniques that we have shown can be easily avoided. There were several themes running through this article.

For analysis, use exploratory techniques to understand the data before you leap into statistical tests. Become friends with your data (Wright, 2002, 2003). Don't just check if a result is statistically significant: look at the size of the effect, ask if it is robust, check to make sure that it is consistent with your graphs, and ask if your finding makes sense.

For graphs, showing technical wizardry and making them 'pretty' can be at odds with the aim of clearly and accurately communicating results. See Wainer and Velleman (2001), and Tufte's marvellous trilogy *The Visual Display of Quantitative Information* (2001, first edition published 1983), *Envisioning Information* (1990), which is about picturing nouns, and *Visual Explanations* (1997), which is about picturing verbs.

For writing styles, thing about your audience: second-year undergraduates should be able to understand what you write. Strunk and White (1979) and Sternberg (2000) highlight numerous ways in which writing styles can be used to improve the presentation of research findings.

The art of conducting and communicating statistics is difficult. Abelson (1995) describes how people should consider what they are trying to persuade the reader about. He gives five MAGIC criteria (Magnitude, Articulation, Generality, Interestingness and Credibility) that you should bear in mind whenever you are reporting a statistical result. You should be excited by your results and convey this to the reader. If you are bored by your results, your readers will be too. If scientific papers were murder mysteries, the results section would reveal the killer.

References

Abelson, R.P. (1995). *Statistics as Principled Argument*. Hillsdale, NJ: Lawrence Erlbaum.

Abelson, R.P., & Tukey, J.W. (1959). Efficient conversation of non-metric information to metric information. *Proceedings of the Social Statistics Section, American Statistical Association*, 226–230.

Agresti, A. (2002). *Categorical Data Analysis* (2nd ed.). Hoboken, NJ: John Wiley & Sons.

Alexander, M.G., & Fisher, T.D. (2003). Truth and consequences: using the bogus pipeline to examine sex differences in self-reported sexuality. *Journal of Sex Research, 40*, 27–35.

Allen, J.J.B., Schnyer, R.N., & Hitt, S.K. (1998). The efficacy of acupuncture in the treatment of major depression in women. *Psychological Science, 9*, 397–401.

Allen, R.E. (1985). *The Oxford Dictionary of Current English*. Oxford: Oxford University Press.

Barnier, A.J., & McConkey, K.M. (1998). Posthypnotic responding away from the hypnotic setting. *Psychological Science, 9*, 256–262.

Berkowitz, L. (1992). Some thoughts about conservative evaluations of replications. *Personality and Social Psychology Bulletin, 18*, 319–324.

Bland, J.M., & Altman, D.G. (1996). Transformations, means, and confidence intervals. *British Medical Journal, 312*, 1079.

Brown, C.K., & Cline, D.M. (2001). Factors affecting injury severity to rear-seated occupants in rural motor vehicle crashes. *American Journal of Emergency Medicine, 19*, 93–98.

Brown, L.H., Silvia, P.J., Myin-Germeys, I., & Kwapil, T.R. (2007). When the need to belong goes wrong: the expression of social anhedonia and social anxiety in daily life. *Psychological Science, 18*, 778–782.

Brown, N.R., & Sinclair, R.C. (1999). Estimating number of lifetime sexual partners: men and women do it differently. *Journal of Sex Research, 36,* 292–297.

Caine, T.M., Foulds, G.A., & Hope, K. (1967). *Manual of the Hostility and Direction of Hostility Questionnaire.* London: London University Press.

Canty, A., & Ripley, B. (2008). *boot: Bootstrap R (S-Plus) Functions.* R package version 1. 2–34.

Chernoff, H. (1973). Use of faces to represent points in *k*-dimensional space graphically. *Journal of the American Statistical Association, 68,* 361–368.

Cohen, J. (1960). A coefficient of agreement for nominal scales. *Educational and Psychological Measurement, 20,* 37–46.

Cohen, J. (1990). Things I have learned (so far). *American Psychologist, 45,* 1304–1312.

Cohen, J. (1992). A power primer. *Psychological Bulletin, 112,* 155–159.

Cook, T.D., & Campbell, D.T. (1979). *Quasi-Experimentation: Design & Analysis Issues for Field Settings.* London: Houghton Mifflin.

Coombs, C.H., Dawes, R.M., & Tversky, A. (1970). *Mathematical Psychology: An Elementary Introduction.* Englewood Cliffs, NJ: Prentice-Hall.

Cuc, A., & Hirst, W. (2001). Implicit theories and context in personal recollection: Romanians' recall of their political and economic past. *Applied Cognitive Psychology, 15,* 45–60.

Cumming, G., Fidler, F., Leonard, M., Kalinowski, P., Christiansen, A., Kleinig, A., Lo, J., McMenamin, N., & Wilson, S. (2007). Statistical reform in psychology: is anything changing? *Psychological Science, 18,* 230–232.

Davison, A.C., & Hinkley, D.V. (1997). *Bootstrap Methods and their Applications.* Cambridge: Cambridge University Press.

Dienes, Z. (2008). *Scientific and Statistical Inference: Conceptual Issues in Psychology.* New York: Palgrave Macmillan.

Dyson, F.W., Eddington, A.S., & Davidson, C. (1920). A determination of the deflection of light by the Sun's gravitational field, from observations made at the total eclipse of May 29, 1919. *Philosophical Transactions of the Royal Society A, 220,* 291–334.

Eddington, A.S. (1920). *Space, Time and Gravitation: An Outline of the General Relativity Theory*. Cambridge: Cambridge University Press.

Efron, B. (1998). R.A. Fisher in the 21st century: invited paper presented at the 1996 R.A. Fisher lecture. *Statistical Science*, *13*, 95–114.

Efron, B., & Gong, G. (1983). A leisurely look at the bootstrap, the jackknife, and cross-validation. *American Statistician*, *37*, 36–48.

Efron, B., & Tibshirani, R. (1993). *An Introduction to the Bootstrap*. New York: Chapman & Hall.

Everitt, B.S. (1996). *Making Sense of Statistics in Psychology: A Second-Level Course*. Oxford: Oxford University Press.

Festinger, L., & Carlsmith, J.M. (1959). Cognitive consequences of forced compliance. *Journal of Abnormal and Social Psychology*, *58*, 203–210.

Field, A.P. (2009). *Discovering Statistics using SPSS for Windows* (3rd ed.). London: Sage.

Fienberg, S.E. (1971). Randomization and social affairs: the 1970 draft lottery. *Science*, *171*, 255–261.

Finley, J.P. (1884). Tornado predictions. *American Meteorological Journal*, *1*, 85–88.

Fisher, R.A. (1921). On the 'probable error' of a coefficient of correlation deduced from a small sample. *Metron, 1*, 1–32.

Fisher, R.A. (1925). *Statistical Methods for Research Workers*. London: Oliver & Boyd (downloaded from http://psychclassics.yorku.ca/Fisher/Methods/).

Fisher, R.P., & Geiselman, R.E. (1992). *Memory-Enhancing Techniques for Investigative Interviewing: The Cognitive Interview*. Springfield, IL: C.C. Thomas.

Fleiss, J.L., Cohen, J., & Everitt, B.S. (1969). Large sample standard errors of kappa and weighted kappa. *Psychological Bulletin*, *72*, 323–327.

Gabriel, P. (1986). *Milgram's 37 (We Do What We're Told)*. The album *So*.

Gaskell, G.D., Wright, D.B., & O'Muircheartaigh, C.A. (1993). Measuring scientific interest: the effect of knowledge questions on interest ratings. *Journal for the Public Understanding of Science*, *2*, 39–57.

Giancola, P.R., & Corman, M.D. (2007). Alcohol and aggression: a test of the attention-allocation model. *Psychological Science*, *18*, 649–655.

Gigerenzer, G. (1993). The superego, the ego and the id in statistical reasoning. In G. Keren & C. Lewis (Eds.), *A Handbook for Data Analysis in the Behavioral Sciences: Methodological Issues (*pp. 311–339*)*. Hove: Lawrence Erlbaum.

Goldstein, H. (2003). *Multilevel Statistical Methods* (3rd ed.). London: Arnold.

Goodare, J., et al. (2004). *Survey of Scottish Witchcraft, 1563–1736* [computer file] (2nd ed.). Colchester: UK Data Archive [distributor].

Gossett, W., writing as 'Student' (1931). The Lanarkshire milk experiment. *Biometrika, 23*, 398–406.

Gould, S.J. (1985). The median isn't the message. Available on http://www.edw ardtufte.com/tufte/gould and http://www.cancerguide.org/median_not_msg.html.

Grice, H.P. (1975). Logic and conversation. In P. Cole & J.L. Morgan (Eds.). *Syntax and Semantics: Speech Acts. Vol. 3* (pp. 41–58). New York: Academic Press.

Grigorenko, E.L. (2000). Doing data analyses and writing up their results: selected tricks and artifices. In R.J. Sternberg (Ed.) *Guide to Publishing in Psychology Journals* (pp. 8–120). Cambridge: Cambridge University Press.

Gudjonsson, G.H. (1997). *The Gudjonsson Suggestibility Scales Manual.* Hove: Psychology Press.

Hand, D.J. (2004). *Measurement Theory and Practice: The World Through Quantification.* London: Arnold.

Helsen, W.F., & Starkes, J.L. (1999). A multidimensional approach to skilled perception and performance in sport. *Applied Cognitive Psychology, 13*, 1–27.

Hoaglin, D.C., Mosteller, F. & Tukey, J.W. (1983). *Understanding Robust Exploratory Data Analysis.* New York: Wiley.

Hole, G.J. (2006). *The Psychology of Driving*. Hove: Lawrence Erlbaum.

Hollands, J.G. & Spence, I. (2001). The discrimination of graphical elements. *Applied Cognitive Psychology, 15*, 413–431.

Hox, J. (2002). *Multilevel Analysis: Techniques and Applications.* London: Lawrence Erlbaum.

Inzlicht, M., & Ben-Zeev, T. (2000). A threatening intellectual environment: why females are susceptible to experiencing problem-solving deficits in the presence of males. *Psychological Science, 11*, 365–371.

James, W. (1890). *The principles of psychology*. Cambridge: Harvard University Press. Retrieved 9 October 2008, http://psycholassics.yorku.ca/James/Principles/

Karlsen, C.F. (1987). *The Devil in the Shape of a Woman: Witchcraft in Colonial New England.* New York: Vintage Books.

Kirk, R.E. (2007). *Statistics: An Introduction* (5th ed.). Belmont, CA: Wadsworth.

Kraemer, H.C. (2006). Correlation coefficients in medical research: from product moment correlation to the odds ratio. *Statistical Methods in Medical Research, 15,* 525–545.

Kreft, I.I., & de Leeuw, J. (1998). *Introducing Multilevel Modeling.* London: Sage.

Kuhn, E.M., Nie, C.L., O'Brien, M.E., Withers, R.L., & Hargarten, S.W. (2000). Victim and perpetrator characteristics for firearm-related homicides of youth during 1991–1997. In P.H. Blackman, V.L. Leggett, B.L. Olson & J.P. Jarvis (Eds.). *The Varieties of Homicide and its Research: Proceedings of the 1999 Meeting of the Homicide Research Working Group.* Washington, DC: Federal Bureau of Investigation.

Landis, J.R., & Koch, G.C. (1977). The measurement of observer agreement for categorical data. *Biometrics, 33,* 1089–1091.

Levine, T.R. & Hullett, C.R. (2002) Eta squared, partial eta squared, and misreporting of effect size in communication research. *Human Communication Research, 28,* 612–625.

Lilienfeld, S.O. (2007). Psychological treatments that cause harm. *Perspectives on Psychological Science, 2,* 53–70.

Lord, F.M. (1953). On the statistical treatment of football numbers. *American Psychologist, 8,* 750–751.

Luckin, J. (2001). An exploration into the effect a proposed football stadium has on the local community. Unpublished manuscript.

Maccallum, F., McConkey, K.M., Bryant, R.A., & Barnier, A.J. (2000). Specific autobiographical memory following hypnotically induced mood state. *International Journal of Clinical and Experimental Hypnosis, 48,* 361–373.

Martin, M., & Jones, G.V. (1995). Danegeld remembered: taxing further the coin head illusion. *Memory, 3,* 97–104.

Masson, M.E.J., & Loftus, G.R. (2003). Using confidence intervals for graphically based data interpretation. *Canadian Journal of Experimental Psychology, 57,* 203–220.

Maxwell, S.E., & Delaney, H.D. (2004). *Designing Experiments and Analyzing Data: A Model Comparison Perspective* (2nd ed.). Mahwah, NJ: Lawrence Erlbaum.

McGill, R., Tukey, J.W., and Larsen, W.A. (1978). Variations of box plots. *American Statistician, 32,* 12–16.

Meehl, P.E. (1967). Theory-testing in psychology and physics: A Methodological paradox. *Philosophy of Science, 34*, 103–115.

Meehl, P. (1978). Theoretical risks and tabular asterisks. Sir Karl, Sir Ronald and the slow progress of soft psychology. *Journal of Consulting and Clinical Psychology, 46*, 806–834.

Miles, J., & Shevlin, M. (2001). *Applying Regression & Correlation: A Guide for Students and Researchers*. London: Sage.

Murphy, A.H. (1996). The Finley affair: a signal event in the history of forecast verification. *Weather Forecasting, 11*, 3–20.

Neath, I. (1996). How to improve your teaching evaulations without improving your teaching. *Psychological Reports, 78*, 1363–1372.

Neisser, U., Winograd, E., Bergman, E.T., Schreiber, C.A., Palmer, S.E., & Weldon, M.S. (1996). Remembering the earthquake: direct experience *vs.* hearing the news. *Memory, 4*, 337–357.

Newton, M. (1998). Changes in measures of personality, hostility and locus of control during residence in a prison therapeutic community. *Legal and Criminological Psychology, 3*, 209–223.

Nightingale, N.N. (1993). Juror reactions to child victim witnesses: factors affecting trial outcome. *Law and Human Behavior, 17*, 679–694.

Northcutt, W. (2000). *The Darwin Awards: Evolution in Action*. New York: Dutton.

Oakes, M. (1986). *Statistical Inference: a Commentary for the Social and Behavioural Sciences*. Chichester: Wiley.

Oppenheimer, D.M. (2006). Consequences of erudite vernacular utilized irrespective of necessity: problems with using long words needlessly. *Applied Cognitive Psychology, 20*, 139–156.

Pelé & Fish, R.L. (2007). *My Life and the Beautiful Game: The Autobiography of Pelé*. New York: Skyhorse.

Pierce, C.A., Block, R.A., & Aguinis, H. (2004). Cautionary note on reporting eta-squared values from multifactor ANOVA designs. *Educational and Psychological Measurement, 64*, 916–924.

Playfair, W. (2005 (1801)) *The Commercial and Political Atlas and Statistical Breviary*. New York: Cambridge University Press.

Porter, T.M. (2004). *Karl Pearson: The Scientific Life in a Statistical Age*. Princeton, NJ: Princeton University Press.

Przibram, K. (Ed.) (1967). *Letters on Wave Mechanics* (trans. M.J. Klein). London: Vision Press.

Reese, R.A. (2005). Boxplots. *Significance*, *2*, 134–135.

Reese, R.A. (2007). Bah! Bar charts. *Significance*, *4*, 41–44.

Reeve, D.K., & Aggleton, J.P. (1998). On the specificity of expert knowledge about a soap opera: an everyday story of farming folk. *Applied Cognitive Psychology*, *12*, 35–42.

Rosenthal, R., Rosnow, R.L., & Rubin, D.B. (2000). *Contrasts and Effect Sizes in Behavioral Research: A Correlational Approach.* Cambridge: Cambridge University Press.

Rothblum, E.D., & Factor, R. (2001). Lesbians and their sisters as a control group: demographic and mental health factors. *Psychological Science*, *12*, 63–69.

Santtila, P., Ekholm, M., & Niemi, P. (1999). The effects of alcohol on interrogative suggestibility: the role of state-anxiety and mood states as mediating factors. *Legal and Criminological Psychology*, *4*, 1–13.

Schkade, D., Sunstein, C.R., & Kahneman, D. (2000). Deliberating about dollars: the severity shift. *Columbia Law Review*, *100*, 1139–1175.

Schrödinger, E. (trans. J.D. Trimmer) (1983). The present situation in quantum mechanics: a translation of Schrödinger's 'Cat Paradox' paper. In J.A. Wheeler & W.H. Zurek (Eds.). *Quantum Theory and Measurement* (pp. 152–167). Princeton, NJ: Princeton University Press. (Original German publication, Schrödinger, E. (1935). Die gegenwärtige Situation in der Quantenmechanik. *Naturwissenschaften*, *23*, 807–812, 823–828, 844–849.)

Schuman, H. & Rieger, C. (1992). Historical analogies, generational effects, and attitudes toward war. *American Sociological Review*, *57*, 315–326.

Shamay-Tsoory, S.G., Tomer, R., & Aharon-Peretz, J. (2005). The neuroanatomical basis of understanding sarcasm and its relationship to social cognition. *Neuropsychology*, *19*, 288–300.

Shariff, A.F. & Norenzayan, A. (2007). God is watching you: priming God concepts increases prosocial behavior in an anonymous economic game. *Psychological Science*, *18*, 803–809.

Siegel, S., & Castellan, N.J., Jr. (1988). *Nonparametric Statistics for the Behavioral Sciences* (2nd ed.). London: McGraw-Hill.

Smithson, M.J. (2003). *Confidence Intervals.* Thousand Oaks, CA: Sage.

Spear, M.E. (1952). *Charting Statistics*. New York: McGraw-Hill.

Startup, H.M., & Davey, G.C.L. (2001). Mood-as-input and catastrophic worrying. *Journal of Abnormal Psychology*, *110*, 83–96.

Sternberg, R.J. (Ed.) (2000). *Guide to Publishing in Psychology Journals*. Cambridge: Cambridge University Press.

Stevens, S.S. (1946). On the theory of scales of measurement. *Science*, *103*, 677–680.

Stevens, S.S. (1968). Measurement, statistics, and the schemapiric view. *Science*, *161*, 849–856.

Stigler, S.M. (1986). *The History of Statistics: The Measurement of Uncertainty before 1900*. Cambridge, MA: Harvard University Press.

Strunk, W.Jr & White, E.B. (1979). *The Elements of Style* (4th edn). Needham Heights, MA: Allyn & Bacon.

Tatar, M. (1998). Teachers as significant others: gender differences in secondary school pupils' perceptions. *British Journal of Educational Psychology*, *68*, 217–227.

Taylor, S.E., Welch, W.T., Kim, H.S., & Sherman, D.K. (2007). Cultural differences in the impact of social support on psychological and biological stress responses. *Psychological Science*, *18*, 831–837.

Terrace, H.S. (1987). *Nim: A Chimpanzee Who Learned Sign Language.* New York: Alfred A. Knopf.

Terrace, H.S., Petitto, L.A., Sanders, R.J., & Bever, T.G. (1979). Can an ape create a sentence? *Science*, *206*, 891–902.

Tipler, P.A., & Mosca, G.P. (2007). *Physics for Scientists and Engineers: Extended Version* (6th rev. ed.). NewYork: W.H. Freeman.

Toothaker, L.E. (1993). *Multiple Comparison Procedures*. Newbury Park, CA: Sage.

Tramo, M.J., Loftus, W.C., Green, R.L., Stukel, T.A., Weaver, J.B., & Gazzaniga, M.S. (1998). Brain size, head size, and IQ in monozygotic twins. *Neurology*, *50*, 1246–1252.

Tufte, E.R. (1990). *Envisioning Information*. Cheshire, CT: Graphics Press.

Tufte, E.R. (1997). *Visual Explanations: Images and Quantities, Evidence and Narrative.* Cheshire, CT: Graphics Press.

Tufte, E.R. (2001). *The Visual Display of Quantitative Information* (2nd Ed.). Cheshire, CT: Graphics Press.

Tufte, E.R. (2006). *Beautiful Evidence*. Cheshire, CT: Graphics Press.

Tukey, J.W. (1972). Some graphic and semigraphic displays. In T.A. Bancroft (Ed.), *Statistical Papers in Honor of George W. Snedecor* (pp. 293–316). Ames, IA: Iowa State University Press.

Tukey, J.W. (1977). *Exploratory Data Analysis*. Reading, MA: Addison-Wesley.

Tukey, J.W. (1986). Data analysis and behavioral science or learning to bear the quantitative man's burden by shunning badmandments. In L.V. Jones (ed.), *The Collected Works of John W. Tukey. Vol. III: Philosophy and Principles of Data Analysis: 1949–1964*. London: Chapman & Hall.

Velleman, P.F., & Wilkinson, L. (1993). Nominal, ordinal, interval, and ratio typologies are misleading. *American Statistician*, *47*, 65–72.

Vicente, K.J., & Brewer, W.F. (1993). Reconstructive remembering of the scientific literature. *Cognition*, *46*, 101–128.

Wainer, H. (1984). How to display data badly. *American Statistician*, *38*, 137–147.

Wainer, H. & Velleman, P.F. (2001). Statistical graphics: mapping the pathways of science. *Annual Review of Psychology*, *52*, 305–335.

Wainer, H. (2005). *Graphic Discovery: A Trout in the Milk and Other Visual Adventures*. Princeton, NJ: Princeton University Press.

Wallgren, A., Wallgren, B., Persson, R., Jorner, U., & Haagland, J.-A. (1996). *Graphing Statistics & Data: Creating Better Charts*. London: Sage.

Wand, M.P. (1997). Data-based choice of histogram bin width. *American Statistician*, *51*, 59–64.

Wilcox, R.R. (2001). *Fundamentals of Modern Statistical Methods: Substantially Improving Power and Accuracy*. New York: Springer-Verlag.

Wilcox, R.R. (2005). *Introduction to Robust Estimation and Hypothesis Testing*. San Diego, CA: Academic Press.

Wilcoxon, F. (1945). Individual comparisons by ranking methods. *Biometrics Bulletin*, *1*, 80–83.

Wilkinson, L. (2000). *Cognitive Science and Graphic Design*. In SPSS Inc., *SYSTAT 10: Graphics* (pp. 1–18). Chicago, IL: SPSS Inc.

Wilkinson, L. (2005). *The Grammar of Graphics*. New York: Springer.

Wilkinson, L. and the Task Force on Statistical Inference, APA Board of Scientific Affairs (1999). Statistical methods in psychology journals: guidelines and explanations. *American Psychologist, 54*, 594–604.

Wright, D.B. (2002). *First Steps in Statistics*. London: Sage.

Wright, D.B. (2003). Making friends with your data: improving how statistics are conducted and reported. *British Journal of Educational Psychology, 73*, 123–136.

Wright, D.B. (2006). Causal and associative hypotheses in psychology: examples from eyewitness testimony research. *Psychology, Public Policy, and Law, 12*, 190–213.

Wright, D.B. (2007). Graphing within subject confidence intervals (WSCI) using SPSS and S-Plus. *Behavior Research Methods, 39*, 82–85.

Wright, D.B., & Hall, M. (2007). How a 'Reasonable Doubt' instruction affects decisions of guilt. *Basic and Applied Social Psychology, 29*, 85–92.

Wright, D.B., & Loftus, E.F. (1999). Measuring dissociation: comparison of alternative forms of the Dissociative Experiences Scale. *American Journal of Psychology, 112*, 107–510.

Wright, D.B., & London, K. (2009). *Modern Regression Techniques Using R: A Practical Guide for Students and Researchers*. London: Sage.

Wright, D.B., & Osborne, J.E. (2005). Dissociation, cognitive failures, and working memory. *American Journal of Psychology, 118*, 103–113.

Wright, D.B., & Skagerberg, E.M. (2007). Post-identification feedback affects real eyewitnesses. *Psychological Science, 18*, 172–178.

Wright, D.B., & Williams, S. (2003). How to produce a bad results section. *The Psychologist, 16*, 646–648.

Wright, D.B., Boyd, C.E., & Tredoux, C.G. (2001). A field study of own-race bias in South Africa and England. *Psychology, Public Policy, and Law, 7*, 119–133.

Wright, D.B., Carlucci, M., Evans, J., & Compo, N.S. (under review). Turning a blind eye to non-blind line-ups.

Wright, D.B., Gaskell, G.D., & O'Muircheartaigh, C.A. (1998). Flashbulb memory assumptions: using national surveys to explore cognitive phenomena. *British Journal of Psychology, 89*, 103–122.

Zelinsky, G.J., & Murphy, G.L. (2000). Synchronizing visual and language processing: an effect of object name length on eye movements. *Psychological Science, 11*, 125–131.

Index